Praise for
Armin A. Brott

"Brott writes honestly and earnestly. His wry sense of humor will be a relief to hassled parents."
—*Time* magazine

Also by Armin Brott in the New Father series

The Expectant Father

"For fathers soon expecting the ultimate gift—a new member of the family —*The Expectant Father* is his best friend." —CNN Interactive

"One would be hard put to find a question about having a baby that's not dealt with here, all from the father's perspective." —*Library Journal*

"...a terrific gift, offering insight into pregnancy and the first few weeks of parenthood." —BabyCenter.com

The New Father: A Dad's Guide to the First Year

"This book would make a great gift for any new dad."
—Lawrence Kutner, Ph.D., columnist, *Parents* magazine

"Read a book? Who has time? But you'd be wise to find some so you can take advantage of a fabulous resource...*The New Father*."
—*Sesame Street Parents*

Fathering Your School-Age Child: A Dad's Guide to the Wonder Years, 3 to 9

"Brott...drolly delivers readable, practical guidance on fathering."
—*Library Journal*

"This, thankfully, is not another one of those goofy, dumbed-down books. . . .
In fact, this is as informative as any traditional parenting book out
there (including those aimed at the moms), and in some ways even better.
Busy dads will be grateful for Brott's accessible tone and
quick-and-painless format..." —*Newsday*

The Military Father:
A Hands-on Guide for Deployed Dads

"As an Army brat I know firsthand that it's not only our military men and
women who serve the country—their spouses and children serve proudly as
well. Armin Brott has contributed his own brand of service with this wonderful book...." —Linda Powell, daughter of General Colin Powell, US Army Ret.,
former Chairman of the Joint Chiefs of Staff

"A much-needed salute to the importance of these unique dads...a 'field
manual' for their most important front of all—the home front."
—Roland C. Warren, President, the National Fatherhood Initiative

The Single Father:
A Dad's Guide to Parenting without a Partner

"Brott...offers the tools to help men become and remain actively involved
parents." —*Fresno Bee*

"Armin Brott steers divorced, separated, gay, widowed and never-married
fathers through every aspect of fathering without a partner."
—*New Orleans Times-Picayune*

Father for Life:
A Journey of Joy, Challenge, and Change

"An essential guide for every dad." —MSN.com

All titles available as e-books

THE
NEW
FATHER

A DAD'S GUIDE TO THE
TODDLER YEARS,
12–36 MONTHS

"Tell the truth, Ezra. Does it look like
he's being a more effective parent than me?"

THE
NEW
FATHER

A DAD'S GUIDE TO THE TODDLER YEARS, 12–36 MONTHS

ARMIN A. BROTT

Abbeville Press Publishers
New York · London

To my sweet Shaundra, who makes me happy and grateful every day

For the previous editions
EDITORS: Jacqueline Decter, Susan Costello
DESIGNERS: Celia Fuller, Misha Beletsky
PRODUCTION EDITORS: Owen Dugan, Molly Dorozenski, David Fabricant
PRODUCTION MANAGERS: Elizabeth Gaynor, Louise Kurtz

For the current edition
EDITOR: Amy K. Hughes
SERIES DESIGN: Celia Fuller
COVER DESIGN: Ada Rodriguez
COMPOSITION: Angela Taormina
PRODUCTION MANAGER: Louise Kurtz

Cover photograph by Joe Epstein.
For cartoon credits, see page 308.

Third paperback edition
10 9 8 7 6 5 4 3 2 1
ISBN 978-0-7892-1323-5

Third hardcover edition
10 9 8 7 6 5 4 3 2 1
ISBN 978-0-7892-1324-2

The previous edition of this book was entitled *Fathering Your Toddler: A Dad's Guide to the Second and Third Years.*

A previous edition of this book was cataloged as follows:
Library of Congress Cataloging-in-Publication Data
Brott, Armin A.
    A dad's guide to the toddler years / Armin A. Brott. — 1st ed.
       p.   cm. — (The new father)
    Includes bibliographical references and index.
    1. Toddlers.   2. Toddlers—Care.   3. Father and child.   I. Title.   II. Series.
HQ774.5.B757   2005
649'.122—dc21   05-32876

For bulk and premium sales and for text adoption procedures, write to Customer Service Manager, Abbeville Press, 655 Third Avenue, New York, NY 10017, or call 1-800-ARTBOOK.

Visit Abbeville Press online at www.abbeville.com.

Contents

*"I was just telling them that there used to be a show called
'Father Knows Best.'"*

Introduction

What image comes to mind when you hear the word *toddler*? Probably that of a child, small, but not nearly as helpless as an infant, walking, falling, walking again. A child brimming with confidence and eager to learn.

Much of the same could be said about the fathers of toddlers as well. You've learned a huge amount over the year or so since your child was born, and you're really getting the hang of this parenting thing. But as confident as you are, something happens every day to remind you that there's still plenty more to learn.

Over the next two years, your child will go from crawling to standing to walking to running, and from one- and two-syllable words to telling you that you don't know anything about anything. Psychologist Lawrence Kutner likens toddlerhood to a musical fugue in which "the themes of intellectual, physical, emotional, and social development intertwine."

But the focus of this book isn't really on that. Sure, we'll spend some time discussing your child's growth and identifying developmental milestones. If you want an exhaustive study of child development, though, you need look no further than your local library or bookstore.

This completely updated edition of *The New Father: A Dad's Guide to the Toddler Years, 12–36 Months* is primarily about *you* and *your* musical fugue, about how fathers develop and grow over time. And that's something you can't find anywhere else.

When writing this book, I talked extensively with dozens of leading experts and studied the research and writings of many more. I also drew from my own experiences as the father of three, as well as from the interviews I've done with hundreds of fathers about their experiences and feelings. It's my hope that giving you access to all this wisdom and experience will leave you far better prepared to meet the challenges of being—and staying—an active, involved father.

The big question, of course, is, why bother to be involved? Three simple reasons: it's good for your kids, it's good for you, and it's good for your relationship with your partner. We'll talk about all of this in detail throughout the book, but let me give you a small taste now.

- **The benefits for your child.** "The evidence is quite robust that kids who have contact with a father have an advantage over kids without that kind of contact," says Norma Radin, who conducted research on fathers for more than twenty years. And these benefits are evident very early in life. In one study, Radin found that children who were raised by actively involved fathers scored higher on verbal ability tests than children raised in more traditional families by less-involved fathers. In another study, toddlers whose fathers took a special interest in childcare were consistently rated two to six months ahead of schedule on tests of development, problem-solving skills, and even social skills. And there's also a strong connection between kids' math skills and the amount of contact they have with their fathers.

- **The benefits for you.** Working fathers also benefit greatly from being involved with their kids. Too many men worry that there's no real way to balance their work and family lives, and that taking an active role at home would be committing career suicide. But the truth is that men who put child-rearing high on their list of priorities are, on average, more successful in their careers at midlife than men who focus only on their work. Fatherhood also seems to "promote men's abilities to understand themselves as adults and to sympathetically care for other adults," says fatherhood researcher John Snarey. Men who take an active role at home are—by the time their children are grown—better managers, community leaders, and mentors. Overall, they're more concerned about the generation coming up than about themselves.

- **The benefits for your partner and your relationship.** Division-of-labor issues are right up there with money as a top marital stressor. Not surprisingly, the more involved you are and the more support your partner gets from you, the happier she'll be in her relationship and the better she'll perform as a parent. And that will make her a happier person, which will make you happier as well and will make your relationship last longer.

HOW THIS BOOK IS ORGANIZED

Because babies (and their fathers) develop so quickly, the previous book in this series, *The New Father: A Dad's Guide to the First Year*, was organized month by month, a format that enabled us to capture the rapid changes that you and your baby were undergoing. But as your baby morphs into a toddler and as you gain in experience, neither of you is developing quite as quickly, and a month-by-month approach would have been too cumbersome. Instead, while we're still going through your child's and your development in chronological order, we've divided the process into three-month blocks. Each of these quarter-year chapters is further divided into several sections.

What's Going on with Your Toddler

In this section we take a brief yet extremely important look at how your toddler is developing physically, intellectually, verbally, and emotionally/socially. In many ways your toddler's growth parallels your own growth as a father. And much of what you'll be experiencing over the next few years will be closely related to your child's development. So knowing the basics of child development will not only help you understand your child but also give you a better, deeper understanding of yourself.

As you no doubt already know, children develop on very different schedules, and the range of "normal" development is quite broad. Dividing the book into three-month sections should take care of most—but probably not all—of the variations, so it might help to imagine that each chapter title is preceded by the word "roughly." The first chapter, for example, would be "Roughly 12–15 Months." You might want to keep extra bookmarks in the chapters immediately preceding and following the one you're reading. If your toddler seems to be two chapters (six months or so) ahead of her age, alert the media. If she's two chapters behind, read the special sections I've added on developmental red flags. If you're still worried, pick up the phone and call your pediatrician.

What You're Going Through

There isn't a lot of social support, or many role models, for fathers who want to be actively involved, which means that most dads don't have very many people to talk to about parenting feelings and concerns. As a result, far too many fathers end up thinking not only that they're absolutely alone in what they're experiencing but that they're abnormal as well. Chances are, however, with very few exceptions, that what you're going through at any particular moment of your fatherhood is fairly similar to what millions of fathers before you have felt and millions more after you will feel. Just as children develop along a more-or-less predictable path, so do fathers. And in this section of each chapter, we'll examine what fathers typically go through at that particular time, so you'll be able to monitor your own physical and emotional development. We'll talk about the emotional ups and downs, the joys, the frustrations, the anger, the confusion, the incredible pride, the ambivalence, and the confidence (or lack thereof) that fatherhood brings to all of us. If what you're reading in one chapter doesn't sound like it applies to you, or there are specific issues you want to learn about, feel free to skip around.

You and Your Toddler

Besides being very important, these sections are undoubtedly the most fun. This is where you'll find the tools you'll need to get to know your child better and to create the deepest, closest possible relationship with her—even if all you have is a half hour a day. We'll deal with activities as diverse as playing games, reading, music, making art, cooking, potty training, technology, discipline, handling your child's fears and imaginary friends, and overcoming gender stereotypes. Every one of these sections is completely different and covers age-appropriate material.

Family Matters

Although the focus of this book is mostly on you and your toddler, the two of you are still very much part of a family, which includes your partner and any other children you might have. For that reason, we've included a separate section that covers all the things that can have a major impact on everyone in your house. We'll talk about finances, family planning, nutrition, looking for preschools, finding dentists, dealing with tantrums, how your child's temperament affects the whole family, improving communication with your partner, sex, and much more. A number of chapters also include a special You and Your Partner section, focused on specific topics that affect your relationship with the mother of your children or your co-parent.

A NOTE ON TERMINOLOGY

He and *She*

As the father of three daughters, I often get annoyed when I read a piece of parenting advice that constantly refers to the child in question as "he." And I'm sure parents of boys feel the same way when the situation is reversed. I'm also not a big fan of using "they" in the singular. So, in an attempt to offend everyone equally, I opted to simply alternate between "he" and "she," one chapter at a time. Of course, some sections in the book apply only to boys or to girls, and in those cases the appropriate pronoun is used. Otherwise, the terms are completely interchangeable.

You're Not in This Thing Alone, You Know

Whether the mother of your child is your wife, your lover, your girlfriend, your live-in companion, your ex, or your fiancée, she plays an important role in your child's and your life—you wouldn't be a father without her. To keep from making any kind of statement about the importance (or lack of importance, depending on how you feel) of marriage, I've decided to keep referring to the mother of your child as your "partner," as I did in *The New Father: A Dad's Guide to the First Year.*

If you happen to be in a two-dad family, keep in mind that the word "partner" is, for the most part, gender-neutral. With the exception of topics having to do with female biology, the majority of "partner" information—especially anything having to do with relationships—applies to any partner, male or female.

IN CASE YOU EXPERIENCE A LITTLE DÉJÀ VU ...

This book, like child and father development, is part of an ongoing process that begins with *The Expectant Father: The Ultimate Guide for Dads-to-Be* (fourth edition) and continues with *The New Father: A Dad's Guide to the First Year* (third edition). And like most ongoing processes, previously mastered skills become the basis for learning new ones. Simply put, this means that while all the information in this book is completely new, some of the topics have been touched on in a different way in previous volumes. In each case I give the exact page reference (of the most recent edition, noted above) to indicate where the idea first came up. If you've got a copy of either or both of these books around, you can check these references. If not, don't worry; everything covered here stands on its own.

YOU CAN BE PART OF THE PROCESS

As you probably noticed, this is the third edition of *The New Father: A Dad's Guide to the Toddler Years, 12–36 Months.* I'm obsessive about research and make every effort to keep all the books in this series, including this one, as current and relevant as possible. If you notice anything that's out of date, or there's a particular issue that you think could help other dads, please let me know. My contact information is on page 293.

THE ALL-IMPORTANT DISCLAIMER

I'm not a pediatrician, financial planner, accountant, or lawyer, nor do I play one on TV (although I do host a radio show). This means that even though all the medical, financial, and legal advice in this book has been reviewed by experts

stack two (maybe even three) blocks, and may occasionally use a spoon or fork to get food from a plate into his mouth as well as for banging (although most of the time he'll use his free hand to take off whatever's on the silverware and pop it into his mouth).

- He loves to play all sorts of physical games. Chase me/catch me, rolling balls back and forth, and wrestling are big favorites, and so are games that involve pouring or splashing water.
- He's trying really, really hard to turn doorknobs. If you're lucky, it'll be a few more months before he successfully puts together grasping and twisting.

Intellectually

- In his ongoing attempt to trash your home, your toddler will be picking up, rotating, dropping, tasting, stacking (then knocking over), and throwing everything he can get his hands on, thus taking a crash course in shape, texture, taste, density, balance, and aerodynamics.

Taking a Walk—or a Crawl—on the Wild Side

On average, babies take their first steps at about twelve months. But, as mentioned above, the range is pretty big, from nine to eighteen months. How early—or late—your child starts to walk depends on a number of factors.

- **Genetics**. If you and/or your partner were early or late walkers, chances are your child will be too.
- **Birth circumstances**. If your baby was born prematurely, he'll probably be a late walker. Researchers have found that preterm infants of very low birth weight learn to walk at an adjusted age of fourteen months. Premature babies usually catch up to their age-mates by the time they're three, but the more premature the baby, the longer it takes to pull even.
- **Older siblings**. Having a brother or sister who's a few years older sometimes gives babies a little extra incentive to walk early.
- **Medical issues**. Your child may learn to walk late if he had to go through a lot of medical intervention early in life, or if he simply got sick or had a bad fall right when he was about to take his first steps. Babies with Down syndrome typically start walking at about twenty-four months.
- **Scheduling issues**. Your toddler has a lot going on now, including learning to speak, trying to identify everything in sight, and establishing his independence. He may simply have decided that walking isn't that much of a priority—especially if he's a fast crawler.

You're Not in This Thing Alone, You Know

Whether the mother of your child is your wife, your lover, your girlfriend, your live-in companion, your ex, or your fiancée, she plays an important role in your child's and your life—you wouldn't be a father without her. To keep from making any kind of statement about the importance (or lack of importance, depending on how you feel) of marriage, I've decided to keep referring to the mother of your child as your "partner," as I did in *The New Father: A Dad's Guide to the First Year*.

If you happen to be in a two-dad family, keep in mind that the word "partner" is, for the most part, gender-neutral. With the exception of topics having to do with female biology, the majority of "partner" information—especially anything having to do with relationships—applies to any partner, male or female.

IN CASE YOU EXPERIENCE A LITTLE DÉJÀ VU ...

This book, like child and father development, is part of an ongoing process that begins with *The Expectant Father: The Ultimate Guide for Dads-to-Be* (fourth edition) and continues with *The New Father: A Dad's Guide to the First Year* (third edition). And like most ongoing processes, previously mastered skills become the basis for learning new ones. Simply put, this means that while all the information in this book is completely new, some of the topics have been touched on in a different way in previous volumes. In each case I give the exact page reference (of the most recent edition, noted above) to indicate where the idea first came up. If you've got a copy of either or both of these books around, you can check these references. If not, don't worry; everything covered here stands on its own.

YOU CAN BE PART OF THE PROCESS

As you probably noticed, this is the third edition of *The New Father: A Dad's Guide to the Toddler Years, 12–36 Months*. I'm obsessive about research and make every effort to keep all the books in this series, including this one, as current and relevant as possible. If you notice anything that's out of date, or there's a particular issue that you think could help other dads, please let me know. My contact information is on page 293.

THE ALL-IMPORTANT DISCLAIMER

I'm not a pediatrician, financial planner, accountant, or lawyer, nor do I play one on TV (although I do host a radio show). This means that even though all the medical, financial, and legal advice in this book has been reviewed by experts and proven to work by real people (including me, in most cases), you should still check with an appropriate professional before trying any of it out on yourself and your family.

And please be particularly careful when trying out any of the recommended games or other activities with your child. Safety should be your number-one concern. Make sure your home is properly childproofed and never, ever leave your child alone during any of these activities—especially any that involve water or small objects. Children can drown or choke much faster than you'd think. And be sure that anything that could possibly end up in your child's mouth is nontoxic and recommended for children under three. Finally, know your child's limitations and don't push her to do anything she's not developmentally ready for. I've made every effort to ensure that the activities in this book are safe when you or another trusted adult is there to supervise. However, neither Abbeville Press nor I can be responsible for any unforeseen consequences.

Getting Off on the Right (or Left) Foot

12–15 MONTHS

WHAT'S GOING ON WITH YOUR TODDLER

Physically

- In his first twelve months of life, your baby grew at an incredible clip, probably tripling his birth weight by his first birthday. This year, the growth rate will slow way, way down. In fact, he'll most likely gain only three to five pounds over the next twelve months. As he gets more mobile, he'll start trimming away the baby fat and will soon be looking less like an infant and more like a little kid.
- By the end of this period, your child will be most comfortable in a fully upright position and can squat down and stand back up again without keeling over. Most babies take their first steps between nine and eighteen months, and once they start, they'll insist on practicing at every opportunity—sometimes holding on to one or both of your hands, sometimes unassisted. And when they're not walking, they're climbing. But even if your child is toddling around by himself, he may still drop into a crawl if he wants to get somewhere quickly.
- Your child's favorite activity now is filling and emptying containers of all kinds (with the emphasis on emptying). He can clean out your dresser drawers, kitchen cabinets, refrigerator, and bookshelves in a matter of seconds.
- He wants to feed himself and may also try to undress himself. He's especially good at removing—and losing—socks and hats.
- His fine motor coordination is greatly improved. He can turn the pages of a book one at a time and now releases objects as accurately and gracefully as he picks them up, a skill he'll find invaluable when he learns to throw a ball. He can also draw a straight line (if you do one first) but prefers to scribble, can

stack two (maybe even three) blocks, and may occasionally use a spoon or fork to get food from a plate into his mouth as well as for banging (although most of the time he'll use his free hand to take off whatever's on the silverware and pop it into his mouth).

- He loves to play all sorts of physical games. Chase me/catch me, rolling balls back and forth, and wrestling are big favorites, and so are games that involve pouring or splashing water.
- He's trying really, really hard to turn doorknobs. If you're lucky, it'll be a few more months before he successfully puts together grasping and twisting.

Intellectually

- In his ongoing attempt to trash your home, your toddler will be picking up, rotating, dropping, tasting, stacking (then knocking over), and throwing everything he can get his hands on, thus taking a crash course in shape, texture, taste, density, balance, and aerodynamics.

Taking a Walk—or a Crawl—on the Wild Side

On average, babies take their first steps at about twelve months. But, as mentioned above, the range is pretty big, from nine to eighteen months. How early—or late—your child starts to walk depends on a number of factors.

- **Genetics**. If you and/or your partner were early or late walkers, chances are your child will be too.
- **Birth circumstances**. If your baby was born prematurely, he'll probably be a late walker. Researchers have found that preterm infants of very low birth weight learn to walk at an adjusted age of fourteen months. Premature babies usually catch up to their age-mates by the time they're three, but the more premature the baby, the longer it takes to pull even.
- **Older siblings**. Having a brother or sister who's a few years older sometimes gives babies a little extra incentive to walk early.
- **Medical issues**. Your child may learn to walk late if he had to go through a lot of medical intervention early in life, or if he simply got sick or had a bad fall right when he was about to take his first steps. Babies with Down syndrome typically start walking at about twenty-four months.
- **Scheduling issues**. Your toddler has a lot going on now, including learning to speak, trying to identify everything in sight, and establishing his independence. He may simply have decided that walking isn't that much of a priority—especially if he's a fast crawler.

- He has a clearer understanding of his own limitations and is getting better at using tools—including adults—to get what he wants. He'll use a stick to get something out from under the couch and will demand that you help him achieve his desire to swing on a swing all day.
- He's much better at distinguishing sizes and shapes and has a well-developed sense of how things "should be." He may occasionally put a square peg in a square hole, and if you turn a familiar object (like a book) upside down, he'll turn it right side up.
- His memory continues to improve, and if you hide an object when he isn't looking and then ask him about it, he can remember it and will look for it. He's also developing a sense of time and sequence, and understands that certain things (like naps) follow others (like meals).
- He's fascinated by hinged objects—especially doors (which he'll open and close over and over and over) and books—not so much for what's in them but for the sheer feeling of accomplishment he gets when he turns the pages.

- **Environmental factors**. Slippery floors, bulky clothing, and parents who gasp every time the baby looks like he's going to fall can contribute to delays in walking.

The whole crawling-to-walking transition is paved with persistent, annoying myths. You may hear, for example, that babies who scoot or slide or roll instead of crawling develop behavior problems later in life, presumably because they missed a major developmental milestone. Or you might hear rumors that early walking is a sure sign that your child is a genius. Or the opposite, that late walkers do better in math and science because a few extra months of crawling helps develop the brain. It's all garbage.

Bottom line? Your child will learn to walk when he's good and ready, and there's nothing you can—or should—do to change his schedule. If you're concerned about your baby's walking ability, be sure to read the rundown of physical development in "What's Going on with Your Toddler" at the beginning of every chapter in this book, which has been vetted by actual pediatricians. If you're still concerned, schedule a visit with your child's pediatrician. In the meantime, stop comparing your baby to other babies you may have heard about (or even met) and resist the temptation to get a walker (there's some evidence that using a walker delays unassisted walking even more).

Verbally

- According to psychologist Fitzhugh Dodson, there are two phases of language learning: passive language learning (what you understand) and active language learning (what you can actually say). Most of the language learning your toddler will do over the course of the next year will be passive. He understands anywhere from two to a hundred words now and will try to increase that by pointing to everything in sight and asking you to tell him what it is.
- By the end of the fifteenth month, he'll identify upon request his shoes, clothes, and body parts; familiar people and objects; and one or two pictures from a favorite book.
- Although he has a speaking vocabulary of fewer than ten words, he'll use them whenever he has a chance, pointing to and naming things he sees. Multisyllabic words may give him some trouble (*peek-a-boo* becomes "boo," and *thermonuclear* becomes "taa"), but by fifteen months he'll be stringing words together two at a time: "Bye-bye, Daddy," and "No, baby," are among his first "sentences." He can also do some pretty good cow, dog, and cat imitations.
- He's becoming aware of the expressive function of language and has developed an uncanny ability to pick out—and endlessly repeat—the one swear word you accidentally slipped into a ten-minute conversation.
- His understanding of the symbolic use of words is growing. If he knows the word *ball*, for example, he may use it when he sees a globe, a coin, an egg, or the moon. He may also call every cat, horse, goat, pig, llama, or other hairy, four-legged animal "dog."

Emotionally and Socially

- He's becoming fiercely independent, demanding to push his stroller instead of riding in it. He'll also insist on feeding himself, but will end up with more food on his face, his cheeks, the walls, the high-chair tray, his lap, and the floor than in his mouth.
- Doing things on his own isn't all there is to being independent. Your toddler wants to separate himself physically from you as well—but not for too long. Pretending to be on a scouting expedition, he'll stroll a short distance away, casually looking back over his shoulder to make sure you haven't gone anywhere. But independence is a pretty scary thing to a one-year-old, so a second or two after you disappear from his view, he'll scamper back and cling to you for all he's worth. He'll repeat the process of going away and coming back at least until he's graduated from college.
- As he slowly becomes secure in the idea that you'll always be there for him, your child's shyness around strangers and his fear of separation should decrease.

- As those fears disappear, however, they'll be replaced by other, even more irrational-seeming ones: the vacuum cleaner and the neighborhood dogs that never bothered him before suddenly terrify him; he now needs a night-light in his room; and he may refuse to take a bath, fearing that he'll get sucked down the drain. (See pages 64–73 for more fears.)
- With all the places he has to go and things he has to do, your toddler won't want to waste his precious time eating and may reject any attempts you make to get him to do so. He'll also regard sleep as a major imposition and may refuse to nap.
- He's a social little creature and will clap and try to sing along with familiar songs. He also loves attention and knows exactly what it takes to get you to focus on him. Sometimes it's something incredibly cute; other times he'll throw in a cough or choking sound just for the shock value.

WHAT YOU'RE GOING THROUGH

Wear and Tear

Being a father can be an exhausting proposition, and I'm not talking about sleep deprivation (which has probably passed for the most part by now anyway). Just trying to keep up with a toddler as he careens happily through his day can be enough to drop even a world-class athlete to his knees.

In our pre-fatherhood days, most of us never did anything to prepare for all the stooping (to get kids into and out of their car seats), bending (to put away hundreds of toys a day), wrestling, pushing (swings or strollers), chasing (to make sure your toddler stays out of trouble), schlepping (all those extra bags of groceries in and out of the car), holding (it's fun, but it's hard to keep up for more than a few blocks), and carrying (sleeping children seem to weigh a lot more than awake ones)—not to mention all that extra laundry and housecleaning. Is it any wonder that just about every father I know has a bad back?

And let's not forget about the psychological pressures that go along with trying to be a good father, partner, friend, employer, provider, and protector all at the same time.

It's crucial to take care of yourself physically as well as psychologically. Not doing so can make it impossible for you to take care of anyone else. Here are a few things you can do:

- **Get plenty of exercise**. Thirty minutes of aerobic activity three times a week not only gets you into better shape but has also been shown to reduce stress and depression. Of course, finding the time to exercise when you have a young child around is easier said than done. So you might want to invest in a jog

17

"Having kids is keeping me young and making me old."

stroller or a child seat (or trailer) for your bicycle and take your toddler along. Remember to stretch before and after your workouts, and be sure to include some special strength-building exercises for your back and abs.

- **Eat right**. Skip the fad diets and make sure you're getting a healthy balance of carbs, proteins, and fats. Go for the good ones—unsaturated and omega-3—and stay away from saturated fats and trans fats (partially hydrogenated oils). Eat more often—five small meals a day is better than three big ones. And try to drink at least eight glasses of water a day. New research has found that coffee, juice, and sports drinks count, but stay away from sugar or artificial sweeteners.
- **Catch some rays**. The neurotransmitter serotonin is a natural antidepressant, and your brain produces more of it on sunny days than on overcast ones.
- **Catch some z's**. Seven to eight hours of sleep per night is optimal for most people. Averaging less than that is associated with a higher risk of heart disease. Interestingly, getting *more* than eight hours a night may be even worse, according to Dr. Chun Shing Kwok, a researcher at Keele University in the UK, who, with his colleagues, analyzed sleep data from more than three million people. Sleeping for nine hours, they found, is associated with a 14 percent higher risk of death, while sleeping for ten hours, increases the risk by 30 percent.
- **Pay attention to your symptoms**. Physical pain is a sign that something's not right. So are headaches, ulcers, muscle tension, chronic depression, feeling angry even when there's nothing wrong, sleep problems, high blood pressure, sudden weight gain or loss, and an unusually short temper.

- **See your doctor regularly**. Sure, you may be feeling fine now, but it's important to have a good relationship with a health-care provider who can take baseline readings and let you know if something's wrong. Oftentimes, the number result you get from a medical test (for blood pressure, cholesterol, PSA—a test for prostate cancer risk—and others) is less important than how much that number changes over time.
- **Skip the quick fixes**. Alcohol and cigarettes may seem like effective ways to reduce your stress, but they're only covering it up for a while. Most of the time, they make things worse.
- **Treat yourself nicely**. Take some breaks, get an occasional massage, buy yourself something special once in a while. If possible, schedule a regular time when you can be without your phone and any other electronic devices. Even a few hours unplugged can feel like a vacation. If you can't spare a few hours, fifteen to twenty minutes of meditating will do wonders.
- **Get some intellectual stimulation**. With all the reading you're doing with your child, don't forget to do some for yourself as well.
- **Leave time for lovin'**. Sex is an important way to stay emotionally and physically connected to your partner. It's also an excellent stress reliever, and some research has shown that regular sex can reduce the likelihood of your developing prostate problems.

A Conflict Between Separateness and Connectedness

As we'll see later in this chapter, your child has been struggling to strike a balance between being dependent on you and independent from you. But your toddler isn't the only one in your immediate family who's dealing with these issues.

As a parent, you're probably wrestling with an adult version of separation anxiety: a conflict between wanting to be needed by your child (wanting to keep him a baby) and wanting to push him toward independence.

The great irony here (to me, anyway) is that the attachment that we try so hard to achieve with our children is inextricably related to separating from them. In fact, says Ellen Galinsky, head of the Families and Work Institute, "the task of becoming attached includes beginning to understand separateness." As a result, the stronger your attachment to your child, the more likely you are to be affected by the separation.

There are, of course, two common ways to deal with this kind of adult separation anxiety: push your child to be more independent, or encourage him to be more dependent on you. Adopting either approach by itself, especially if you are forceful or extreme in your manner, will guarantee disaster for your child and everyone else in your family. As with just about anything else to do with parenting, the trick is to find the right balance between the available extremes. And the first step is to become aware of what might be motivating you to move in whichever direction you're heading.

WHY YOU MAY BE PUSHING YOUR CHILD TO BE MORE INDEPENDENT

- Your child may be quieter than you'd like him to be.
- He may not be as curious as you think he should be.
- You may be afraid that your child is too clingy or dependent and that if he doesn't start learning to take care of himself, he'll grow up to be a wimp.
- You may be afraid that your child is controlling you, that you're losing *your* independence, and/or that he's making too many demands on your time and affection. This is especially common among fathers who have a child with a "difficult" temperament.
- If you're a stay-at-home or very involved dad, you may be afraid that besides having lost your career, you've also lost your prestige and your masculinity.

Pushing early self-reliance tends to be thought of as a "dad thing," but mothers are far from immune from trying to make their kids more independent. Either way, remember this:

- If your child seems clingy, there's probably a reason for it. Until he feels secure in your relationship, he won't be ready to separate from you.
- Learn to take pride in what he does, rather than in what you think he should do. He's your child, but he's not you, and he won't do exactly what you wish he would.
- If you feel that your toddler isn't growing up as quickly as you'd like, you may end up pushing him to go places or do things he isn't ready for, says psychiatrist Stanley Greenspan. This can lead to your being even more disappointed when he fails to live up to your towering expectations and to him feeling guilty and inadequate because he can't make you happy.

Some potential negative side effects of pushing independence on your child too much or too soon:

- You may find yourself working longer hours, coming home later, or doing just about anything to stay away from home more.
- You might begin distancing yourself from your partner as well as your toddler, feeling that you have to make up for all the time you haven't been getting for yourself since the baby came.
- You may become less affectionate with your child and less responsive to his emotional needs—especially if you have a boy.

"Please, Jason. Don't you want to grow up to be an autonomous person?"

- Your child may come to feel unloved and uncared for, as though you're trying to get rid of him.
- You may not supervise your child as well as you should, or you might not help your child when he really does need some help. Unsupervised kids get into more accidents and suffer more injuries than well-supervised ones.

WHY YOU MAY BE SUBTLY ENCOURAGING YOUR CHILD TO BE MORE DEPENDENT

- You may be sad that your baby is growing up so quickly. As young as he still is, he's already outgrown certain adorable behaviors and gestures, and you may almost wish that he'd stay this age forever.
- You may be afraid of being rejected or abandoned by your child. You'll get a sharp jolt of this feeling when you want to sit quietly and snuggle with your child, but he's got places to go and things to do and would rather squirm off your lap and run away.

Although it's usually thought of as more of a "mom thing," plenty of dads have trouble letting their kids go. If you're one of them, consider this:

- Don't think that your toddler doesn't need you or love you. He may not show it, but he actually needs you more than ever. Your support and love let him know that growing up (which he's going to do whether you like it or not) is okay.

21

- Your feeling that your baby's youth has somehow been "lost" runs parallel to his feelings of exploring unknown territory. Taking pride in his independence and all the "big kid" things he can do is an important part of building his self-esteem and independence.
- You may wistfully wish that your child would stay a baby forever, but is that what you *really* want? To be changing his diapers for the next fifty years? I didn't think so.

Here are some of the potential negatives of limiting independence:
- You might hover (hence the term *helicopter parent*) too much, never allowing your child to make the mistakes he needs to make in order to learn. Or, you might be overprotective and not give your child enough room to explore. As a result, he could end up lacking the confidence he'll need throughout his life to persevere in the face of adversity.
- You might limit his contacts with other people, feeling that any free time he has should be spent with you.
- You might refrain from setting limits or disciplining your child for fear of driving him away.
- You may spoil your child, or you might become excessively aggressive in trying to win his love.
- Kids whose parents don't support and encourage their independence may have trouble managing their emotions, according to Nicole B. Perry, a researcher at the University of Minnesota. Limiting independence also may harm their physical and mental health and negatively affect their later academic success and ability to form healthy social relationships.

RECOGNIZING YOUR LIMITATIONS

Before Clint Eastwood (as Dirty Harry) was throwing down the gauntlet with the line "Go ahead, make my day," he was advising people that "a man's got to know his limitations."

According to the research of family and parenting experts Phil and Carolyn Cowan, one of the factors that differentiates fathers from nonfathers is that fathers do a better job of discriminating between what they can and can't control. This skill—as absolutely basic as it sounds—is something that actually takes years to develop.

"We heard men working on it when they discussed their struggles with wanting it all—job advancement, involved relationships with their wives and children, time for themselves—while accepting the fact that no matter how hard they tried, some things had to be put aside for the time being," write the Cowans. Men who weren't parents, however, seemed to have fewer competing roles to juggle, didn't seem to be as aware of their limitations, and were "more invested in maintaining at least the illusion of personal control."

YOU AND YOUR TODDLER

Play

The first few months of your child's second year have been full of dramatic changes, and the way he plays is no exception. Only a few months ago he depended on you to pick the toys or games he'd play with, and he could focus on only one object (or person) at a time.

But in just the past few weeks, your toddler has begun to assume a more active role in his own entertainment. Play is now serious business. And there's a lot more to it than just having fun: Play is how your toddler is going to learn about the world around him. It's how he's going to try out new skills and perfect them; it's how he's going to improve and perfect his communication, counting, large motor skills (running and walking), fine motor skills (picking up a single grain of rice), balance, imagination, problem solving, and more.

But play isn't only for kids. Playing with your child is a great way to get to know him, see how he reacts to challenges, and learn about his likes and dislikes, attention span, and natural aptitudes. So set aside some time every day—try for a minimum of twenty to thirty minutes (it doesn't have to be in one chunk)—to get down on the floor and play with your child. Actually, the phrase *play with* isn't entirely accurate. At this age, your baby is too young to play *with* anyone. Oh, sure, he may hand you a toy he's been using or snatch something from you, or he may excitedly want to show you what he's accomplished. But he doesn't understand sharing or taking turns or rules or the give-and-take flow of games. What he's doing is called "parallel play," which simply means playing next to someone.

This doesn't mean you can't have fun together—I'll tell you a lot of ways to do just that below. What it does mean is that you might not be able to play with your child exactly the way you'd hoped—at least not yet. Most dads want to interact with their children, teach them strategy, show them the best way to pass a football, hit a baseball, shoot a basket, dig a hole, ride a bike, catch a fish, build a tower, program a robot, fold a paper airplane, or move a chess piece. You'll be able to do all that, just not right now. First, you'll have to master one of the most important—and hardest—ways of playing with your child: watching.

You'll want to decide what he should play with and how. And you're going to be tempted to jump in to save the day or wrestle away a toy so you can show your child the "right" way to use it. Don't. Remember: your child is the real play expert. He doesn't tell you how to do your job, so don't tell him how to do his.

Offering choices ("Do you want to play with the blocks or take a walk?") and making occasional encouraging suggestions ("Can you put one more block on your tower?") is fine. And so is teaching by example, such as building a tower of your own right next to the one your child is working on. But be sure to spend at least part of your time together just watching what your child is doing. Once you get used to it, you'll be amazed at how much fun it is. I can't count the number of hours I spent watching my children play, marveling at how they'd overcome obstacles—trying one solution after another until they got it right—and admiring their capacity to find joy in the littlest things.

Here are some toys and activities that will keep you and your toddler entertained for the next six months or so.

TWELVE TO FIFTEEN MONTHS

TOYS

When looking for toys, pick those that:

- Are age- and developmentally appropriate, which means look for toys that are challenging but not impossible for your toddler's current abilities. The age ranges printed on most toy boxes are pretty accurate. But remember, they're only guidelines, so use some common sense and think about what's best for your child. If the box says the toy inside is for kids twelve to fifteen months, but it introduces a skill your toddler has already mastered and will only bore him, get something else. At the same time, if a toy introduces a skill your toddler isn't ready for, put it away and bring it out again in a few months.
- Your toddler can safely chew on, throw, or sit on without damaging anything or anyone (soft plastic or padded blocks, for example).
- Can be washed.
- Can survive in water, like cups, sponges, boats, cars, and anything else your child might want to bring into the bath.
- Stimulate the senses by incorporating lots of different noises, textures, and colors—the more the better.
- Encourage manual dexterity by requiring the child to twist, turn, poke, flick, open, close, and/or snap them to get a response.
- Encourage the use of both hands. Duplo (the bigger Lego blocks), toy farms with animals, and the like are great.
- Have wheels or can easily be pulled, pushed, dragged, or shoved. Toy lawn mowers, buggies, strollers, wagons, and "popcorn poppers" are all good. If your

When Less Is More (Really)

About 3 percent of the world's children live in the United States, but we account for about 40 percent of the world's toy market. American parents spend an average of $480 per child per year on toys, and each one of those children owns about 100 toys (with some families admitting to having more than 250 per child). The good news is that we can—and should—cut way back. University of Toledo (Ohio) researcher Carly Dauch and her colleagues divided thirty-six toddlers into two groups and had them play with either four or sixteen toys. The kids who had more toys flitted distractedly from one to the next. Those with fewer toys had longer attention spans, spending more time playing with each toy, and were more creative, coming up with different ways to play. You've probably already noticed that your child is often more interested in the box something came in than whatever was in the box. And why not? A box can be a box or a car or a spaceship or a bed or any one of a hundred other things.

My recommendation, supported by Dauch's research, is to cut back your in-home toy store to about fifteen to twenty toys and rotate through them so your child has no more than four or five to play with at any one time. Have a nice mix of familiar and unfamiliar toys. (Take a look at the toy and activity guidelines on pages 24–31 for suggestions on variety.)

child still isn't very steady on his feet, make sure to get toys that won't fall over, roll away, or collapse if he leans on them.

- Develop sorting and categorizing skills, such as containers or toy trucks for filling and dumping, nesting toys, measuring spoons, and shape sorters (although it'll be a few months before your toddler will be able to get the round block in the round hole very regularly).
- Stimulate the imagination. Stock up on costumes and props for dress-up and fantasy play.
- Are real. Old phones (without cords) and even that extra computer keyboard and mouse you've got lying around, for example, are more interesting to many kids than their fake counterparts.
- Bounce. Just about any kind of ball will amuse just about any kind of kid.
- Offer variety. Your child's toy collection should include a good mix of big and little, indoor and outdoor, wet and dry, noisy and quiet, electronic and nonelectronic.

ACTIVITIES

Choose activities that:

- Encourage manual dexterity and hand-eye coordination.
  - Blowing bubbles. Try to chase down the bubbles and catch them before they hit the floor.
  - Touching games, such as "This little piggy went to market" and "Round and round the garden went the teddy bear."
- Promote awareness of size, shape, color, and/or spatial concepts (*in/out*, *up/down*, and so forth).
  - Emptying, dumping, and refilling everything from buckets and bathtubs to kitchen cabinets builds awareness of *in* and *out*.
  - Toys that nest and stack. These are great for teaching about size, as are large boxes your toddler can crawl into.
- Encourage large motor skills.
  - Playing ball. For now, this means rolling a ball back and forth. Your toddler will be able to heave a ball in a few months but won't be able to catch one for another year. The first time you play ball, start just a few feet apart and

The Scientist in the Playpen

As you spend time looking for toys and activities for your child, you may come across the terms *STEM*, which stands for science, technology, engineering, and math—skills most experts believe kids will need to thrive in the world of tomorrow—and *STEAM*, which adds arts to the equation. Whether it's STEM or STEAM, isn't it too early to be talking about teaching your child science, tech, engineering, and math? Actually, this is the perfect time. But instead of breaking out the textbooks and teaching him about quadratic equations and the laws of thermodynamics, we'll begin with the basics: talking with your child as he's playing and exploring his world in a way that encourages curiosity and observation, which are at the heart of the scientific method.

Talk about how things feel (wet vs. dry, warm vs. cold, heavy vs. light), how they look (big vs. small, long vs. short), how they smell (an orange vs. an onion), and taste (sweet vs. sour).

Math is about sequencing, categorizing, and shapes. Your toddler isn't ready for counting yet, but he definitely understands the concepts of *big* and *little*, *more* and *fewer* (such as a group of three blocks next to a group of six blocks), and he can probably organize things (put the rectangular things like blocks in one pile and round things like balls in another). As your child gets older, he'll

increase the distance a little every time you play. By varying the speed and bounciness, you'll be teaching your child about timing and anticipation.
  • Obstacle courses. Arrange pillows, furniture, boxes, and toys that your toddler will have to go over, through, around, and under.
• Develop balance.
  • Blanket sledding. Fold a blanket in half and lay it out lengthwise on the floor. Sit your toddler about two feet from one end with a pillow behind him. Then take the other end and gently pull your toddler toward you. The first few times you do this, he'll probably fall over backward (that's why the pillow is there). But it won't take long for him to develop the sense of balance he needs to stay upright. A few notes: Hardwood floors are best, but you can play this game on carpet as well. Always make sure your toddler is sitting solidly before you start, and don't jerk the blanket. And never, ever do this near stairs.
  • Push/pull toys such as toy lawn mowers and shopping carts. These are great for improving balance.
  • If your child walks well, have him try to kick a large ball. It's harder than it looks (since it requires balancing on one foot), so be patient.

be able to perform more sophisticated tasks. For example, if you have a big object and a little one, what happens if you add a third item that's even bigger or smaller (introducing the idea of *biggest* and *smallest*) or in between?

Engineering is about how things work, and it requires a lot of experimentation. If you drop a ball on the floor, what happens? How about if you drop a block? If you're at the park, and you and your child go down two slides next to each other, which one of you will reach the bottom first? What happens if it's your child on one slide and a ball on the other? If you're building a block tower at home, is it better to stack large blocks on top of small ones or the other way around?

And don't forget about nature. Look at things through a magnifying glass. Talk about how babies become grown-ups, kittens grow up to be cats, and saplings become trees. And what happens when you put water in the freezer— and then when you leave a piece of ice on the counter?

While there's an element of teaching in all of this, the most important thing is to keep it fun. So get excited as you talk, keep your expectations reasonable, and, as always, take your cues from your child. You want your toddler to associate learning with fun.

- Teach about consequences.
  - Tie a string to a favorite toy, hand the other end of the string to your toddler, and ask him to get the toy. Will he pull the string?
  - Have your child turn the lights on and off. Does he understand the connection between flipping the switch and what happens next?
  - If your child is able to blow bubbles, show him the difference between blowing softly (you get a small number of larger bubbles) and hard (you get a lot of smaller ones).
- Stimulate the imagination.
  - Have a pretend phone conversation with your child.
  - Ask him to feed and diaper one of his stuffed animals.
  - Have him read you a bedtime story instead of the other way around.
  - Stick out your tongue or make a silly face and ask your toddler to imitate you. If he does, try picking up a toy and putting it away. He'll probably go along with the imitation game for a little while, but as soon as he figures out that you're making him work, it's over.
- Are low-key.
  - Take a walk around your neighborhood and talk about everything—the trees, the flowers, the difference between a pickup, a car, a motorcycle, and a garbage truck. Stop and watch a spider spin a web or an ant carry a bread crumb across the sidewalk. Try to look at the world through your child's eyes. Everything he sees or hears or smells is new and fascinating.
  - Snuggle up on the couch and read (see pages 37–41 for more on reading).
- That are really and truly fun—for your toddler.
  - Let's face it: most dads love to play, and it's oh-so-easy to get caught up in something you're doing and forget about your playmate. I remember getting really annoyed at one of my daughters after I'd spent a bunch of time building a gorgeous Lego skyscraper, only to have her angrily knock the whole thing down. She'd been trying to tell me for quite a while that she was tired of playing with Lego, but I was too preoccupied to get the hint. So pay close attention to your child's mood—when he's not having fun anymore, it's time to move on to the next activity.

FIFTEEN TO EIGHTEEN MONTHS

TOYS

All of the above, plus toys that:

- Your toddler can pound, smack, beat, and smash. Hammer-and-peg boards and sandbox toys are always big hits at this age.

- Your toddler can ride on. Four-wheelers are better (more stable) than trikes. Make sure when he sits astride it, his feet touch the ground so he can scoot himself along. Skip the battery-operated or motorized toddler vehicles (they are potentially dangerous—and besides, your child hasn't been walking long enough to need a break) and forget the pedals (it's way too early).
- Encourage sorting. Your toddler is getting much better at putting the right block in the right hole on his shape sorter. He should also be able to stack a series of different-size rings on a cylinder in the right order, putting the largest at the bottom.

ACTIVITIES

All of the above, plus those that:

- Encourage body-part identification.
  - Games like "Where's your nose?" or "Where's Daddy's belly button?" And don't limit yourself to people. Animals and toys have body parts too.
- Continue to encourage manipulation play (turning, twisting, and so on) with his hands.
  - For some strange reason, all of my kids entertained themselves for hours by locking and unlocking the doors to the car and the house.
- Continue to promote awareness of size, color, and spatial relationships. And take things up a notch if your toddler is ready.
  - Have your child pour some uncooked rice or beans from one bowl into another. Then have him try to pour the same stuff into a narrow-necked bottle.
- Promote independence.
  - Let your child ask you for help before you jump in—at this age he should be able to give you some pretty clear signals. See how long it takes him, or how many tries he needs, to learn new skills. For example, watch as he figures out how to sit down on a child-size chair. In the beginning, he'll climb on front-first. But after a few falls he'll figure out that backing onto the seat works better.
- Use real tools.
  - Let your toddler sweep, push the vacuum cleaner, wipe up the floor, and even shave you. An electric razor is no problem, but if you use a razor and shaving cream, you might want to leave the blade off the handle the first few times. The lathering is the most fun for him anyway. You can then shave one side of your face and let him feel the difference between the smooth side and the scratchy side.

- Stimulate memory.
  - Play your own version of the shell game. Get three identical cups (plastic yogurt or margarine containers work well) and have your child put a small ball underneath one of them. Then move the containers around and have him guess where the ball is.
  - Have a treasure hunt. With your toddler watching, hide several of his toys in various parts of the house. Then ask him to find them.
- Stimulate the senses.
  - Take a "texture tour." Take off your shoes (and your child's too) and walk around your house testing out all the different surfaces—tile, wood, carpet, vinyl. If it's safe, you can take the tour outside as well, trying out grass, sand, concrete, and mud puddles.
- Make your own orchestra (or at least a percussion section), with pots, pans, xylophones, cymbals, drums, and wooden spoons. This game is also a great way to start introducing him to music.
- Promote art awareness (see pages 41–44).
- Encourage physical fitness, such as dancing to music, chasing, wrestling, and early attempts at gymnastics. For much more on the importance of physical play, see pages 229–31.

PLAYTHINGS TO AVOID FOR THIS GENERAL AGE GROUP

- Things that are too small. A good rule of thumb is that anything that can fit through a cardboard toilet-paper tube is too small and poses a choking hazard.
- Anything with springs, pinch points, sharp edges, or small detachable pieces.
- Complicated things. Simplicity is the key here. Your child doesn't need fancy attachments, smartphones, video cameras, and the like. Busy boxes are generally unappreciated by kids this age. You can have a huge amount of fun with whatever you happen to have in your house.
- Antiques. Unless they're exceptionally sturdy, conform to today's stringent safety standards, and aren't covered in lead paint, leave them in the attic.
- Anything that has a heating element or an electrical cord (battery-operated toys—provided that the battery can't be accessed by the child—are okay).
- Balloons. They're among the leading causes of toy-related fatalities.
- CDs and DVDs—unless you don't need them anymore. The disks may look indestructible, but toddlers have an amazing capacity for find ways to destroy things. LPs, if you have any, are very destructible and pose serious risks if they get broken.
- Passive toys. You want a toy that will make your child want to get up and dance rather than one that will encourage him to sit quietly and watch.

- Gender-specific toys. There is absolutely no reason why boys can't play with dolls, vacuums, brooms, and kitchen sets, or why girls can't play with cars, walkie-talkies, and balls. In fact, one of my younger daughter's favorite activities was shooting her fifty Hot Wheels cars one at a time down her loop-de-loop track. Don't push any particular toys at your child—just make them available and try to incorporate them into your playtime. If your child sees you using them, he'll want to do the same.

Technology for Toddlers, Part I

I know that your child has been walking for only a few months, but have you thought about whether it might already be time to introduce him to some of the high-tech equipment he's likely to encounter as he grows up?

A lot of parents have legitimate questions about the sensibleness and worthwhileness (and even the danger) of starting kids on television, smartphones, tablets, and other such things at such an early age. Making the right decision—assuming there is such a thing—is nearly impossible, given the heated debate among researchers, medical professionals, and advocacy groups.

On one side, there are qualified experts who claim that it's almost never too early to get children comfortable with using technology. And the Internet is filled with images of babies swiping at images on their parents' iPads and other tablets. On the other side, people with equally impressive résumés say exactly the opposite, that introducing children to technology too early can be dangerous. Below I'll show you how the arguments stack up. But before we get to that, it's important to distinguish between television and other types of screens.

Television is, for the most part, completely passive—we watch it rather than interact with it. While those purportedly "educational" videos or TV programs may keep kids entertained for a while, there is absolutely no question that for children under three, television and video games do more harm than good. A variety of studies show that children learn more and solve problems more quickly when they're interacting with an actual human than when being taught on-screen. And studies by Dimitri Christakis, Ling-Yi Lin, and many other researchers have found that the more time young children spend watching "educational" videos, the smaller their vocabularies, the more likely they are to be diagnosed with attention problems at age seven, and the higher their risk of cognitive delays. There's a good reason the American Academy of Pediatrics (AAP) recommends zero screen time (other than video chatting) for children under eighteen months. For children eighteen to twenty-four months of age, the AAP recommends that parents limit screen-based media to "high-quality programming/apps" (which is a fairly meaningless phrase) and—this is important—"they

31

use them together with children, because this is how toddlers learn best. Letting children use media by themselves should be avoided."

Okay, so no TV or videos until eighteen months. And then very limited, joint exposure until twenty-four months. We'll revisit this a little later in the book. But what about smartphones and tablets? This is where things get more complicated, because there's not much solid research out there on the effects of smartphones and tablets on children under age two. However, what there is

ARGUMENTS IN FAVOR OF TECH USE

- Tech is everywhere, and our kids see us interacting with screens in every aspect of our lives. Kids who don't have superior tech skills will be at a disadvantage as they grow up. Young children can use app-based technology to learn about shapes and letters and numbers. And it makes intuitive sense that children who enter preschool and kindergarten with that knowledge will have a leg up.

- It's only for a few minutes at a time. What harm could there be in that?

- Although computer-, tablet-, and smartphone-based apps aren't nearly as social as reading, apps are far more interactive than television.

- Children as young as a year can use computers to learn shapes, colors, numbers, and opposites, and many apps offer opportunities for creativity, without all the mess of, say, finger painting.

- Two-dimensional images are also safer, because they can't be put in the mouth or swallowed

- As kids get older, apps can assist them in learning upper- and lowercase letters, recognizing words and patterns, spelling, reading, doing arithmetic, and developing reasoning skills and hand-eye coordination.

- Apps are colorful and engaging and kids love them. And apps keep them from getting bored.

paints a pretty grim picture. I've summarized the arguments from both sides in the table below.

App use in moderation shouldn't be a problem. However, too many parents don't supervise their children's mobile-device usage or impose adequate time restrictions. As a result, too many kids are spending time on a screen when they should be running around. It's no coincidence that rates of obesity and over-weight are rising, now reaching 20 percent in infants and toddlers.

ARGUMENTS AGAINST

- Children are being pushed by their parents to grow up too quickly. What they need is time to relax, enjoy life, and be kids. And the research is clear: young children learn everything better by interacting with their parents than from a machine. They also need to physically interact with their world, something they can't do with two-dimensional images on a phone or tablet.

- Researcher Karin Archer found that 62 percent of children under one year old and 89 percent of children under two and a half had been introduced to at least one mobile device. Pediatrician Catherine Birken and her colleagues found that 20 percent of children under eighteen months were using hand-held devices an average of twenty-eight minutes per day. They also found that the more time a child spent on a device, the higher the risk of an "expressive speech delay," meaning the child has trouble using words and language.

- Kids under about two and a half aren't old enough to be able to understand the symbolic nature of what's on the screen—in other words, that the two-dimensional image of a dog is not a real dog.

- Children under about thirty months don't have the physical dexterity to easily manipulate objects on-screen. Clicking and applying consistent pressure to drag and drop, for example, is a pretty complicated act.

- Toddlers learn by actively engaging with the world: touching, feeling, pushing, pulling, throwing, tasting, and so on. Two-dimensional images don't allow kids to learn about an object's weight, texture, and how it looks from a variety of angles. In addition, dragging and dropping blocks to make a tower on a screen is very different from trying to balance actual blocks on top of one another.

- No child this age should be getting bored. The world and everything in it is new and exciting.

I've also heard from several pediatricians that some of their young patients who spend a lot of time on devices have poorer fine motor skills and muscle tone than their less digitally savvy patients. And doctors in England's National Health Service are reporting that many children are starting preschool without the hand strength and dexterity to hold a pencil. They blame overuse of touchscreen devices.

Technology and Special-Needs Children

Although the topic of technology for toddlers is very controversial, there's one group that almost everyone agrees can definitely benefit from computer technology: children with special needs, including those with Down syndrome, cerebral palsy, intellectual and developmental disabilities, blindness, and autism.

Assistive technology (AT), including computers, software, modified keyboards, and especially tablets and apps, can help special-needs children learn or improve their skills in a number of important areas, including:

- Social skills, such as sharing and taking turns
- Communication
- Focus and attention span
- Fine and large motor skills
- Self-confidence and independence
- Literacy

If you have a child with special needs, the sooner you introduce him to AT, the better. If you're worried that relying on technology will discourage your child from learning certain skills on his own, don't be. One of the big risks disabled children face is what researcher Catherine Burke calls "learned helplessness"—where children learn to wait for their parents or other people to initiate communication, play, or other interactions. AT can help children become more empowered initiators in play and communication regardless of their age, according to Burke.

Another advantage of AT is the effect it could have on you, your partner, and the other people who love and care for your child. As the Parent Advocacy Coalition for Educational Rights (PACER) puts it, "With assistive technology, parents learn that the dreams they had for their child don't necessarily end when he or she is diagnosed with a disability. The dreams may have to be changed a little, but they can still come true."

PACER defines AT as "a device or service that helps children with disabilities participate more independently within their environment at home or

So, will letting your child play with your phone or tablet make him antisocial, destroy his coordination, or cause all sorts of other problems? Possibly. But whether that happens or not is largely within your control. You and your partner need to make a serious commitment to restricting your toddler's access to screens and to making sure that anytime your child is on a device, you're right

school." In addition to the high-tech options mentioned above, there are plenty of low-tech ATs, including:

- Switches, or specially adapted knobs or buttons, that promote cause and effect, enabling a child to open drawers and doors, turn devices off or on, or get a toy to move. Even children with severe disabilities can use switches. For example, one can be placed near a child's head so that every time he moves in a certain direction, a mobile or other toy will start to move.
- Velcro wrist or ankle bands can be attached to bells, rattles, or other toys that the child has trouble holding onto without assistance.
- Augmentative communication devices allow children who can't speak, or who aren't speaking yet, to communicate. These could be anything from holders that help children keep books open to touchscreen devices to picture boards and special pointers that can activate prerecorded messages, such as "I'm hungry."

Some parents worry that augmentative communications technologies might actually keep their child from learning speech. But according to Catherine Burke, using augmentative communication within a spoken language framework has the exact opposite effect. "We typically see children become more verbal in response to spoken language paired with signs and communication boards because they understand more about what words mean and how to use them with the people in their lives," she says.

If you think your child could benefit from AT devices, your first step should be to get in contact with the agencies in your state that provide information, services, and evaluations for special-needs children and their families. Depending on the results of the evaluation, you may be able to receive AT devices and any necessary training at no charge. If your child isn't eligible for free services, he may still be covered under your health insurance policy.

If you aren't already in contact with the right agencies, the Center for Parent Information and Resources (https://www.parentcenterhub.org) will be able to point you in the right direction.

there with him. As long as you don't try to make a device and its apps replace all of your child's other toys, it'll be just another toy on his shelf.

After thoroughly investigating the pros and cons, I have come to the conclusion that you should keep your year-old child away from devices, including TVs, for a while longer, ideally until he turns two. That said, I'm well aware that we all need to make a phone call, take a shower, or keep a hungry child occupied while we're stuck in traffic, and giving a child a mobile device is an easy—and very effective—way to achieve our goal. As long as these exposures are brief and rare, no harm, no foul.

For those of you who plan to disregard my advice and let your child use your smartphone or tablet, at least stick to the following guidelines, please. And read "Technology for Toddlers, Part II," on pages 190–95.

- **Your child must be ready**. He should have a firm grasp of cause-and-effect relationships (I push the ENTER key, and something happens on the screen).
- **He must be interested**. One way to increase the chances he'll be interested is to let him watch you work on your device. Another is to let him bang around on an old keyboard (if you don't have one, you can probably buy a used one at a flea market). Or sit down with him and watch a movie together.
- **Never use the television or device as an electronic babysitter**. You must be willing to be there, with your child sitting on your lap, every time he's playing or watching something on a screen. When he's a little older, he can graduate to sitting next to you.
- **Keep it interactive**. Talk about what you're seeing on the screen, why your child is making the choices he is, and so on, just as you would if you were reading a story or playing a game.
- **Have fun**. At this age, the goal of exposing your tot to technology isn't to teach him anything, and it's not to boost his IQ or get him into an Ivy League school before he's out of diapers. It should really be just another way the two of you can play together. As with any other activity, pay attention to your child's cues. If he's bored or isn't interested, shut down the computer and go for a walk or pick up a book.
- **Never put a device or a television in your child's room**.
- **Make sure you select good equipment**. Common Sense Media (https://www.commonsensemedia.org) has reviews and recommendations of apps, games, movies, and other media.
- **Limit screen time**. At this age, chances are good that your toddler won't be interested in playing on a device for more than five or ten minutes at a stretch. But if he's easily mesmerized, cut him off at fifteen minutes per day.

Reading

By about fifteen months, your toddler will have put his passive reading days behind him, and he'll become a real participant. He'll babble along with you now as you read out loud and will make unsolicited (but often appropriate) animal sounds. And if you pause briefly while reading a familiar story, he'll often fill in a missing word or two—usually the last word in a sentence or rhyme. Over the next few months, he'll try to seize control of your reading sessions by pointing to illustrations and insisting that you identify them.

But no matter how great your child's interest in reading, his newfound mobility—the thrill of being able to go where and when he wants—is so consuming that he'll start squirming within seconds after he sits in your lap. Don't be offended or try to limit his movements. If he wants to go, let him. He'll be back soon enough. (At bedtime, though, this dynamic may change, and your toddler might demand book after book after book as a way to avoid having to go to sleep.)

To encourage your toddler's interest in books and to give him more control over his reading material, consider making a low bookshelf for him, one in which the books face cover out, so he can bring you his current favorites. Having a toddler-accessible bookshelf will also allow your child the opportunity to pull a few books down and "read" by himself.

If your toddler has developed enough hand-eye coordination to turn the pages of a book without shredding them, you may want to break out some lift-the-flap books. But don't go overboard with them. It seems intuitive that giving a child a way to physically interact with books would encourage and support a love of reading. But while lift-the-flap books are fun and will encourage children to pick up books (which is definitely a good thing), University of London researcher Jeanne Shinskey found that when it comes to teaching kids factual information about the world (such as the names of unfamiliar fruits, as Shinskey tried to do in her studies), lift-the-flap books fall short. If you're feeling particularly brave, you may want to introduce a pop-up book (again, purely for the fun factor, not for educational purposes). But pay close attention to your child's reaction. Some kids this age may be frightened by the sudden appearance of a three-dimensional object in the middle of a book. Others may try to smash, shred, or eat the object. Before you read any interactive book to your toddler for the first time, go through it once yourself and test all the flaps and pop-ups; unopened (and hard-to-open) flaps can frustrate even the most eager little fingers.

Books that feature pictures of babies, families, animals, and real-world themes (like trucks, farms, and boats) are big hits.

At this stage, children crave familiarity and will request the same two or three books over and over. For variety—as well as your own sanity—try to slip in a new one every few days. But watch out: your toddler's literary tastes can turn on a dime, and the book you had to read to him seventeen times yesterday may be pushed away today before you even get a chance to open it. And what gets pushed away today could be back on the A list next Tuesday.

Whatever you're reading to your toddler, keep these points in mind:

- **Make reading part of your child's daily routine**. And be sure to select a time when he's neither exhausted nor bouncing off the walls.
- **If your toddler hasn't already made a selection, offer two or three choices**.
- **When you read, use a pleasant, conversational manner and be theatrical**. Adopt a different voice for each character.
- **Be interactive**. Your toddler won't be interested in plot for a few more months, so don't be afraid to interrupt your reading to "discuss" what's happening in the story or the illustrations. If there's a picture of an apple tree, pretend to pick an apple or two and share it with your toddler. Occasionally, it's also fun to replace a book character's name with your child's (when reading to my younger daughter, for example, I turned Goldilocks into Zoëlocks).
- **Encourage participation**. Make an occasional mistake and see whether your toddler corrects you. And when reading familiar books, stop occasionally and let him finish your sentences.
- **Read your toddler's cues**. Some kids will be happy to snuggle up with you and read for an hour. Others will insist on running around the room while you're reading. There's no law that says you have to read a book from beginning to end, or even that you have to finish it at all. If your toddler is losing interest, offer another book or take a break.

BENEFITS OF READING TO YOUR TODDLER

People often ask me why I make such a big deal about reading with toddlers. Here are just a few of the many reasons:

- Reading offers one of the best opportunities to snuggle up and spend time with your child, and it helps the two of you create wonderful memories and a stronger bond.
- It helps kids learn about their world: letters, colors, animals, seasons, shapes, what people do and how they behave, and much more.
- It's one of the best ways to expose children to spoken language. And numerous studies show that hearing people speak helps children develop an interest in reading, builds their active and passive vocabularies, and sparks a love of learning, all of which helps prepare them for school and everything that comes after.
- It helps develop children's power of concentration by getting them to focus on specific objects on the page.

- It helps build creativity and imagination, especially when you deviate from the written text and ask your child questions about what's happening on the page and why the characters are doing what they're doing.
- It helps children develop empathy. By talking about the characters in a story and what they're experiencing, children begin to appreciate others' feelings and emotions.
- A number of studies, including those conducted by Elisabeth Duursma and by Meredith Rowe and her colleagues, have found that father-child reading time may be more predictive of children's later cognitive outcomes than mother-child time.
- As Groucho Marx put it, "Outside of a dog, a book is man's best friend. Inside of a dog, it's too dark to read."

ADDING TO YOUR LIBRARY

Keep reading your child's favorites until either he gets sick of them or they fall apart (but if the latter happens before the former, you may have to go out and buy another copy). Hopefully, you've been reading to your child for a few months, and you've probably put together a pretty good basic book collection. (If you need some suggestions, take a look at the lists on pages 304–6 of *The New Father: A Dad's Guide to the First Year*.)

As you introduce new books, keep in mind that toddlers like rhyme and rhythm and books about things and activities they know, such as animals, going to the store, getting ready for bed, and so on. They also love bold, bright colors and illustrations that contain lots of hidden objects. Below are some of my favorites for this age. If you have any recommendations to add, please let us know. Our contact info is on page 293.

FAVORITES

Airport, Byron Barton

Are You There, Bear? Ron Maris

Baby Happy, Baby Sad, Leslie Patricelli

Crash! Bang! Boom! (and others), Peter Spier

The Cupboard, John Burningham

Daddy Hugs, Karen Katz

Dear Zoo, Rod Campbell

Duck, David Lloyd

Freight Train (and many others), Donald Crews

The Going to Bed Book, Sandra Boynton

Goodnight, Goodnight (and others), Eve Rice

Goodnight Moon, Margaret Wise Brown
Happy Egg, Crockett Johnson
Have You Seen My Duckling? (and many others), Nancy Tafuri
I Love My Daddy Because . . ., Laurel Porter-Gaylord
In Our House, Anne Rockwell
Jesse Bear, What Will You Wear? Nancy White Carlstrom
Listen to the Rain, Bill Martin Jr. and John Archambault

Poetry for Toddlers?

Generally speaking, children's taste in poetry is pretty unsophisticated. (I find it to be just about as lowbrow as my own.) Back in the 1990s, researchers Karen Kutiper and Patricia Wilson discovered that children tend to like:

- Poems they can understand
- Narrative poems or poems that tell a story
- Poems with rhyme, distinctive rhythm, strong sound patterns, and a sense of excitement
- Poems about animals or familiar experiences
- Limericks of all sorts

On the other hand, they don't like:

- Poems with a lot of abstract or figurative language and imagery
- Highly abstract poems that don't make sense to them or don't relate to their own experiences
- Haiku

Keeping all that in mind, if you start introducing your child to a variety of types of poetry now, he'll eventually develop a taste for it. Here are a few suggestions to get you started:

The Owl and the Pussycat, Edward Lear
Every Time I Climb a Tree, David McCord
A Light in the Attic (and others), Shel Silverstein
Scranimals (and others), Jack Prelutsky

A lot of people are intimidated by poetry. Don't be one of them. You don't have to be a college professor; in fact, you don't even have to be able to tell the difference between a sonnet and a couplet. All you have to do is find poems you like, read them with enthusiasm, and have fun.

Max's Ride, Rosemary Wells

Mommy, Buy Me a China Doll, Harve Zemach

My Brown Bear Barney, Dorothy Butler

Piggies, Don and Audrey Wood

Press Here, Hervé Tullet

Tickle, Tickle (and many, many others), Helen Oxenbury

Toolbox, Anne Rockwell

Two Shoes, New Shoes (and many others), Shirley Hughes

The Very Hungry Caterpillar (and many, many others), Eric Carle

CONCEPT BOOKS

Animal Dads, Sneed B. Collard III

Dogs (and many other photography books), Seymour Simon

Everybody Has Feelings, Charles Avery

In the Morning, Anne Rockwell

I Touch (and many others), Rachel Isadora

100 First Words to Say with Your Baby, Edwina Riddel

Slam Bang, John Burningham

Art

As soon as your child has gotten past the everything-I-pick-up-goes-directly-into-my-mouth stage, it's safe to introduce him to art. His first tools will be a crayon, a marker, or a pencil, and he'll start with scribbling. At first, the art he produces will look like a bunch of random marks on the page, which is exactly what it is. But in the same way that the random sounds your child used to make turned into babbling and then actual words, those scribbles will eventually become drawing and writing. And the way that's going to happen is just as predictable as his physical, intellectual, verbal, and social development. Here's how the sequence goes:

1. Starting now, the first marks he'll make on a piece of paper (or the wall, if you happen to turn your back for two seconds) will be dots—the result of banging.

2. Over the next few months, as you encourage him and he tries to imitate you, he'll make some sweeping lines. The edges of the paper mean absolutely nothing to him.

3. Next, he'll start making back-and-forth scribbles and may occasionally draw a single line if you make one first. He's paying a little more attention to the size of the paper.

4. Eventually, he'll discover that making marks can be fun. He'll try to draw with anything he can get his hands on and will scribble so energetically that sometimes he'll wear through the paper. If he can't find any drawing tools, he'll use

his fingers, often dipped in ketchup, mashed-up food, or anything else he can get his hands on (yes, even that, so make sure you change his diapers the second he's done filling them).

Painting skills also evolve along a fairly predictable sequence, from simple, random marks to big swaths of individual colors to putting so many colors on top of each other that the result looks like mud.

GETTING READY; OR, FRANKLY, MY DEAR, I DON'T . . .

Making art with a toddler can be incredibly fun—and incredibly messy. Now that you've been warned, if you don't take the necessary precautions, you're on your own.

- **Cover every surface—walls, floors, tabletops, chairs—with paper**. If you're still concerned, move the whole show outside onto the sidewalk or into the backyard, where you can just hose everything off.
- **Clip the drawing paper to an easel or tape the paper right to the table**. It's far too frustrating for a toddler to have to hold the paper steady and draw on it at the same time.
- **Observe the dress code**. Kids this age usually don't like to wear aprons, so have them either work naked (always fun) or wear old clothes that are okay to trash.
- **Use tiny amounts**. A thin film of paint or glue on the inside of a shallow container is fine. You can refill it as often as you need to, and if it tips over, there won't be much to clean up.
- **Dilute**. Most of the paint you get at craft stores is quite concentrated. Diluting it 25–50 percent with dishwashing liquid will help the paint wash out of the clothes later and also tends to deter kids from putting the paint in their mouths (and the paint will last longer too).

SO, WHAT'S YOUR ROLE IN ALL THIS?

The first thing you have to do is let go of the idea that you're teaching. At this point—and for the next few years—all you need to do is encourage and support your toddler. Here are some tips that will make doing art projects with your child fun for both of you:

- **Don't give too many choices**. Asking "Do you want red or green?" is okay. Asking "What colors do you want?" is an invitation to a power struggle (unless you're prepared to give in to your child's every demand).
- **Stay away from coloring books**. And don't encourage tracing or copying.
- **Don't ask what anything is**. Your child is drawing or painting because it's fun. The idea that he can create something that looks like something else won't occur to him until he's at least three years old.

- **Pay attention**. Your child's attention span ranges from about three seconds to fifteen minutes. If you notice any indications of boredom—he walks away or starts crying or eating the supplies—offer another art-related activity or shut things down for the day.
- **Don't interfere**. Showing your toddler once or twice how to use a brush or marker is okay. But telling him which colors to pick, showing him where or what to draw, or making any kind of correction is completely inappropriate. Again, the object here is not to give your toddler art lessons or to create the next little Picasso. It's simply to introduce your child—in a no-pressure, no-expectations kind of way—to the creative process and to the idea that making art can be fun.

Art Projects: The Basics

- **Safety first**. Make sure everything your toddler uses in his art projects is absolutely nontoxic, washable, and too big to be a choking hazard.
- **Drawing implements**. Large, nontoxic markers are the best bet. They come in a wide variety of sizes, colors, scents, and flavors. Ordinary crayons aren't practical at this age—they crumble and can get ground into carpets and floors. You can introduce crayons in a few months when your child is doing more controlled scribbling and less banging.
- **Pencils**. Save these for when your child is older. Pencils require too much adult involvement—either to sharpen them or to make sure your toddler doesn't stab himself, you, or the dog with the sharp point.
- **Painting implements**. Use long-handled (eight inches minimum), wide (at least three-eighth inch) brushes. Little kids can't—and won't—do much with anything smaller. But let's not forget about painting with his fingers, which will probably be your child's first choice.
- **Paper to draw, paint, or glue on**. Construction (thick) paper is the staple here. It's available at toy, art-supply, and stationery stores. Children's art projects also provide a great opportunity to start a recycling program at home and at work. Instead of tossing out all those old reports, flip them over and let your toddler create on the other side.
- **Things to learn from**. At this age, your child is still exploring the world with all his senses. So give him art supplies that stimulate as many senses as possible, such as scented markers and textured papers.

- **Monitor your expectations**. Even if your child is, in fact, the next Picasso, there's a good chance that he won't create anything remotely recognizable (except perhaps a line, a circle, or a spiral) for another year.
- **Stop caring**. The more concerned you are about the mess or about your child wasting or destroying the supplies (toddlers love to shred paper, put glue in their hair, and use markers as hammers), the less fun you'll let your toddler have. So do what you can to prepare. Then take a deep breath and relax.
- **Praise your child**. Your praise is not for the artistic merit of what he's produced but for the effort he put into it. ("Wow, you worked really hard on this! Can I hang it up in my office?")

Given your child's age, attention span, interest, and level of hand-eye coordination, the range of age-appropriate art projects is fairly limited. Here, though, are some big hits and the supplies you'll need:

- **Drawing**. Paper, markers.
- **Collages**. Objects that will help your toddler use all his senses: smelly seeds (fennel, coriander, and so forth); anything that has an interesting shape or texture or that makes an interesting sound when touched (sandpaper, aluminum foil); glue; cotton balls and cotton swabs; and just about anything you might otherwise be tempted to throw away—egg and juice cartons, cereal boxes, bottle caps, Bubble Wrap.
- **Painting**. Paint, paper, potatoes or sponges (for cutting out patterns and making prints), toy cars, sticks, or anything else that can be dipped in paint and makes an interesting mark on paper.

DISPLAY

Whatever your child creates, be sure to display it someplace—on the fridge, on a bulletin board, taped to the wall. You don't have to compliment the work very much; just having it up where he can see it himself is enough to make him feel proud of himself.

FAMILY MATTERS

Separation Anxiety

Try to think about things from your toddler's perspective for a second. For most of your life you've controlled everything that happened in the world: who and what came and went, how long they stayed, what they did while they were there—at least that's the way it's seemed. But over the past few months, your grip has been slipping. People and objects come and go whenever they please. And everyone you thought you could always count on to be there for you has developed a nasty habit of disappearing just when you need them most. Even worse, people you don't know—and aren't sure you want to know—keep pinching your cheeks, making silly sounds in your face, and trying to pick you up and take you away. The universe is clearly in chaos, and given the way things are going, you can't really be sure that the people you're most attached to will ever come back.

Welcome to separation anxiety. In your toddler's mind, the best way to restore order and put himself back in the driver's seat is to cry. "That's it," he says. "If I turn on the tears, my parents won't leave. I just know it."

DEALING WITH SEPARATION ANXIETY

Some babies experience separation anxiety, others don't. Kids who have had regular contact with lots of friendly, loving people often have an easier time adapting to brief separations than those who've spent all their time with one or two people. They're more comfortable with strangers and more confident that their parents and other loved ones will return eventually.

In an unusual but far from uncommon manifestation of separation anxiety, many kids about this age develop some sleep problems, almost as if they view going to sleep as yet another assault on their ability to control the world. Note that it can also be confusing and frightening for a child to go to sleep in the dark and wake up in the light or to see you wearing one thing when you put him to bed and something else in the morning. To him, staying awake can seem like a surefire way to make certain that everything (and everyone) stays right where it's supposed to.

Here are some things you can do to help your child manage his separation anxieties:

- **Be firm but reassuring**. Tell your toddler where you're going and that you'll be back soon.
- **Don't say you'll miss him or that you're sad to be leaving**. He'll only feel guilty that he's making you unhappy. He'll also wonder why you would do something to deliberately make yourself unhappy. And finally, if you act dejected or upset at leaving him, your toddler will use that as a model for how to react to separation.
- **Don't sneak away and don't linger**. If you're leaving your child somewhere, say goodbye like a grown-up and walk out with your head high. Tiptoeing away while he's not looking will undermine your toddler's trust in you, and taking

twenty minutes to say goodbye or repeatedly coming back to make sure everything's okay will just make your departure harder for both of you.

- **Don't give in to crying**. If you're sure your toddler is in good hands, leave—with a smile on your face.
- **Don't force**. Let your toddler stay in your arms for a while longer if he needs to and don't make fun of him if he wants to bury his head in your shoulder.
- **Try to use sitters your toddler knows**. If you have to use someone new, have him or her arrive fifteen to twenty minutes before you go out so he or she can get acquainted with your child while you're there. And make sure the new sitter is completely up to speed on your toddler's bedtime ritual.
- **When you're going out in the evening, leave while your toddler is awake**. Waking up in the middle of the night to a strange or even a familiar but unexpected sitter can be terrifying to a child.
- **Be patient**. Don't trivialize your toddler's feelings about your leaving. You know you'll be back; your child isn't so sure. So give him plenty of time to adjust to any new situation.
- **Play**. Object-permanence games (games such as peek-a-boo that reinforce the idea that objects and people still exist even though they can't be seen) help reassure your child that things—and especially people—don't disappear forever.
- **Establish routines**. Having a regular schedule or rituals (such as dropping the toddler off at day care immediately after breakfast or reading two stories right before bed) can help your child understand that at least some things in his life can be counted on.
- **Develop a strong attachment**. Singing, playing, reading, and talking together all help build a strong, loving bond between you and your toddler and help him feel more secure. The more secure he is, the less he'll worry about being abandoned.
- **Ask questions**. You'll have a better chance of finding out what your child is afraid of if you ask. Most kids' biggest fear, for example, isn't the dark but being alone. So make sure your child has a favorite toy or other security object at night. And leave a light on so he can see he's not alone.
- **Give the toddler plenty of space**. If you hover, he'll get the idea that you're afraid to leave him by himself and that there's actually something to fear from being alone.
- **Distract**. Encourage independence by suggesting to your toddler that he play with his train set while you wash the dishes.
- **Relax**. Young children will pick up on your mood; if you're nervous they'll figure that they should be too.

- **Let your toddler follow you around**. This builds a sense of security and confidence that you're there—just in case he needs you.
- **Know your toddler's temperament**. (For a thorough discussion of temperament, see pages 118–25.) If your child has a low frustration tolerance, he won't want you to leave and may cry all day after being separated. Your slow-to-adapt child won't want you to leave either, but when you do, he'll usually cry for only a few minutes. He may cry again when you return, though, because your coming back is as much of a transition as your leaving was.

INDEPENDENCE VS. DEPENDENCE

From your toddler's perspective, separation anxiety can be a real problem. But from a child-development perspective, it's a positive (albeit frequently frustrating) sign, marking the beginning of your toddler's struggle between independence and dependence.

It's a scary time for your toddler, and you can see his ambivalence dozens of times every day as he alternates between clinging and pushing you away. At this stage, says British childcare expert Penelope Leach, "his own emotions are his worst enemy"—just when it seems that your toddler should be needing you less, he actually needs you more.

As the grown-up, it's up to you to help your toddler make some sense of his conflicting emotions, as well as to nurture his independence while supporting his dependence. But beware: it's extremely easy to get trapped in a vicious circle of dependence and independence. Here's how it works:

IF YOU ...	HE FEELS ...	WHICH, IN TURN, MAKES HIM FEEL ...
Interfere with his independence and his developing ego	frustration, anger, and hate	anxious and afraid
Interfere with his need to be dependent on you and his desire to cling	anxiety and fear	frustrated, angry, and hateful

Health and Safety Update

Now that your child is vertical and moving around on his own, he can get into a lot more trouble a lot more quickly than he could just a few months ago. That means that in addition to thoroughly childproofing every room in your home (which, hopefully, you've already done), you're going to need to take some extra precautions to make sure your home is a safe—and fun—place for your toddler to explore. (If you haven't childproofed, and/or you need a review of what needs to be done, check out pages 199–205 of *The New Father: A Dad's Guide to the First Year*.)

GENERAL SAFETY

- **Take CPR and first-aid classes**. Check with your local Red Cross chapter or YMCA or similar facility.
- **Do a car-seat safety review**. The old standard of moving kids from rear-facing car seats to front-facing ones used to be twelve months or twenty pounds. In 2018, the American Academy of Pediatrics changed its recommendation to two years. More recently, the group changed it again, removing the age reference and suggesting that children ride in rear-facing seats "as long as possible." So check your car-seat owner's manual, labels on the actual seat, or the manufacturer's website to find out the height and weight limits. It's unlikely that you'll be making the switch any sooner than a year from now. If your toddler is outgrowing his seat, get a bigger one. Either way, it's a good idea to recheck your seat to make sure it's still properly installed. Many state highway patrols, fire departments, police departments, and even some toddler-equipment stores do inspections for free. The National Highway Traffic Safety Administration (NHTSA; https://www.nhtsa.gov) has some car-seat- and car-safety-related resources. Aside from proper installation of a car seat, the most important thing to do is keep your car clear of debris. The rule of thumb is: don't bring anything into the car that you wouldn't want to get hit in the head with if it suddenly becomes a flying object.
- **Be cautious around pets**—whether they're yours or not—and never leave your child alone with one. Animals may not be as responsive to your child's hugs, kisses, yanks, grabs, pokes, and pinches as you'd like them to be. If you have pets of your own, make sure their shots are up to date and their claws are trimmed. Wash your child's hands thoroughly after he touches any pet. And be sure to exercise and play with them (your pets, I mean). Jealous or tense animals don't always express their feelings in the most civil ways.
- **Lower the temperature of your hot-water heater to 120 degrees Fahrenheit**.

Even after you've done that, always check the temperature of the water before you wash your toddler or immerse him in it.

- **Remember the twelve-inch rule**: to keep babies from grabbing things from counters and tabletops, make sure you keep everything at least twelve inches from the edge.
- **Never leave your child alone**—or with another child younger than twelve years old—in or near water, even if he seems to be sitting up nicely by himself in the bathtub. And while we're on the subject, be sure to dump the liquid out of any buckets or pans you happen to have standing around. About fifty children drown every year after falling into large buckets. Over three-fourths of these children were supposedly being supervised by at least one parent and had been missing for five minutes or less, according to the US Consumer Product Safety Commission.
- **Prevent accidental shootings**. The only completely foolproof way to do so is never to have firearms of any kind in your home. But if you do, at least store them unloaded in a locked safe or gun cabinet. Keep the ammunition in a

*"I need something sturdy enough to
withstand the scrutiny of other parents."*

separate locked location and put the keys someplace where the kids can't get to them. And to be extra careful, put on trigger locks.

- **Keep furniture away from windows, so that your child won't be able to use it to climb up onto the sills.** For upper-floor windows, install child safety window guards, which can be installed and modified by adults but not manipulated by a child. Your local fire department should be able to recommend the best bars for your home. If you don't have bars, keep windows closed and locked any time your child is in the house. A screen is not a reliable barrier to keep a child from falling out a window.
- **Make sure all window-shade and drapery cords are rolled up or permanently attached to the floor or wall.** For your child's room or play area, you might consider getting cordless window coverings. Every year about a dozen

Green Toddlers

People generally select the products they buy based on price, quality, availability, and brand. In recent years, though, consumers are paying more attention to how products impact the environment, whether it's their home environment or the larger one we all live in. One recent Nielsen survey found that 66 percent of all consumers (and 73 percent of Millennials) would pay more for sustainable and/or eco-friendly products. And a similar study by Cone Communications found that 89 percent of Americans would switch brands to one that's associated with a good cause. Eighty-seven percent of consumers said they'd "purchase a product because a company advocated for an issue they cared about," and over 75 percent said they'd "refuse to purchase a product if they found out a company supported an issue contrary to their beliefs."

What does this have to do with you and your toddler? Plenty.

You might be concerned that the paint you used in the nursery could emit toxic fumes. Maybe you're worried about the bleach you add to your laundry load, or you'd prefer that your toddler wore only organic fabrics or clothes made by people who earn a living wage. Or perhaps you're concerned about how disposable diapers are impacting the environment or whether the moisturizer your partner uses is cruelty-free. Whatever your concern, there are alternatives out there to just about any product you're currently using. And in most cases, you can get them delivered right to your front door.

babies get tangled up in cords and strangle. In some cases, it might be easier to just replace your window coverings altogether. But if you really love the ones you have, you may be able to retrofit them to current safety standards. You can order free retrofit kits from the Window Covering Safety Council (www.windowcoverings.org).

- **Check your child's toys**. Nesting cups should have ventilation holes in case your toddler gets one stuck in his throat or over his mouth and nose. Toy chests should have hinges that keep the lid from closing and vent holes in case your toddler develops a fascination with Houdini and locks himself inside.
- **Check for toy and baby/toddler equipment recalls**. The Consumer Product Safety Commission's website (www.cpsc.gov) is probably the most comprehensive and up-to-date resource.
- **Install safety gates at the top and bottom of each stairway**. Pressure-mounted gates are usually okay for the bottom of the staircase but not the top; hardware-mounted gates are usually okay for both. However, check the manufacturer's recommendations to be sure. Stay away from accordion-style gates. The diamond-shaped holes can trap little heads or hands, and they're tempting footholds.
- **Teach your toddler to climb down stairs backward**.
- **Keep the National Capital Poison Center phone number handy**: (1-800) 222-1222. The center also has a handy online tool that can help in nonemergency situations (https://www.poison.org).
- **Pad the corners and sharp edges of anything your toddler could run into or fall onto**.
- **Ensure that televisions, bookshelves, dressers, and other heavy objects can't be pulled over (or fall in an earthquake)**. And make sure that DVD/CD players and all other electronics are high enough that your child won't be able to insert a slice of cheese or a handful of oatmeal.
- **Keep all automatic or self-closing doors either locked or secured in the open position**. Kids can (and do) get stuck.
- **Scuff up the soles of your toddler's new shoes with sandpaper**. Slippery shoes and slippery floors aren't a good combination.

ESPECIALLY IN THE KITCHEN

- **Never leave your child unattended in his high chair**. Always keep waist and crotch belts securely buckled.
- **Consider keeping a playpen in the kitchen**. It's nice to have a safe place to put your toddler while you're cooking.

- **Don't give your child grapes, nuts, or hot dogs unless you've cut them into small pieces**. Those three foods, plus hard candies, cause almost half of all childhood choking deaths.
- **As soon as your toddler is tall enough to reach stove knobs, take them off or buy covers for them**. If oven doors are low enough, get a lock for them too.
- **Use back burners** as much as possible and keep pot and pan handles pointed toward the rear of the stove.
- **Never drink anything hot while a child is in your lap**, and keep hot foods away from the edges of the counter and sink.
- **Put your placemats and tablecloths in storage**, at least until your toddler is old enough to master the party trick of yanking the tablecloth off the table without dumping everything on top of himself.
- **Install locks on drawers and cabinets**. As a distraction, keep at least one unlocked cabinet filled with pots, pans, measuring cups, and other safe objects that your child can play with.
- **Keep your garbage can and recycling away from where your toddler is**. Three-day-old food, sharp metal cans, broken glass, and babies are not a good combination.
- **Remove refrigerator magnets that are small enough to be choking hazards**, including the small magnets that are glued to the backs of the larger part on display.
- **Cover electrical outlets**. They're incredibly tempting for little fingers.

Cleaning out Your Laundry Area

When childproofing, we tend to spend most of our time and efforts in the living room, kitchen, and bedrooms—where babies and toddlers spend most of their time. But don't forget about your laundry room. Every year, thousands of toddlers who are simply on a quest to learn more about their world get hold of liquid laundry packets (or pods) and put them in their mouth or eyes. Those accidental exposures often cause serious harm.

The best solution is to lock up those packets in a cabinet. But because your toddler is likely to see a locked cabinet as a challenge, it's important that you use one that's far, far out of your youngster's reach. In addition, the American Cleaning Institute (https://www.cleaninginstitute.org) recommends that you: never let your children handle laundry packets, no matter how much they want to help you; never puncture or pull packets apart; and always keep packets securely closed and in their original container.

- **Never leave chairs or stools near counters or tables.**
- **Lock up cleaning supplies, chemicals, and alcohol, or put them on out-of-reach shelves.**

ESPECIALLY IN THE GARAGE, BASEMENT, WORKSHOP, AND OUTSIDE

- **Keep all dangerous chemicals, paints, thinners, gas, oil, pesticides, weed killers, fertilizers, and so forth securely locked up.**
- **If you have an extra refrigerator or freezer, make sure it is locked** (not just shut). It's easier than you think for a toddler to pull open the door, climb in after something particularly attractive, and get stuck inside. If the refrigerator/freezer isn't being used, take the doors off.
- **Be particularly careful when backing your car out of the garage or driveway.** Your toddler might run after you to say one more goodbye or to get one more kiss and . . .

ESPECIALLY AROUND SWIMMING POOLS

- **Never let your child into the pool area** without at least one adult present.
- **Put a fence around the pool, although not an electrified one.** (Don't laugh; I actually heard of a couple who installed an electrified fence around their pool to keep the dog out but succeeded in electrocuting one of their children.) The fence should be at least five feet high, have no footholds, and be equipped with self-closing, self-latching gates.
- **Keep furniture, plants, toys, or anything else that can be climbed on away from the fence.**
- **Keep pool chemicals and cleaning tools locked up.**
- **Get a pool cover that's strong enough for an adult to walk on.**
- **Make sure you have the proper poolside safety equipment** (life preserver, poles, and so on).
- **Keep a phone nearby** for emergency purposes.
- **Be very, very careful when using air-filled flotation devices** such as water wings or blow-up rings. They're sometimes advertised as "swimming aids," but they're really toys. Most important, they are not a substitute for your supervision.
- **Apply plenty of waterproof sunscreen.**
- **If you have a wading pool, be sure to empty out the water** every time you've finished using it.
- **If you have a spa or Jacuzzi, water temperature shouldn't ever be above 104 degrees Fahrenheit.**

ESPECIALLY IN THE BATHROOM
(OR WHEREVER YOU KEEP MEDICATION)

Most adults have numerous prescription and/or over-the-counter medications, vitamins, supplements, and other pills or compounds that our children may see us consume. Some of those items can be fatal to a toddler—as little as one pill or one teaspoon—according to researchers Gideon Koren and Ari Nachmani. So spend extra time making sure that anything remotely medical that your child could possibly fit in his mouth is stored away safely. This includes any kind of prescriptions, including antidepressants, as well as theoretically safe items like iron supplements and aspirin.

While you're in the bathroom, if you haven't already done so, stow away or lock up all those intriguing, sharp or pointy little tools—razors, tweezers, nail scissors, and the like.

Keeping Communication Open

WHAT'S GOING ON WITH YOUR TODDLER

Physically

- As if making up for the lull in motor development of the past few months, your toddler will be a blur of activity, rushing from room to room, investigating everything, often while carrying something in each hand.
- Right now her walking will still be somewhat clumsy: getting herself into motion is difficult, her legs are far apart and move stiffly, and she'll hold her arms away from her body for balance. Most of the time she'll stop by falling. But by the time she's eighteen months old, starting and stopping will be no problem (although she'll still have a tough time negotiating corners upright).
- Her balance is also improving. If she holds on to something, she can actually stand on one foot. If she's been walking for a while, she may be able to do this without holding on to anything.
- She'll climb anything and everything and has figured out the concept of using a chair to get onto the kitchen counter. She may also have figured out how to climb out of her crib, so if you can't lower her mattress any further, at least put something soft on the floor for her to land on.
- She can crawl up stairs on her hands and knees and might walk up if you hold one of her hands. Fortunately, she's also getting used to the idea of climbing down backward and may actually do so without having to be reminded.
- She adores ride-on toys and loves to show off her strength, often grunting theatrically as she struggles to pick up, push, or drag around the biggest objects she can get her hands on.

- She may be able to throw a small ball but can't catch one. And although she'd like to kick a ball, more often than not she ends up stepping on it (and then falling over) instead.
- She's developing a clear preference for one hand over the other, uses cups and spoons, can turn the pages of ordinary books without doing too much damage, and can possibly turn on faucets and turn doorknobs.

Note: If your child isn't walking unassisted by the end of her eighteenth month, check with your pediatrician. Also, see "Developmental Red Flags" (page 58).

Intellectually

- A lot of your child's cognitive development in this period will come from lessons she learns while playing. Climbing under, over, around, and through, she'll learn how objects look from different perspectives. Dropping and throwing food, bottles, and utensils off her high chair will teach her not only about gravity but also the sounds that different things make when they hit the floor. She's also learning about cause and effect: "I drop something, and one of those big people picks it up and brings it back. Cool."
- She'll continue to use trial and error to solve problems and will expand her use of tools to retrieve out-of-reach items. (If a toy is on a blanket, for example, she may pull the blanket toward her instead of walking over to get the toy.)
- She still struggles with the conflict between autonomy and dependence—refusing your requests to do even the most basic things but wanting to keep you well within sight as she explores new places.
- Her memory is getting better, and she may remember where she left a toy a day or two before. She's also beginning to associate objects with their owners and may announce "Daddy!" when picking up one of your shoes.
- She may give you some hints that she needs a diaper change but is nowhere near ready to work on potty training.
- She has a very short attention span and flits from activity to activity. Expecting a lot of rational thought from a child of this age is a waste of time, as is giving her long explanations of whys and why nots.
- Toddlers love routines and rituals. Establishing patterns now, such as bath-story-bedtime and park-lunch-nap, will help minimize some of the problems you're likely to encounter later on.
- She's developing an imagination. She'll crawl on the floor, pretending to be a dog, and she'll "eat" food pictured in a book. The downside to this is that if your child continues imagining things after she falls asleep (and most do), she may begin to have nightmares. Since kids can't really tell the difference between

dreams and reality, nightmares at this age can be particularly frightening. (See pages 72–73 for more on nightmares.)

Verbally

- Your toddler continues to discover the power of language. She tries as often as possible to combine words, and she knows that phrases like "up me," "gimme ba-ba," and "book read" will get her picked up, fed, or read to.
- She probably understands about a hundred words now, although her active vocabulary is probably closer to a dozen. Her mimicking skills, however, are moving into high gear, and she'll try to repeat any word you throw at her.
- She likes books but may be happier to point out familiar pictures than to have you read a whole story.
- She loves singing and will join in on familiar songs wherever and whenever she can. Although far from fluent, your toddler is beginning to understand the humorous uses of language. My middle daughter had the "moo-moo," "woof-woof," "quack-quack" parts of "Old MacDonald's Farm" down at fifteen months but insisted that the chorus was "E-I-E-I-EEEEEEEEE."
- She may also sing, hum, chatter to herself, and bounce to music when she's alone.

Emotionally and Socially

- The first half of the second year may be marked by great frustration, a feeling that frequently results in tantrums. Unable to express their wants in words, kids this age often become enraged. They also "get angry both when their parents withhold help and when they proffer needed assistance," write the child-development experts Frank and Theresa Caplan. Overall, "they get angry because they are not big or strong enough for the tasks they set for themselves." Some tantrums, especially the ones that involve breath-holding, can be quite spectacular. (See pages 111–18 for more on tantrums.)
- She's expressing other emotions besides frustration, with joy, love, and pleasure topping the list. Just watch as she hugs and kisses a favorite toy or how her whole body shakes with excitement when she sees you at the end of the day. At the same time, she's also learning about anger. If she can't get a toy to move, a page to turn, or a piece of food to stay on her spoon, she may just slam the whole thing down and scream.
- Most of the time, however, she's a pretty happy soul and is easily entertained. Her sense of humor is developing nicely, and she's truly amused by her own movement—sliding, dropping things, and falling down on purpose.

- She can also understand verbal humor, particularly when it deals with incongruities. For example, after emphatically refusing your lunchtime offer of a

Developmental Red Flags

As we've discussed elsewhere, the developmental milestones you're reading about in this book are guidelines only, and the range of "normal" or "average" is relatively broad. That's why I suggested in the introduction to this book that you add the word *roughly* to each chapter title—this one would be "Roughly 15–18 Months." Keeping all that in mind, if one or more of the following statements are true about your child, call your pediatrician as soon as possible:

My child...
- Doesn't transfer objects from hand to hand.
- Doesn't use a pincer grip (thumb and first finger) to pick up small items.
- Doesn't sit on her own.
- Doesn't seem to know the difference between strangers and people she sees all the time.
- Can't follow simple directions, such as "Give me the book" or "Touch your nose."
- Speaks fewer than fifteen words. (If she can say more than fifteen, but you and your partner are the only ones who understand them, that's okay, just as long as you know what she means and she uses the words consistently.)
- Doesn't try to imitate words I say.
- Seems emotionally flat: no anger, no joy, no frustration, no delight, no fear.
- Shows little or no interest in toys or play.
- Doesn't like being held or cuddled.
- Can't push a toy with wheels.
- Doesn't stand by herself.
- Hasn't started walking or walks on her toes.
- Doesn't make eye contact.
- Doesn't respond when I whisper.
- Doesn't turn toward me when I call her name.
- Doesn't look in the direction of something I'm pointing at.
- Doesn't make any attempt to initiate communication with me or others.

banana, a bowl of cereal, or a cheese sandwich, she may laugh hysterically if you suggest a spoonful of dirt.

- She still plays alongside, not with, other toddlers, although she may occasionally share a toy with a playmate. In fact, the only people she really wants to socialize with are you and your partner, and she'll try to get one or both of you involved in everything she does.

WHAT YOU'RE GOING THROUGH

Thinking about Sex

After childbirth, about 90 percent of couples have resumed having sex by the time their baby is four months old. But even a year and a half into parenthood, there's a big difference between "resuming sex" and "resuming a normal sex life," whatever that means to you. There are all sorts of reasons you have not been able to re-create the intimate life you once had, with fatigue and lack of time in the top two slots. It's also important to understand that sex may mean very different things to you and to your partner.

YOU MAY...	YOUR PARTNER MAY...
• See sex as a way of setting the stage for verbal intimacy.	• See verbal intimacy as a way of setting the stage for sex.
• Want sex as a way of feeling closer to your partner.	• Want sex when she is already feeling close to you.
• Need sex to establish an emotional connection with your partner.	• Need an emotional connection with you before being interested in sex.

OTHER POTENTIAL CONFLICTS

YOU MAY...

- Resent your partner's lack of seductive behavior or failure to take the initiative, in addition to wishing for better sex, more often.
- Feel alienated or separated from your baby by your partner and want to have sex as a way of reconnecting with your partner.
- Be embarrassed to admit that you feel too exhausted, unsure, or overwhelmed by family responsibilities to even think about sex.
- Feel guilty about what pregnancy did to your partner's body.

- Feel guilty about the discomfort and pain she was in during pregnancy, labor, and the delivery, and be afraid of her having to go through the same thing again. (This is a common fear, even if you're using birth control.)
- Feel that your partner prefers the baby to you if she rejects your advances.
- Find it difficult to contemplate sex—especially oral sex—after remembering all the blood from the birth and the emerging baby. You may be feeling that she's somehow been disfigured, and you get turned off as a result.

YOUR PARTNER MAY...

- Complain that you don't talk to her, you aren't affectionate enough, you take her for granted, you don't understand her or her feelings. For women, sexual desire is often increased (or sparked) by feeling loved and wanted—using her definitions.
- Be withholding sex as a way of getting back at you for not doing more around the house and with your child or for spending too much time at work.
- Be "affectioned out" from taking care of the baby, especially if she's still breastfeeding.
- Be too tired to show much sexual interest in you.
- Have less interest in sex, find intercourse painful, or have difficulty reaching orgasm. Twenty-five percent of women experience pain during sex a full eighteen months after giving birth, according to Australian researcher Ellie McDonald. McDonald also found that women who had a C-section or delivered vaginally with vacuum extraction were twice as likely to experience pain than those who delivered without complications.
- Still be suffering from postpartum depression (if she had it). About 80 percent of new moms get "baby blues" after the birth of their baby. Those symptoms, which may include sadness, fatigue, mood swings, irritability, anxiety, and inability to concentrate, usually last only a few weeks at most. For about 15 percent of new moms—and approximately 10 percent of new dads, who also get baby blues—those symptoms may linger and develop into postpartum depression (PPD). With treatment, most PPD symptoms will fade by the time the baby turns one. But as many as 30 percent of women who don't get clinical treatment continue to have symptoms of PPD as long as three years after giving birth, according to researchers Nicole Vliegen, Sara Casalin, and Patrick Luyten. One common symptom of PPD is decreased sex drive.
- Not be feeling enough of a connection with you. After focusing predominantly on your toddler, she may have lost track of what she and you have in common.
- Think that you find her less attractive than you used to. She also may find herself less attractive and less desirable.

- Be more comfortable interacting with your toddler because the child expects less of her.
- Feel like a failure as your partner and/or as a mother and, to make things worse, may feel guilty about not being able to "have it all" or "do it all."

BOTH OF YOU MAY ...

- Find it hard to admit to the other your basic need for support, comfort, and love. The result can often be mutual blaming and resentment, which you carry around until it boils over into a fight.
- Be reluctant to allow yourselves to get aroused. You might be afraid of being interrupted by your toddler, or you might feel guilty about thinking about satisfying your own needs when you should really be doing something to take care of your child.
- Have stopped touching each other because you're afraid that a kiss or a touch might be misinterpreted as a sexual overture. A new mother "may think her mate is obsessed with sexual desires," says psychologist Aaron Hass, "when what he really needs is reassurance that she still loves him and he has not been replaced by the baby."

YOUR TODDLER MAY ...

- Have developed an uncanny ability to know exactly when you and your partner are starting to get frisky and will choose that exact moment to either wake up screaming or, if she's old enough to climb out of her crib, barge into your room.

SOME POSSIBLE SOLUTIONS

Getting your sex life back to normal is going to take communication, planning, and lots of patience.

- **Make sure there are opportunities for verbal as well as sexual intimacy**. And while you're at it, get rid of the idea that there's always a connection between the two.
- **Stop thinking about it** (for a while). Spend some time getting used to being affectionate with each other in a nonsexual way.
  - Hold hands
  - Stroke her hair
  - Kiss her when walking through the kitchen
  - Give each other massages, back rubs, and so forth
  - Make out
- **Schedule sex**. It doesn't have to be as spontaneous as it once was. (See page 91 for more on this.)

- **Go on dates**. See "Dating Your Partner," opposite.
- **Go for quality over quantity**. You may be able to make love only a few times a month, but make them count.
- **Get used to quickies**. Those three-hour marathon lovemaking sessions may not be possible for the next decade or so. But you'd be amazed by what you can pack into five minutes if you really set your mind to it.
- **Try to keep it regular**. Your sex organs are muscles, and they need some regular working out to operate at peak capacity.
- **Get out of the house**—or at least the bedroom. Your house and your bedroom are filled with too many distractions. So have sex in the back seat of your car, in the shower, or on top of the washing machine. (You get the point.)
- **Flirt**. Remember when you and your partner were just falling in love? Recapturing some of those feelings isn't as hard as you think. When you see her getting

The Ultimate Aphrodisiac?

Over the years, I've done hundreds of interviews and led dozens of workshops with moms and dads. And by far the most frequent complaint I hear from women is that their male partners aren't involved enough with the children. Actually, it goes a little beyond that. From her point of view, if you don't love the kids, you don't love her. From there, it's only a hop, skip, and a jump to all-out resentment.

The solution? Be an active, involved father.

"There is no more powerful aphrodisiac to a mother than to see her husband lovingly engaged with their children," Aaron Hass writes:

When your wife sees your involvement with her children, she will want to see you happy. She will, therefore, want to satisfy your sexual desires. She will be more likely to suggest that just the two of you get away for a night or a weekend so that you can have more intimate time together. She will be more open to sexual experimentation.... She will be more sexually creative. She will take pains to make sure the children are tucked away early in the evening so that you can have uninterrupted time together. And, of course, when your wife is happier, her own libido is more likely to assert itself.

Whew! If that doesn't make you want to quit your job and take care of your children full-time, nothing will.

Dating Your Partner

New parents have more than their fair share of marital problems (see pages 90–94 and 261–64 for more on this topic). One of the biggest culprits is not spending enough time together. It's awfully easy for you and your partner to get so focused on your toddler and doing everything for her that you forget to focus on each other as individuals or on your relationship. The result is that you can lose track of the interests, passions, hobbies, philosophies, and other things that made you who you are and brought the two of you together in the first place.

Perhaps the best solution to this problem is to schedule some dates. Yep, just as you did in the good old days, before you had kids. The basic idea is the same: the two of you go out and spend a few hours together staring into each other's eyes and getting to know each other. A few of the ground rules have changed, though:

- **Don't try to make up for lost time**. Packing too many things into a single evening can put a lot of pressure on both of you.
- **Make it clear that there are no strings attached**. Either of you may be suspicious that the "date" will be used as a way of getting the other in the sack. If lack of sex has been an issue for you, however, you may want to schedule a date to do nothing but that.
- **Don't talk about your toddler**. Let's be realistic: that adorable little child of yours is exactly what you and your partner are trying to get away from, in part because she's the one who has consumed so much of your time that the two of you have neglected each other.

out of the shower, tell her how good she looks; let her catch you looking down her shirt or staring at her butt; put some love notes in her wallet so she'll find them when she's at work. Do a little sexting.
- **Take turns pleasuring each other**. She may not want to "go all the way," but she might be interested in trading a back rub for a somewhat more intimate kind of rub. And of course the same holds true if she's in the mood at a time you aren't.
- **Try something new**: new techniques, positions, new role play.
- **Just do it**. Despite the exhaustion and everything else, sometimes just starting to go through the motions—touching, stroking, kissing—can be enough to get you aroused.
- **Put a lock on your bedroom door**.
- **Leave your child with a babysitter and go to a hotel**.

YOU AND YOUR TODDLER

Dealing with Your Toddler's Fears

Even though your toddler's world is growing at an incredible clip, it's still a fairly small, well-managed, and—above all—safe place. But the more she separates from you and the more independent she becomes, the scarier her world gets.

Toddlers may seem fairly unpredictable to us, but they're essentially creatures of habit, who crave familiarity and routine. And just about everything your child will fear in her first three years of life will be the result of a break in her routines or an unfamiliar, unanticipated, or surprising event. Even seemingly minor changes to familiar objects or people can panic a child. For example, if your toddler has seen you only with a beard, and one day you come home clean-shaven, she might get very upset and not believe it's you. Or if you rearrange the furniture in your living room, she might have some doubts that she's really in her own home.

Separation anxiety (pages 44–47) and the fear of strangers were undoubtedly your child's first fears. At about fifteen months, fear of the bath and fear of getting their hair washed top most kids' lists (see the chart on pages 68–71 for a list of some of the most common early-toddlerhood fears, a little about what they might mean, and a few suggestions for handling them). By the time they're twenty-one months old, most kids have graduated to being afraid of dogs, the dark (and associated monsters), and loud noises (sirens, vacuum cleaners, cars backfiring, and so forth)—in that order.

Many of your child's fears, writes child psychologist Selma Fraiberg, are "essentially a fear of his own impulses which are transferred to objects or phenomena outside himself. . . . Normally the fear will subside when the child has learned to control successfully the particular impulse which is disturbing him."

FIGHTING FEARS

Here are some general guidelines for helping your child deal with her fears:

TRY TO DISCOVER THE CAUSE

Starting when she was about eighteen months old, my middle daughter, who used to love taking long walks with me, suddenly started crying hysterically every time I put her down on the sidewalk. After a few days, I figured out that she was afraid that the cars would hop the curb and run us down—a perfectly reasonable fear. I explained to her that cars live in the street and that they aren't allowed where people walk. That seemed to take the edge off the fear. But a few days later, when we were out for a walk, a car pulled into a driveway right in front of us, and my daughter went ballistic again. In her view, I'd been lying to her, and cars really *were* after her.

It's also important to remember that small children don't always make a distinction between animate and inanimate objects. In their minds, toilets and cars and stuffed animals and trees are as alive as they are—they just don't happen to be moving right now. Who knows, maybe they're asleep. If they are, they could wake up any second. And if they do, they might attack without warning.

Once you've figured out what's troubling your child, keep the following in mind as you address the issue:

- **Acknowledge that your child's fears are real**. Say something like, "You're right: barking dogs can be scary." Let her know that everyone has fears and that being afraid is perfectly normal. You might want to tell your child about some of the fears you had when you were a kid.
- **Read to her**. There are plenty of excellent books about how kids triumph over all sorts of potentially scary situations.
- **Don't tell her she really isn't—or shouldn't be—afraid** of any particular thing, place, or person, or that "big kids aren't afraid of things like that." Instead, comfort her and tell her that you'll always be there to help her.
- **Never force your child to confront her fears**. Gently demonstrating that vacuum cleaners and baths really won't hurt your toddler is okay, but don't force the issue.
- **Be creative**. At about eighteen months, my middle daughter developed a morbid fear of sirens. Considering that we lived just a few blocks away from a firehouse, that was a big issue. One day we walked over to the firehouse, and a friendly firefighter let her sit in the front seat of one of the fire trucks and play around with all the buttons and switches, including the one that turns on the siren. The first time the siren went on, she screamed and jumped out of the truck and into my arms. But a few seconds later, she wanted to do it again— and again, and again. Sirens were never a problem after that.
- **Never laugh at or tease a fearful child**. That will only make things worse.
- **Be patient**. Most childhood fears are outgrown within a few months.

CONTROL YOUR OWN REACTIONS

Thrust into a situation she's never been in before—especially a scary one— your toddler probably won't know how to react. So she'll look to you for some visual or verbal cues as to how you think she should respond. In one classic study, researcher James Sorce and his associates conducted a series of experiments to see whether parents' facial expressions—happy, fearful, interested, or angry—have any influence on their children's behavior in potentially dangerous situations. Sorce placed the children and one of their parents on opposite sides of a "visual cliff"; between them, traversing the gap, was a long piece of sturdy but transparent Plexiglas—a dangerous-looking (to the children, anyway) surface. He then tried to get the children to crawl across the span to retrieve a tempting toy from the parent. The results were illuminating: Of the seventeen children who saw a fearful expression on their parent's face, none crossed the cliff. Only two of the eighteen confronted with an angry expression did. Of the nineteen who saw happy faces, however, fourteen crossed, and so did eleven of the fifteen whose parent's expression was one of "sincere interest."

As fascinating as Sorce's studies were, they didn't really go far enough. Who's going to try to get a baby to do—or not do—something just by making faces at her? That might work in a lab experiment but not in your kitchen. Researchers Amrisha Vaish and Tricia Striano took Sorce's experiments to the next level by adding vocal cues. They found that children who heard encouraging words would cross the visual cliff more quickly than those who saw only encouraging faces. More surprising, it didn't even matter whether the parents were looking at the children at all when they spoke!

Facial expressions and words aren't the only ways you'll influence your child. When she's learning to walk, for example, she'll probably fall down twenty times a minute and get right back up without the slightest complaint. But if you gasp and lunge across the room to "save" her, she'll probably start crying, thinking that since you're scared, she should be too. In just a few years she'll be able to overreact on her own, without your help. When you were a kid, you could probably take a pretty good tumble, get right up, and forget all about it. But if you saw blood, you'd start crying.

PLAY IT OUT

One of the things babies and toddlers are most afraid of is being out of control. Letting them play through scary situations—either ones that just happened or ones they're anticipating—can help them regain that important feeling of being in charge. If your toddler is afraid of doctors, get her a toy doctor's kit, complete with stethoscope and syringe, so she can examine—and give shots to—all her stuffed animals. If she's afraid of real animals, try a small but ferocious-looking stuffed one she can "tame."

EXPECT THE IRRATIONAL—AND TRY NOT TO LAUGH

Your child may develop various fears during her toddlerhood. The things she is afraid of may surprise you. They may amuse you (privately, of course). And they will not always make sense to you—or immediate sense, anyway. But even the strangest fears may have an underlying logic. A friend of mine told me about taking her two-year-old daughter, Arielle, to the barber for her first haircut. They'd talked things over, read some books about haircuts, given the stuffed animals trims, and everything was going fine—until the barber made the first cut. Arielle winced and let out an incredibly loud *Ouch!*—a wail she repeated with every snip of the scissors. There wasn't anything wrong, but little Arielle, who knew that cutting her finger hurt, figured that cutting her hair should hurt too.

Watch What You Say

The words you use can have a huge influence on how your child deals with scary situations. Here's how you can help her:

- **Bring up and discuss potentially scary situations in advance**. Say things like, "We're going to the aquarium, and we're going to see the alligator. But I'm going to hold you the whole time, and if you don't like the alligator, we can visit the dolphins instead."
- **Well-intentioned warnings, such as, "Oh, there's nothing to be afraid of," usually backfire**. In your child's mind, if there really wasn't anything to be afraid of, you wouldn't have brought it up at all.
- **Don't say things like, "Be careful, this might be a little scary."** Your child will think you actually want her to be scared.
- **Don't go overboard on safety issues**. Warnings like the ones you heard from your parents ("Don't talk to strangers," "Don't take candy from strangers," "Don't get into a car with strangers") can give a child a nearly irrational fear of, well, strangers.
- **Think about potential mixed messages**. Now that you've scared your toddler away from the hot stove, do you think she's going to be happy about eating some hot breakfast cereal or, even worse, getting into a bathtub filled with hot water?
- **Dump the crystal ball**. Remember all those warnings we got when we were kids? "If you don't stop playing with that, you'll put your eye out." Or, "Be careful going across that street; you're going to get run over by a truck." Well, in most cases, you didn't put your eye out or get run over by a truck. Giving your toddler a bunch of warnings that never come true teaches her that she can't trust what you say. And that will make her less likely to pay attention to the rest of your warnings—even the ones she really should listen to.

FEAR	WHAT IT MIGHT MEAN
Bath/hair washing	• Fear of getting washed down the drain and thrown away (if soapsuds go down the drain, the hair can go too, and if the hair goes, why not the whole body?). • Fear of the noise of the water. • Fear of the hot water. • Fear of getting things in the eyes and losing vision—if you can't see the world, you can't control it.
Vacuum cleaner	• Fear of being sucked in by the hose and disposed of, just like the dust (similar to fear of the bathtub drain, above). • Fear of loud noises, of being yelled at.
Haircuts	• Fear of being disposed of (just like soapsuds, above). • Fear that the haircut will hurt
Monsters	• Fear of the unknown. • Fear of being separated from you. • Fear that there is something so powerful and unpredictable that even you (the all-powerful parent) can't control it.

WHAT TO DO ABOUT IT

- Get a special toy that your toddler can play with only in the bathtub.
- Have her give one of her washable stuffed animals a bath.
- Take baths with your child.
- Show her that big things (like you and she) can't go down the drain.
- Have her get in one toe at a time, then a leg, then the bottom.
- Wash her with a washcloth instead of sticking her head underwater.

- Have your toddler explore the vacuum, and perhaps even push it around a little while it's off.
- Have one of her toys go for a "ride" on the vacuum cleaner.
- Hold your child while vacuuming, but don't force her to be held.
- Let her turn the vacuum cleaner on and off, thus giving her control over the noise.

- Have your child check out the barber first and watch a few strangers get haircuts.
- Take her (with another adult) to watch you get a haircut.
- Find a child-friendly barber who has lots of experience with kids.
- Learn to cut hair yourself.
- Let your child cut the hair of her dolls, bears, and so on to practice.
- Have her sit in your lap during the haircut.
- Skip the hair washing at the barbershop—too many fears combined.

- Read *There's a Nightmare in My Closet* by Mercer Mayer.
- Don't tell your child that monsters don't exist or that they aren't hiding under her bed—it won't work. "Your child will simply reply that the monsters are hiding and will come out later," writes psychologist Lawrence Kutner. "He's right, of course, since his fears reside in his head, not in his room."
- Write and post a "No Monsters Allowed" sign (or one warning of a monster-eating kid inside the room).
- Have a large, sturdy toy "stand guard" over your toddler's room.
- Give her a magic wand or a special magic button to push that makes monsters disappear instantly.
- Cut down on scary things (including stories, growling, and making faces) before bedtime.
- Leave on a night-light.

continued on page 70

FEAR *continued*	**WHAT IT MIGHT MEAN**
Sleep or the dark	• Fear of losing control. • Fear that loved ones and loved things won't be there later.
Scary stories	• Similar to monsters, dark.
Animals	• Fear of the unfamiliar (not human). • Fear of being eaten. • Fear of being bitten. • Fear of not being able to control her own impulses or live up to her parents' expectations.
Doctors/ dentists	• Fear of strangers. • Fear of new situations, smells, sights. • Fear of pain. • Fear that there's really something wrong (you wouldn't go to the doctor if there weren't, right?).

WHAT TO DO ABOUT IT

- Establish a comfortable bedtime routine.
- Tell her that everyone else she knows is sleeping (name them one at a time).
- Tell her that you—and everyone else—will be there in the morning.
- Leave a light on.

- No scary stories before bed; if the problem is severe, no scary stories at all, even during the day.
- Cuddle while reading.
- Edit or cut out any scary parts.
- Make sure she knows the story isn't real, although she won't fully grasp this concept for another few years.
- Use a night-light.

- Read lots of books about friendly animals (the Carl books, by Alexandra Day, are great for this).
- Ease her into a familiarity with animals. Start by petting a toy dog, then have her approach a friendly real one.
- Teach your toddler the proper way to behave with pets: no fingers in animals' noses, no tail pulling, and so on. Take her hand and show her the right way to pet an animal.
- Teach her to recognize inviting and hostile animal gestures.
- Ask pet owners if their animal is friendly before letting your child anywhere near it.
- Hold your toddler's hand near unfamiliar pets.
- Never force her to touch animals if she doesn't want to.

- Talk about the doctor, about how pediatricians love kids and want to make them feel good.
- Play through it (see page 66): have your toddler do to her dolls or stuffed animals what the doctor will do to her.
- Do not lie—don't say there won't be shots or that the shots won't hurt.
- Schedule appointments for times when your child tends not to be cranky.
- Switch to a same-sex doctor. (Don't worry about offending your current practitioner; he or she is very familiar with these requests.)
- Read some books about going to the doctor to your toddler.

SECURITY OBJECTS

About half of all kids need, want, use, or demand some kind of security or transitional object: blankets, pacifiers, toys, and so on. (Remember Linus from the *Peanuts* comics and his most trusted and reliable companion—his blue blanket?) If your child has a security object, don't discourage her—she'll give it up when she's ready to. Trying to break a security-object habit can make your toddler feel even more needy than before. Doing so can even create a pattern that may result in your child using, in later years, such "adult" security devices as cigarettes, alcohol, and drugs. So if you think your child is developing a real fondness for a particular object, it may be worthwhile to go out and buy one or two more identical ones to keep in the closet. The extra might come in handy if the first one gets lost, shredded, or so filthy that it can't be salvaged.

Coping with Nightmares and Night Terrors

As if being scared of things during the day weren't enough, many toddlers have bad dreams at night. Your toddler can't tell the difference between reality and fantasy, and a scary experience during the day or an image from a bedtime story or video can get lodged in her brain and resurface hours later as a nightmare.

You can reduce the chances that nightmares will happen by not telling scary stories or showing scary videos right before bedtime. Having a calm, secure bedtime ritual can help too. But no amount of preparation will eliminate nightmares altogether. Here's what to do when your child has one:

- **Make sure you can always hear her if she cries out in the night**. Get a monitor if you need to. If a babysitter stays with your child, make sure he or she knows how to comfort her.
- **Get to your child as quickly as you can and wake her gently**, if she's not already awake.
- **Reassure her in a calm, soothing voice** that it's safe to go back to sleep.
- **Take it easy**—really. Your child has an uncanny ability to read your emotions, and sensing your tension will upset her even more.
- **Stay with her until she's settled down**, or let her know you're nearby. Reading a story is a great way to ease her back to sleep.
- **Discuss the nightmare—but only if your child is open to it**. If she remembers her dream in the morning, encourage her to talk about the frightening parts and to make up a happy ending to it.

Talking *with* (not *at*) Your Toddler

The amount of time you spend speaking with your child is one of the biggest predictors of how well she'll do in life—intellectually, linguistically, socially, and especially academically. To start with, the more live language (coming from a real live human, as opposed to a TV or a mobile device) children hear, the bigger their vocabularies. Actually, it's not just the number of words they *hear* but the number of words that are directed specifically at them that makes the difference.

Janellen Huttenlocher, a researcher at the University of Chicago, and her colleagues have found that at twenty months, children whose parents spoke with them frequently knew 131 more words than children whose parents didn't speak to them very much. By the time those same kids were two years old, that gap was almost 300 words. Huttenlocher tracked those same children for several

NIGHTMARES AND NIGHT TERRORS: WHAT NOT TO DO

- **Don't let your toddler sleep with you**, especially after a nightmare. You may end up giving her the impression that she should be afraid of her own bed or of being alone in her room. And if she gets used to sleeping with you, it may also become a habit that is difficult to break.
- **Don't tell her that nightmares aren't real**. They seem real to her, and blowing them off as trivial will only upset her more.

Nightmares and night terrors (sometimes called "sleep terrors") are very different things and should be dealt with differently. Nightmares happen during the dream phase of sleep known as REM (rapid eye movement), and they usually end up waking the child.

Night terrors, on the other hand, happen during a much deeper sleep phase. They can last anywhere from a few minutes to an hour. Technically, your child is asleep the entire time, even though her eyes will be wide open. When a night terror is over, though, she won't remember anything about it. But while it's going on, it'll scare the hell out of you.

It's going to be tough, but if your child is having a night terror, it's important that you don't wake her up. You can try to comfort her by stroking her head or putting an arm around her shoulders, but that may make her more upset. So just stay nearby to make sure she doesn't hurt herself, until she slips back into a more peaceful sleep.

more years and found that the ones who heard the most words when they were one and two scored higher on IQ and language tests. And when they were in the third grade, those children still had greater language skills than the ones with less chatty parents. Other researchers, including Stanford's Adriana Weisleder and the University of Chicago's Erica Cartmill, have found similarly strong connections between the amount of child-directed speech kids hear at eighteen months and the size of their vocabulary at ages two and three.

Don't Be a Sexist

Most of us would like to believe that we'd treat our sons and daughters the same way, but, unfortunately, most of us fall short. Dads (and, to a lesser extent, moms) respond much more quickly to distressed girls than to equally distressed boys. Jennifer Mascaro, a researcher at Emory University, and her colleagues found that dads spend 60 percent more time actively responding to daughters, five times more time singing and whistling with girls, and use a much more emotion-based vocabulary, including words such as *cry*, *tears*, and *lonely*.

It's hard to pinpoint the effects of the different ways dads treat boys and girls. But Mascaro suspects that by using a richer emotional vocabulary with girls, dads may be helping them develop more empathy than boys. At the same time, "the fact that fathers may actually be less attentive to the emotional needs of boys, perhaps despite their best intentions, is important to recognize," she says. "Validating emotions is good for everyone—not just daughters."

If you've got a daughter, keep doing what you're doing. But if you have a son, pay close attention to how you respond to him and the language you use when you do. Over the centuries, the whole "big boys don't cry" thing has done a tremendous amount of damage to boys and men by filling their heads with the idea that they need to be strong and stoic, ignore their feelings and their physical and emotional pain, and always "man up."

Teaching boys to repress their emotions—which is exactly what we're doing when we ignore their fears or anxieties and don't help them recognize and cope with them—is a terrible thing to do. Repressed emotions have been linked with a variety of negative health outcomes in boys and men, including increased risk of heart attack or stroke, depression, anxiety, aggressive or violent behavior, and substance abuse. Is that really what you want your legacy to be?

Unfortunately, far too many parents talk *at* their children instead of talking *with* them. If you've got any old videos from when you were a baby, you may be able to see what I mean. Chances are there's a scene that sounds like this:

Dad or Mom: Can you say "elephant," Jenny? Elephant? Come on, Jenny, you know how to say "elephant," don't you? *E-le-phant.* You know what an elephant is, don't you? And where does an elephant live? In the zoo, right? Can you say "zoo"? *ZOOOO.* What else lives in the zoo? Bears, right? What do bears say? Do they say "grrr grrr"? Sure they do, Jenny. And what does an elephant say? Can you say "elephant," Jenny? Jen? Elephant?

Even if you don't have any old family videos around, you can see the same type of scene live anyplace that parents are trying to show off how smart their kids are. But no matter where these scenes happen to occur, they all have one thing in common: little Jenny doesn't say a word. Thanks to Dad or Mom's constant chattering, she couldn't even if she wanted to.

And that's a problem. When you don't let your child respond to what you're saying, you're not giving her the opportunity she needs to hear the rhythm and the give-and-take nature of speech. Most important, you're not giving her the context she needs to build her vocabulary. For example, when you're out with your toddler, pointing out new objects and situations is great. But if she's in a stroller and has no idea what you're pointing to or talking about, she's not learning anything.

Here's what you can do to help your child develop her vocabulary and her conversational abilities:

- **Get down to your toddler's level**, on your hands and knees, or have her sit on your lap facing you. Having a clearer view of your mouth will help your toddler see how sounds are produced.
- **Identify**. Point, but make sure your toddler is actually looking at what you're pointing at before you launch into an explanation.
- **Explain**. Label everything; talk about what you're doing. ("I'm taking your dirty diaper off. Now I'm wiping your butt. Now I'm putting a clean diaper on you.") Tell her where you're going and what you're going to do, whether it's open a door, turn on a light, or ring a doorbell. Besides building vocabulary, you're also giving her lessons in cause and effect and in sequences.
- **Don't correct grammar or pronunciation mistakes**. Instead, repeat the word or idea, pronouncing it properly, in a new, grammatically correct sentence.
- **Prompt**. When your child points to something she clearly doesn't know the word for, tell her what it is. If she tries to pronounce something but makes a mistake ("baba" for bottle), say something like, "Good job! That is a bottle."

- **Expand**. If your child says, "Truck drive," you say, "Yes, the truck is driving by." Or if she says, "Milk gone," say: "That's right, the milk is gone, because you spilled it on the floor."
- **Expand even more**. If your child seems interested in something (dogs, for example), point out other examples and talk about the differences between them. (Chihuahuas and Great Danes are dogs, but, boy, are they different.)
- **Sing**. Nursery rhymes are great. But feel free to change the lyrics to personalize them for your child. For example, I'd sometimes replace the words to "London Bridge" with, "Zoë's climbing up the stairs, up the stairs, up the stairs. Zoë's climbing up the stairs, in her PJs."
- **Don't talk so much**. As important as it is to speak to your child, it's perhaps even more important to listen. (My grandmother always said we have two ears and only one mouth to help us do exactly that.) After a sentence or two, stop talking and let your toddler get in a few words. If she doesn't respond, say something else and give her another chance to join the conversation.
- **React**. Whenever your baby makes a sound, whether it's a word or a delighted squeal, say something. Children who don't get responses to their conversation starters stop trying after a while.
- **Stay away from yes or no questions**. Your toddler is just discovering the word *no*, and she'll be looking for any opportunity to use it. So instead of "Do you want to go for a walk?" try something like, "Do you want to go to the park or the swimming pool?"
- **Watch for some interesting word associations**. A friend once told me that whenever she recited "Wee Willie Winkie" to her son, she'd make a knocking gesture in the air during the "rapping at the windows" part. One day she was talking to her toddler about wrapping birthday presents, and she was surprised when he smiled and made the very same knocking gesture.
- **Avoid baby talk**. Toddlers imitate what they hear. And even though sentences like "does widdole baaaabee want wawa in her baba?" sound cutesy-wootsie, they don't challenge your child, and they may actually slow down her language development. When you speak in complex sentences (sentences with multiple nouns, verbs, or clauses), you're setting a much better example of what language really is, and you're helping improve your toddler's language and grammar skills. So speak clearly and normally.

YOUR UNIQUE ROLE IN YOUR TODDLER'S LANGUAGE DEVELOPMENT

Men and women, moms and dads, tend to speak to children differently. I'll talk more about that in a second. But what's especially important to understand is that many, many researchers have found that dads have a bigger influence on their children's language development than moms do.

So what are the differences? To start with, dads naturally do a lot of the things I just suggested in the previous section. We generally use less baby talk than moms do, and we ask fewer binary (yes/no) questions. We also tend to use bigger, more complex, and more abstract words than moms do, and we repeat ourselves less. All of those factors encourage children's language development and both their passive and active vocabularies. That, in turn, better prepares them for school.

After you've had a few moments to congratulate yourself on how influential you are in your child's life, spend a little time thinking about whether you'd speak differently to your toddler if his or her sex were reversed. As I discussed in "Don't Be a Sexist" (page 74), dads tend to speak differently with sons and daughters, using more emotionally rich words with girls. According to researcher Jennifer Mascaro, dads also use a more abstract, analytical language with girls, including words like *all*, *below*, and *much*. With boys, however, we use more power- and achievement-oriented words like *win*, *best*, and *super*. And with girls we use more body-related words, like *belly*, *cheek*, *face*, *fat*, and *feet*. These differences may seem very subtle—and they're usually made unconsciously—but over a lifetime can be hugely important. For example, Mascaro and her colleagues wonder whether dads' innocent use of more body words with girls contributes to some of the body-image problems that many girls develop as teens.

SIGNING WITH YOUR TODDLER

A few decades ago, researchers began to notice that children whose parents were hearing-impaired and taught their children to sign were able to communicate before they were nine months old. Children with two hearing parents don't usually have much to say until after their first birthday. If you think about it, using the hands to communicate makes a lot of sense. After all, toddlers have a lot more control over their fingers and hands than they do over their tongue and mouth. And they start waving goodbye and pointing at things they want long before they can say "bye-bye" and "parapsychologist."

If you haven't started teaching your child sign language, there's no reason not to start right now—especially if your child is getting frustrated that you can't understand what she wants. (And of course, if you've already started, there's no reason to stop.) Be aware, though, that once your child realizes she can use words to communicate, she may refuse to sign.

There are a number of signing methods, and I recommend that you do a little research to find the one that's right for your family. Most are based on American Sign Language (ASL), which is a nice thing—if you're going to learn a language,

Raising a Bilingual Toddler

If you and your partner are fluent in different languages, and you want your child to grow up knowing both, it's not too late. Same goes if you just feel like teaching your child a second language. Several experts have told me that to the extent possible, you should try to compartmentalize the two languages. That means each adult should speak to the child in the language he or she knows best. Although babies can already tell the difference between languages, especially if they were spoken in their presence before they were born, your toddler will create some simple rules—English with Daddy, Russian with Mommy, French with the babysitter—to help her make sense of things and keep them straight. You might also want to get foreign-language children's books or DVDs, so your child can start learning about the culture as well. Learning two languages at the same time will probably slow down the pace of your child's spoken-language development, but that's no reason to drop the second language. By the time she starts school, she'll have caught up in both languages. And according to researchers at Cornell University, she may enjoy a number of benefits, including better focus, attention, memory, and critical-thinking and problem-solving skills, and even better test scores in reading, writing and math.

you might as well learn a real one. A toddler who knows some ASL will be able to communicate with children and adults who have also learned it.

Where the methods differ most is in their adherence to the rules of ASL. Some signing methods are very rigid, others are more flexible, and some encourage parents to modify the signs as they see fit or to even invent their own. You and your partner will need to decide which approach works best for your family.

Nutrition Update

BALANCED MEALS? GOOD LUCK!

Getting your toddler to eat a balanced diet is one of the most frustrating tasks you'll have during her second year of life. For a week, it may seem that no matter what kind of delicacies you prepare, she won't eat anything but plain rice and soy sauce. Then, all of a sudden, she'll refuse to eat rice and won't be satisfied with anything but macaroni and cheese. Believe me, this happens all the time.

Part of the problem, of course, is that you and your toddler haven't agreed on what, exactly, a balanced meal is—and you won't for quite a few years. Fortunately, you may not have to. In a classic study (done more than ninety years ago!), pediatrician Clara Davis allowed a group of year-old toddlers to choose freely from a sampling of foods (which carefully omitted high-sugar foods, including candy, cookies, and soft drinks). She found that on a day-to-day basis, the toddlers' diets were indeed out of balance. But over the course of a few months—a far more critical time frame—their diets were actually quite well balanced.

Still, having a kid eat nothing but bananas for two weeks at a stretch (as my middle daughter did) can be a little disconcerting. The only time this kind of eating truly is a problem is if the child has absolutely no fruits or vegetables for more than a week—a situation that's probably more your fault than your child's. If this happens, call your pediatrician; he or she may be able to suggest some alternative sources of those crucial nutrients.

Despite the fact that toddlers' diets aren't as unbalanced as they may seem, the sad truth is that 60 percent of children don't eat the recommended amount of fruit, and 93 percent don't eat the recommended amount of vegetables. Besides reducing obesity, a diet rich in fruits and vegetables is also associated with reduced risk of developing cancer or diabetes or of having a heart attack or stroke. Here are some guidelines to help increase your toddler's fruit and veggie intake:

- **Regular food is fine**. Unless your pediatrician says otherwise, your child doesn't need baby food anymore. Just cut the same food that you're eating into bite-size pieces and stay away from very salty or spicy dishes. You've probably noticed that your child often turns up her nose at what is on her high-chair tray and lunges for whatever is on your plate instead.

The Three R's of Toddler Eating

Researcher Clare Holley and her colleagues divided 115 toddlers into five groups to test a variety of possible strategies designed to increase toddlers' consumption of foods they claim not to like. The strategies were: repeated exposure to the disliked food; role modeling by the parent plus repeated exposure; a nonfood reward (like stickers) plus repeated exposure; role modeling plus a reward plus repeated exposure; and no intervention at all. Every day for fourteen days, parents exposed their toddler to the same disliked vegetable. At the beginning of the study, the toddlers consumed an average of 0.6 grams of the yucky stuff. But the end, though, the kids in the 3R group—Role modeling + Reward + Repeated exposure—had increased consumption to 4 grams of the formerly dreaded vegetable. The 2R group—Repeated exposure + Reward—was a close second.

- **Save liquid for later in the meal**. If your toddler fills up on milk or water, she'll be less interested in trying a new food.
- **Introduce a wide variety of foods**—even if she won't touch any of them.
- **Serve small portions**—roughly a tablespoon of each kind of food for every year of age. Large servings can be a little intimidating.
- **Keep a log of what your toddler eats over the course of a week**—just to see.
- **Don't make a huge battle out of eating**.
- **Try different textures**. Toddlers are often more sensitive to the way a food feels in their mouth than in the actual taste.
- **Don't give up after only one try**. It can sometimes take as many as twenty tries before your child will agree to take a taste.
- **Give her some flatware**. For some reason, toddlers often seem to find that the sense of accomplishment they get from skewering their food on a fork makes it taste better. The fork also enables them to fling the food farther across the room than a bare hand.
- **Don't beg**; it gives your child an inflated view of her ability to control you.
- **Don't punish your toddler for not eating what you serve**.
- **Don't expect her to eat the same amount every day**.
- **Don't use dessert as a bribe**. (For more on dessert, see page 199.)
- **Be sure to read "Food and Your Child's Temperament,"** on page 202.

"Your mom cooks the chicken, but your dad makes it dance."

Weaning Your Child from the Bottle and/or Breast

At this point in her life, your toddler is probably less interested in drinking from a bottle or in nursing (if your partner has continued to breastfeed) and more interested in imitating you by drinking from a cup. If she's started to wean herself, great. If not, you should get the process going now.

As mentioned earlier, if your child fills up on liquids, she may lose interest in the solid foods she needs for that ever-elusive balanced diet. In addition, children who feed from bottles are more susceptible to ear infections and/or tooth decay. Finally, it's easy for bottles to become security objects (see page 72), and some experts believe that a child's overdependence on the bottle can interfere with physical and mental developmental milestones, and advise that she give it up entirely by eighteen months.

If your toddler is still nursing, she's already gotten most of the health benefits that breast milk confers. Like bottle feeders, she also may start (or may already be) using the breast as a comfort or sleep aid, thus delaying the development of her ability to comfort herself or fall asleep by herself. Tread lightly around this one. If your partner wants to nurse for a bit longer, that's fine. Besides providing some nutritional value to your child, nursing can also provide a lot of emotional value to both child and mom.

Here's how you can start the weaning process:

- **Phase out the bottles**. Start by replacing midday bottles with cups. Then, over the course of a few weeks, eliminate the morning bottle altogether, followed by the right-before-bed bottle.
- **Cut back on milk**. Your toddler shouldn't be drinking any more than twenty-four ounces of milk daily (unless your pediatrician says otherwise). If you're giving her more than that, replace the excess milk with bottles of water. Reducing the amount of milk your toddler drinks will increase her food intake, which should reduce her desire for the bottle.
- **Be patient**. Trying to wean your child in a day or two from bottle or breast will be a traumatic experience for everyone involved.

Taking Care of Those Pearly Whites

Hopefully, you've been cleaning your toddler's teeth at least once a day since they started coming in. If you haven't, start now. There's not much to it, really. All you need is a toothbrush and sixty seconds. Skip the toothpaste until your toddler's able to spit—most toothpastes have fluoride, which can upset your child's stomach if swallowed. If your child will let you brush her teeth, do it for a total of one minute—thirty seconds (about as much time as it takes to sing the "ABC" song all the way through) on the top, thirty on the bottom.

Be warned: Not all toddlers will willingly go along with having their teeth brushed. Although they still love to put things in their mouth, they aren't nearly as happy to have anyone else put something in there, unless it's edible. So if your toddler won't let you brush her teeth, make sure she's around when you're brushing yours, and give her a toothbrush of her own to play around with—even if it's an adult-size one—but keep an eye on her the whole time so she doesn't run around with it in her mouth. The combination of wanting to imitate you and chewing on the toothbrush will probably get her teeth pretty clean. If that doesn't work, try making it more fun: she brushes your teeth, and you brush hers; sing her favorite song while you brush her teeth, and so on.

One important reminder: Never put your child to sleep with a bottle or sippy cup of milk, or even a breast. Any kind of sugar, including the lactose in milk, will cause tooth decay.

OPEN WIIIIIIDE

Unless your child needs dental work, her dental exams probably won't last any more than a minute or so until she's three. Still, like most new things, the first trip to the dentist can be a scary experience. So start preparing your toddler several weeks in advance. Tell her you're going to a special doctor who is going to count her teeth and take some pictures of them. You might also want to check out of the library one or two books on going to the dentist. Though you shouldn't ever lie to your child about what's going to happen at the dentist's office, stay away from words that might frighten her, such as *drill, needle, shot,* and *pain.* And save your personal dental horror stories until she's a teenager.

If your dentist is pretty child-friendly or you belong to a family practice, bring your child along on one of your routine exams. The dentist will probably let her ride up and down in the chair a few times, give her a sugar-free lollipop and a couple of stickers or a toy, and maybe take a very quick look at her teeth. That's it. See you both in six months. After three or four visits like that, your child may actually look forward to seeing the dentist. And the fact that you are seeing the same dentist will reinforce the positive experience.

If your dentist doesn't see children, if the office might be scary to a little one, or if your child won't let him or her anywhere near her mouth, find a local pediatric dentist. At my daughters' dentist, the waiting rooms are filled with toys and bowls of fruit. The furniture is all bright colors and kid-friendly patterns. In the examining room there are televisions mounted on the ceiling so kids can watch videos while their teeth are being cleaned. And in the X-ray area, kids sit on a horse—complete with saddle and stirrups—instead of a regular chair. What I want to know is, where were all the pediatric dentists when I was a kid?

Despite all the attempts to distract her during her dental exam, your child may still scream, squirm, and try to escape. Don't be embarrassed. Any good pediatric dentist and his or her staff have seen the same little show a hundred times before.

Some dentists think it's a good idea to have parents in the examining room with their children; others don't. You know your child better than anyone, so you know whether you need to hold her hand or stay in the waiting room.

Food Allergies or Intolerances

Correctly diagnosing and treating food allergies, even for professionals, is tricky. In fact, according to the Mayo Clinic, a lot of primary care physicians and pediatricians don't know what the most common food allergies are and don't feel confident in their ability to help their patients manage their allergies.

Allergies can produce a variety of symptoms, ranging from the minor and annoying (itching, minor rash or swelling, nausea, sneezing, stuffy nose) to the serious and even life-threatening (major swelling, widespread hives, significant drop in blood pressure, passing out, complete inability to breathe).

There also may be a connection between food allergies and other conditions. For example, children who have severe eczema before six months of age are more likely than other children to develop allergies to peanuts, milk, and eggs. And asthma and food allergies often go together (studies have shown that 44 percent of children diagnosed with asthma also have at least one food allergy, and kids with food allergies are four times more likely to have asthma).

One thing that makes allergies difficult to diagnose and treat is that some of the symptoms—particularly the minor ones—overlap with food intolerances. The difference between the two conditions is subtle but very important. Allergies are immune-system reactions to foods that the body has decided are harmful. Intolerances don't involve the immune system and usually happen because of an inability to digest something in a particular food, such as the sugar lactose in milk. The symptoms, which may include diarrhea, gas, indigestion, and headaches, sometimes mimic allergic symptoms, but they're rarely anything more than unpleasant. To complicate things even further, there's celiac disease, which is a severe intolerance to the protein gluten that also involves the immune system.

If you suspect your toddler is allergic or has an intolerance, but her reactions aren't severe, keep a detailed diary, documenting what she eats, what the symptoms are, how often the symptoms appear, and how soon they appear after she eats the suspected food. Of course, if the symptoms are severe, cut out the offending food immediately and get your child to the doctor.

If the doctor suspects a food allergy or intolerance, he or she will most likely refer you to an allergist for more detailed diagnostics, which might involve skin and/or blood tests. Treating food allergies and intolerances always starts with identifying exactly which foods are causing which problems. Unfortunately, since trace amounts of the most common triggers are present in many foods, pinpointing the single offending ingredient won't be easy. Casein (a milk protein), for example, is sometimes found in tuna and even in nondairy ice creams. Chili recipes often include peanuts; gluten is everywhere; and good luck trying to find a packaged product that doesn't contain corn or at least corn syrup.

Allergists used to believe that allergies were incurable and recommended complete avoidance of foods that produce an allergic or intolerance reaction. But some researchers are finding that controlled introduction of the offending foods may help a person overcome allergies. (In 2017, for example, the National Institute of Allergy and Infectious Disease, the American College of Allergy, Asthma and Immunology, and twenty-four other organizations changed their recommendations for introducing peanuts. They now suggest that instead of waiting until their children are twelve months old, parents should introduce peanut-containing foods as early as six months.) That said, allergies are serious business, and you should *never* attempt to introduce potentially allergenic foods or treat a suspected allergy *unless* you're under the supervision of a trained medical professional who has experience diagnosing, managing, and treating these conditions. (That may or may not be your child's pediatrician.) That's especially important if you or your partner have a family history of food allergies.

MOST ALLERGENIC FOODS	MOST COMMON FOOD INTOLERANCES	LEAST ALLERGENIC FOODS
• Cow's milk* • Eggs* • Wheat* • Soy* • Peanuts • Tree nuts (e.g., almonds, cashews, walnuts, hazelnuts) • Fin fish (e.g., cod, sole, tuna, salmon) • Shellfish (e.g., crab, lobster, shrimp, oysters) *Allergy usually outgrown in early childhood	• Dairy (usually related to the body's shortage of the enzyme lactase) • Gluten (found in wheat, rye, barley, triticale) • Caffeine • Salicylates (natural chemicals produced by plants) • Sulfites (often found in dried fruit and wine) • FODMAPs (carbohydrates that can cause digestive upset, found in apples, beans, lentils, bread, and honey)	• Apples • Pears • Sweet potatoes • Cherries • Carrots • Rice • Avocado • Mango • Peaches • Lamb • Other red meats

Dealing with the Disappointment of Disability

One of the major themes in this book is the constantly evolving need to deal with the disparity between the way you dreamed your child would be and the way she actually is. A lot of the differences between reality and expectations have to do with choices and interests—the child choosing to join a motorcycle gang instead of going to medical school like you wanted her to, or the child having no interest in sports, let alone in living out your dream to win an Olympic medal in the luge.

In most cases, parents manage to get past these things, and learn to accept their children as they are. But what happens if your child can't live up to your expectations or hopes because she's disabled or chronically ill?

You're likely to feel a wide range of emotions, from shock, disbelief, and denial to shame, depression, anger, ambivalence about having a child at all, resentment at having to spend so much time and money on treatment, and even wishing that your child had died. Many of these more negative feelings will immediately be followed by profound guilt at ever having had the thought in the first place. Whatever your feelings, having a child with a disability may do serious damage to your self-esteem.

To make matters worse, you and your partner will have to deal with a tremendous number of unexpected challenges, ranging from simple exhaustion and burnout (above and beyond what you'd feel if your child did not have a disability) to struggling to find the right resources for yourselves and your child to financial issues, social isolation, and relationship strain.

Not surprisingly, mothers and fathers tend to react to a child's disability differently. Mothers typically worry more about the emotional strain of caring for a physically or intellectually challenged child, how they'll have to reorganize their life around the child, and whether that will make them neglect other members of the family, according to researchers Jaipaul Roopnarine and Brent Miller.

Fathers tend to worry more about practical things, such as the cost of providing care and whether the child will be able to function in school. Dads also tend to be more concerned with their disabled children's (especially boys') social status and employment prospects, says fatherhood researcher Michael Lamb. Some fathers of children with disabilities feel inferior, says Lamb. They get less pleasure from their children, and "they end up with fewer reminders of their own value." Overall, Israeli researcher Malka Margalit and her colleagues found, fathers of children with disabilities derived less satisfaction from family life, perceived fewer opportunities for independence, personal growth, and intellectual and recreational activities for their children, and had less confidence in themselves than fathers whose children were not disabled.

How (and how well) you and your partner cope with a disabled or chronically sick child depends on a fascinating collection of factors.

- **When you become aware of the condition**. The earlier the condition comes to light, the easier it is for parents to begin to cope. It's harder for parents to acknowledge a problem with a child who seemed perfect for a while (which is often what happens with children on the autism spectrum, who are rarely diagnosed any earlier than eighteen months of age).
- **How obvious the disability is**. Fathers, according to Michael Lamb, generally feel more scrutinized by society, which makes them particularly sensitive to any perceived "imperfections" their child might have, especially visible ones (including Down syndrome).
- **Birth order**. Fathers tend to be more involved with firstborn children who have a disability than with ones born later.
- **The type of condition**. Physical or mental disability seems harder for parents to adjust to than chronic illness.

Parenting with a Disability

In the United States alone, there are more than four million parents who have one or more disabilities, which may have been congenital or caused by stroke, spinal cord or brain injury, multiple sclerosis, cerebral palsy, or something else. If you're a dad with a disability, you probably want to do everything in your power to be there for your child, to protect her, keep her safe, and ensure that she grows up to be a fantastic adult. But in addition to any challenges your disability itself may pose, there are a number of other obstacles that may interfere with your ability to be a parent. The most tragic of these is government regulations.

The Americans with Disabilities Act (ADA) was designed to protect the rights of people with disabilities and to ensure that they're treated fairly in all situations. However—and this is a really big *however*—nearly three dozen states have laws on the books that allow them to terminate your parental rights simply because you have a disability, even without any evidence of abuse or neglect on your part, according to the National Council on Disability (ncd.gov). NCD and the Christopher and Dana Reeve Foundation have published a booklet, *Parenting with a Disability: Know Your Rights Toolkit*, that's filled with extremely important and valuable information and resources. (You'll find information for downloading the booklet in the Resources section of this book.)

- **The sex of the child**. Sadly, since a lot of parents (especially fathers) have higher expectations for their sons than their daughters, they may react more negatively to a boy's disability or chronic condition than to a girl's. Families with an intellectually disabled son, for example, often have more problems than families with an intellectually disabled daughter.
- **The couple's relationship**. Couples who are more content with each other and who have more social support are more likely to have favorable reactions to kids with disabilities than those who aren't as stable, according to Roopnarine and Miller.
- **How the father's parents respond**. Acceptance of the child with a disability by the father's parents has a big influence on how well the father himself accepts the child.
- **Whether you join a support group or not**. Men who get involved with other fathers of children with disabilities feel less sadness, fatigue, pessimism, guilt, and stress, and have more feelings of satisfaction and success, fewer problems, and better decision-making abilities than dads who don't join groups, according to researchers Patricia Vadasy, Rebecca Fewell, and their colleagues.

There's no question that having a child with a disability or chronic illness puts a lot of stress on the entire family. Conflict, tension, and even divorce are more common in families with a child with a disability. That's why it's especially important for you and your partner to get as much support as possible and that you communicate with each other constantly. When one parent backs off, that leaves the other parent with twice the burden. If your friends are able to step in, that'll certainly help. But you absolutely must explore every other possible resource.

Start by getting some couples therapy. Then check with your child's pediatrician, parent support groups, and your local school district (yes, your child is too young for school, but schools typically know about resources.) Exceptional Parent (eparent.com) has a ton of information, opportunities for support, and resources for parents and families of children with disabilities. You'll find links to more information in the Resources section of this book.

Your child's disability will undoubtedly have an impact on how you treat her. You may respond by being overprotective, or you may be more lenient and lax with setting limits and enforcing them. Try not to do either, if you can. Naturally, you'll need to adapt to your child's individual capabilities, but remember this rule: as with any child, if you treat her as though she's weak and fragile, she'll grow up thinking of herself in exactly those terms.

Keep in mind that while having a child with a disability will be challenging, it doesn't have to be a negative experience. Most families get great pleasure out of

Coping with the Death of a Child

Losing a child is every parent's worst nightmare, something no one who hasn't experienced it can possibly imagine. A child's death can bring up feelings of grief, anger, denial, and even guilt at not having been there enough or inadequacy at not having been able to prevent the death.

Researcher Wendee Kim Schildhaus studied how couples adapt to and cope with the loss of a child and keep their marriage alive. She found that, as in most areas of parenting, men and women cope with the loss of a child differently. Women had two basic coping mechanisms: one was to focus on the surviving children, if any; the other was to use support systems. Men did what men usually do: they tried to ignore their feelings, and they dove headlong into their jobs. The rationale for that kind of approach, as several of the men I interviewed said, is that since they'd failed in their societally approved role as protector of the family, they knew they could at least succeed at being a breadwinner. Unfortunately, that isn't an effective way of coping with grief—either in the short or the long term. "Grief will change you," advises Amy Hillyard Jensen, author of *Healing Grief*. "But you have some control over whether the changes are for better or worse."

Men, traditionally, are brought up to be tough, strong, competent, knowledgeable, and in control of their emotions. Weakness—especially tears—is discouraged. Anger and frustration are okay, but sadness and pain are not. This kind of socialization is very effective in a lot of ways. But when we face an emotional upheaval such as the loss of a child, too many of us have no idea how to react.

Dawn Hawthorne, a researcher and professor at Florida Atlantic University, and her colleagues found that grieving fathers tend to isolate themselves from friends and family, while grieving mothers talk more about the death with others. Instead of acknowledging our grief and dealing with it, we men ignore it. Instead of getting help, we pull away from the people closest to us. (The fact that dads try to cope on their own may explain Hawthorne's findings that religious and spiritual activities seem to be more effective in helping men than women.)

The results of isolation and denial can be dangerous. "If feelings are left buried, they cause prolonged turmoil, bitterness, family problems, and even ill health," writes *Healing a Father's Grief* author William Schatz. Jiong Li, a researcher at the University of Aarhus in Denmark, and his coauthors found that parents who lose a child are far more likely than other parents to commit suicide or die in an accident. In the case of mothers, the likelihood of dying of cancer or infectious disease is also higher.

Besides being devastating to the parents, losing a child can also destroy the marriage itself. But it doesn't have to. Wendee Schildhaus identified a number of factors shared by couples who adapted to their loss and stayed together. These couples:

- Accept different ways of grieving and allow each other space in the relationship without making judgments. Men and women accept each other's individual style.
- Believe in and utilize a support network, asking for help when it's needed, accepting when it's offered.
- Focus on their other children.
- Focus on their work and career.
- Agree that the death of their child was the most tragic loss imaginable and that the thought of losing their spouse too is unbearable.
- Develop new friendship networks that include other parents who have lost children.
- Get therapy.
- Keep the memory of the deceased child alive.
- Communicate with each other.

DON'T TRY TO SPARE YOUR PARTNER

Many parents who have experienced the loss of a child spend more energy, with the best of intentions, trying to spare their partner increased grief than worrying about themselves. It turns out that this approach might actually make things worse. Margaret Stroebe and her colleagues at Utrecht and VU universities in Amsterdam interviewed more than two hundred couples who had lost a child and asked each individual how much they agreed with statements such as, "I stay strong for my partner," "I hide my feelings for the sake of my partner," and "I try to spare my partner's feelings." Those attitudes are part of what Stroebe calls partner-oriented self-regulation (POSR), and while a lot of us believe that POSR will help protect our partner, it backfires, increasing not only our own grief but also our partner's. To start with, repressing your own feelings makes it harder for you to work through your grief, which you're going to have to do in order to heal. At the same time, your partner may misinterpret your stoic behavior as a sign that you aren't grieving or that you've already forgotten your child (neither of which is probably true), and she may end up feeling as though she's alone in her grief (which is also probably not true).

raising such a child, and many even go out of their way to adopt one. In addition, several studies have shown that children with disabilities may have a positive effect on families, says Michael Lamb. At least one researcher found that some fathers reorder their priorities to put their family first, discover new values, and experience personal growth as they adapt to their children's disabilities.

YOU AND YOUR PARTNER

Communication

One of the most common traps new parents fall into is that they stop communicating—or at least change the way they do it. Half the time these changes are permanent, according to researchers Jay Belsky and John Kelly. Here are some factors Belsky and several other researchers have identified as contributing to the problem:

- "A new child deprives a couple of many of the mechanisms they once used to manage differences," says Belsky. For example, a couple that had disagreements about who did what around the house might solve the problem by getting a housekeeper. But with a toddler around the house, strained finances might not allow for a cleaning person, which means you'll have to deal with the once painless who-does-what disagreements.
- The lack of spontaneity. Before your baby was born, if you wanted to go to a movie or just sit around and talk, you could just do it. But now, as parents, you don't have that luxury. If you want to go out, you have to get a sitter a day or so in advance, make sure the baby is fed, and be back at a certain time.
- Physical exhaustion. Your toddler may now be sleeping through the night, but having a child around can be incredibly tiring. So even if you and your partner stay home together, there's a better than even chance you'll be too tired to stay awake for an entire conversation.
- There's a general decline in intimacy-promoting activities such as sex, getting together with friends, and so forth.
- With so much time and energy focused on your toddler, you and your partner may find that your pool of common interests is shrinking fast.
- There's a lot less time and money left to pursue individual interests and activities outside the home. As a result, many new parents find that their communication skills have "rusted." They don't have nearly as many new things to talk about, and they've lost (partially, at least) the ability to hear and understand each other.

- If you or your partner has left the workplace, you've lost a rich source of conversational topics; there are now a lot fewer stories to tell about people at the office.

Here are some things you and your partner can do to keep (or get) communication on track:

- **Get a family calendar**. This can keep double-booking and scheduling miscommunications to a minimum.
- **Set aside at least fifteen minutes a day to talk about things other than your child**. It's harder than you think. See "(Re)Learning to Talk," below, for more.
- **Go out on dates (with your partner, of course)**. Spending time alone with your partner is absolutely critical to the long-term health of your marriage. Get a sitter if you can, or ask friends or relatives to step in. You might also want to set up an informal babysitting cooperative with a few other parents in your neighborhood; they need to get out as much as you and your partner do.
- **Do something special for each other**. But be flexible and understanding. If you've made surprise plans, and your partner is too exhausted to go through with them, it doesn't mean she doesn't love you. Try again another night, or put the "surprise" on the calendar.
- **Schedule sex**. It sounds terribly unromantic, but just having the big _S_ on the calendar may actually make it more fun, adding the excitement of anticipation. Besides, if you're still interested, this may be the only way it's going to happen. Weekdays may be out, but if you use your weekends wisely, you should still be able to rechristen every room in your house.
- **If your partner is at home with your child during the day, try to give her some time every day when she can be completely alone and doesn't have to take care of anyone but herself**. If you're the primary caretaker, do the same for yourself.
- **Don't blame your toddler for your troubles**. Too many couples interpret their communication problems as a sign that their child pushed them apart and that they shouldn't have become parents.
- **Talk to other people**. Talk to other couples with kids to find out what they've been through, what works, and what doesn't. You might also join a new parents' or new fathers' group.

(RE)LEARNING TO TALK

"I get the picture sometimes of two people who may be very much in love and very much together, having private dreams that shape their lives, but not letting each other know the content," writes fatherhood researcher Phil Cowan, coauthor of *When Partners Become Parents*. Frequent, open, and honest communication is "the key to an effective transition from couple to family," he adds. But because so many couples seem to forget how to communicate, let's go over the basics:

- **Open your mouth**. Although many men have been socialized to think that we don't have strong feelings or emotional needs, this obviously isn't true. Nevertheless, many men are reluctant to talk to their partners about their needs and feelings, fearing that they'll seem weak in the eyes of their partners and will be letting them down.

- **Now close your mouth and open your ears**. One of the most widespread stereotypes about men and women is that women are more open than men about discussing their feelings and emotions. If your partner is a natural talker, great. But plenty of new mothers need some gentle, supportive encouragement. "A great deal of needless suffering goes on because mothers and fathers are ashamed to express feelings they have that seem 'unmotherly' or 'unfatherly,'" writes Phil Cowan. So encourage her to talk, ask her about her deepest feelings about the baby, tell her you love her, reassure her that you'll be there for her.

- **Speak the same language**. Sounds silly, but it's not. Some of the biggest communication breakdowns come because people don't (or can't or won't) agree on the definition of some very basic words. For example, does the word *love* mean the same thing to you and your partner? Do the two of you show your love for each other in the same way? Probably not. Men commonly express love for their partners and other people by doing things for them (which may be how the whole "good provider" thing got started). Women, however, are more likely to express their love verbally. Unfortunately, most people want to be spoken to in their own language. Consequently, what you do may not be loving enough for your partner, and what she says may not be enough for you. Learning to express—and accept—love differently is like learning a new language. Granted, it's a little more complicated than high school French, but it can be learned.

Here are some ground rules for putting your communication skills to work:

1. **Schedule a special time and place for your discussions**. Let's face it: if you can't have sex without a calendar, you won't be able to have a serious conversation without one either.

2. **Tell her what's on your mind**. Tackle one issue at a time, and stay away from phrases like "You always," "You never," or any others that start with an accusation or an attempt to blame your partner for something. Those are guaranteed to put a quick end to your conversations. You'll also have more

productive conversations if you use *I* more than *you* (such as, "I feel angry when I don't get phone messages," rather than "You never tell me when someone has called for me.")

3. **Ask her to tell you what she heard you say**. It isn't enough to just say, "I understand what you're saying." It's important to have your partner tell you in her own words what you've just told her.

4. **Confirm for her that she heard you correctly**. Tell her what you said again if she didn't.

5. **Go back to step 2 but switch roles: she talks, you listen**.

6. **Listen—really carefully**. Most people use the time in a conversation when they aren't talking to plan out the next thing they want to say, the next killer point that will score big and maybe win the argument. The problem with that approach is that scoring isn't worth much in a marriage. And while you're busy plotting, your partner is saying something that you really should hear.

7. **Learn to compromise**. Understanding each other's concerns is a great place to start, but it doesn't do much good if you can't figure out how to bridge the gaps.

8. **Get some professional help if you need it**. Set up a monthly or quarterly appointment with a marriage counselor to give you and your partner a safe place to discuss your relationship, differences, problems, worries, and so forth.

"All parents fight."

FIGHTING CAN BE A GOOD THING

Parenting approaches are the source of just about as many marital spats as money and division of labor. Naturally, you should avoid having huge fights in front of your children. Kids are scared and confused when their parents yell at each other, and researchers have found that the angrier the parents, the more distressed the children.

But this doesn't mean that whenever the kids are around, you and your partner always have to see eye to eye (or at least seem to). In fact, just the opposite is true: "Children of parents who have regular and resolved fights have higher levels of interpersonal poise and self-esteem than those whose parents have chronic unresolved fights or those whose parents appear not to fight at all," writes psychologist Brad Sachs.

Children can also learn plenty from watching their parents disagree—provided they do it civilly. Seeing you and your partner handle your disagreements respectfully will encourage your children to do the same. It may also help them learn some negotiation and bargaining skills that will come in handy when they are trying to communicate their point of view to others. So let your child see you and your partner squabble about easily resolvable things, and schedule weekly or, if necessary, daily meetings away from the kids to discuss the bigger issues.

Big or small, if you do ever have a disagreement in front of your child, pay close attention to how you make up afterward. "It is probably useful for young children to observe how adults renegotiate their relationship following a squabble or moments of hostility," child psychologist and educator Lilian Katz advised in her *Parents* magazine column. "These observations can reassure the child that when distance and anger come between her and members of the family, the relationship is not over but can be resumed to be enjoyed again."

GO AHEAD, GET ANGRY

Don't go too far out of your way to avoid fighting with your partner. As odd as it sounds, a little spousal fighting now and then may actually be good for you. Internalizing your anger for long periods can cause all sorts of problems, including ulcers, high blood pressure, and depression. And if you don't let off a little steam now and then, your anger can come out in more subtle ways. "The phone message that we forget to deliver to our partner, the medicine we forget to give to the baby, the check we forget to deposit," writes Brad Sachs, "can all be passive aggressions directed against our spouse when we're afraid of what we're feeling."

Still Wild (or Mild) after All These Months

WHAT'S GOING ON WITH YOUR TODDLER

Physically

- No longer content just to walk forward, your toddler can now walk backward and sideways. He may even be able to run. (Well, sort of: it really looks more like a clumsy, straight-legged speed walk.) And as his ability to balance on one leg at a time improves, so does his ability to climb stairs.
- He can kick a ball without stepping on it and can, at long last, throw overhand.
- He can draw a pretty good straight line, brush his teeth, and even wash and dry his hands (although he may not want to).
- As his hand-eye coordination improves, your toddler loves piecing things together. He does simple puzzles (the kind where each piece fits in a separate hole) and can build some pretty impressive towers, five or six blocks high. He'll also put blocks, Duplo, or Lego pieces together to make long, straight walls. There's still room for improvement; when using a toy hammer, he finds it nearly impossible to keep the head of the hammer straight, and more often than not it lands sideways.
- He's getting really good at undressing himself. But his dressing skills are still largely confined to not squirming for a few seconds and allowing you to slip something on him. He may be able to put his shoes on, but they'll often end up on the wrong feet.
- He's experimenting with using forks and spoons but probably not the way you'd hoped. He holds his fork in one hand, picks up a piece of food, and pushes it onto the tines with the other. His liquid-handling skills are getting better,

though: he can pour water from one container to another without spilling much, and can drink from a cup without completely drenching himself.

- He's doing better at turning the pages of a book but may still tear them.

Intellectually

- Although he's made major intellectual advances over the past eighteen months, your toddler is still a fairly egotistical little creature, believing that he's the source of all action. Child psychologist Selma Fraiberg beautifully describes the typical toddler's attitude toward the world: "The magician is seated in his high chair and looks upon the world with favor. He is at the height of his powers. If he closes his eyes, he causes the world to disappear. If he opens his eyes, he causes the world to come back. . . . If desire arises within him, he utters the magic syllables that cause the desired object to appear. His wishes, his thoughts, his gestures, his noises command the universe."

- Despite his self-centered view of the world, your toddler is becoming aware of the ownership of objects. He can (but may not want to) distinguish between *mine* and *yours*.

- His sense of object permanence is becoming more sophisticated, and he now anticipates where objects "should" be. If a ball rolls under the couch, for example, he'll run to the back of the couch, knowing the ball will be there soon. And as you pass the gas station down the block from your house and turn onto your street, he'll begin to get excited, knowing he's almost home.

- Your toddler is developing a mind of his own and is increasingly negative and contrary: the first word out of his mouth in any given situation is usually *no*, he'll refuse to do almost anything you ask, and he deliberately dawdles when he knows you're in a hurry. For a toddler to do just the opposite of what you want him to do "strikes him as being the very essence of his individuality," writes Selma Fraiberg. In the right mood, though, your toddler may be able to follow two-stage directions, such as "put down that crystal vase and back away from the table."

- He still has some difficulty with time concepts: *now*, *later*, *yesterday*, and *tomorrow* mean nothing to him. But he can now identify several colors by name, and he recognizes himself in the mirror.

Verbally

- At about eighteen months, your toddler's passive vocabulary (the words he understands) will start growing by a word or two every day. By twenty-one months, his active vocabulary (the words he can say) will kick into overdrive, and he'll learn as many as five new words every day. Once he can say fifty to sixty words (not including animal sounds, or air-raid siren and airplane imitations), he'll start experimenting with two-word (and possibly three-word) sentences, such as "Up me" or "Down me."

- He now makes a serious effort to repeat what you say, using a kind of shorthand. For example, if you say, "No, you can't pour your milk on the floor," he'll probably reply, "Pour milk floor." Language expert James Britton has found that toddlers repeat the words that carry the most information, while omitting the less important ones.
- He's learning about *what* and *why* and will frequently ask you to identify unfamiliar (and sometimes quite familiar) objects. And when you're reading to him, he'll name every object or character on the page.
- Kids this age are beginning to grasp the concept of pronouns and can make subtle distinctions: "Don't hit *him*" is different from "Don't hit *her*."
- For the first time, your toddler is capable of engaging in "conversation." Instead of responding physically to your questions (by going somewhere, pointing to something, or doing something), he may use words.

Emotionally and Socially

- He still has some trouble telling the difference between inanimate objects and people, and he treats other toddlers accordingly—poking, hitting, biting, and pushing them. This kind of behavior usually is not hostile, though; he's just learning some valuable lessons about actions and reactions.
- Although he's expressing some interest in interacting and socializing with other kids, your toddler prefers to play alone, pausing once in a while to defend his property rights or to snatch something away from a "playmate." He may even hide his toys so other kids won't be able to play with them. Despite his seeming lack of interest, he's learning a huge amount by imitating his friends (and they, presumably, are also learning from him).
- He loves cuddling, and he will hug and kiss you (and his favorite toys) frequently.
- If they haven't already, this is about the time when girls discover their vagina and boys their penis. Boys may even get, albeit rarely, an erection. Genital exploration is absolutely normal for kids this age, and every attempt should be made not to make a big deal of it (see pages 255–57 for more on this topic).
- He knows what he wants, and you'll see plenty of tantrums when he doesn't get it.
- Your toddler may exhibit an early interest in toilet training by occasionally letting you know when he has a wet or soiled diaper. But it's going to be a while before he's ready to use the toilet.

WHAT YOU'RE GOING THROUGH

Being Rejected by Your Toddler

One of these days, you're going to run to comfort your crying toddler. Yes, you've done it before, but this time it'll be different. This time, instead of running to meet you, he'll see you and scream, "No! I want Mommy!" or "I hate you" or "You're a bad daddy!" There's not really anything I or anyone else can say that will make you feel any less rejected or despised when those horrible words pop out of your child's mouth. The first time (and the tenth and the twentieth) my older daughter said something like that to me, I nearly cried. And those feelings came flooding back as each of my other children went through the same phase.

Remember, though, that your child has no idea that he's hurting you with words. Feelings are still something new to him, and he may just be experimenting to see how you'll react. Rather than withdraw completely or punish your child (even subtly) for wounding you, here are a few possible approaches:

- **Acknowledge that your child is upset**. Say something like, "You're really mad, aren't you?"
- **Reassure him that you love him**.
- **During a calm moment much later, talk with him a little about how it feels when your feelings are hurt**. But don't go on too long about this; the last thing

*"When I was your age, things were hard
for my dad when he was my age."*

you want to do is put your child in charge of your self-esteem (or make him feel as though he is).

- **Try some sarcasm**. Saying, "Yep, you're right. I'm the world's worst father, and everyone hates me," may shock your child so much that he'll rush to your defense.

Eventually, you'll learn to ignore (or at least pay less attention to) your child's slings and arrows. And you'll find that things have a way of coming full circle. When my middle daughter was about eighteen months old, she went through a stage when she wouldn't let me put her down. In fact, she wouldn't let anyone else—my wife included—come near her. On one occasion, after I'd been carrying her around for about eight hours straight, my legs and shoulders had gone completely numb and I needed a break. So I told my daughter I was going to take her to Mommy for a while and did exactly that. The handoff went fairly well, but the moment I turned to walk away, my daughter shrieked, "Daddy! Help me, Daddy! Save me!" I'll admit it: that felt wonderful.

Why Bother Being an Involved Father Anyway?

At some point in his life, every father asks himself whether his priorities are in the right order, and one of the biggest issues he'll think about is whether he's spending enough time—or could it be too much?—with his family. On pages 103–5, I talk about the costs and benefits of fatherhood. But here, let me give you some very compelling reasons to stay (or get) as involved as possible.

IT'S GOOD FOR YOUR CHILD

- He'll have better friendships. Three-year-olds who have positive relationships with their fathers have better friendships when they're five. The more negative the father-child relationship, the worse the quality of the kids' friendships.
- He'll be cooperative and self-reliant. Children whose fathers regularly look after them during infancy and the toddler years are more self-disciplined and have better social skills than those whose fathers spend less time alone with them, according to Kay Margetts, a researcher at Melbourne University in Australia. And researcher Karin Grossman and her colleagues found that "sensitive and challenging father-child play at two years predicted teenagers who were more comfortable with uncertainties and complexities, were less likely to seek reassurance from others and less likely to withdraw in the face of frustration and adversity."
- He'll have an easier time separating from Mom. From the time your child is eighteen months old until he turns three or so, you—and only you—are gently

helping him safely and securely separate from the intense dependency he has on his mother. "Healthy though dependency on their mother is for children at the beginning of their life," says child psychiatrist Kyle Pruett, "they will not experience, let alone practice, their own competence and mastery skills if they do not strike off in search of their own physical and emotional autonomy."

- He'll develop better problem-solving skills. The combination of a father's more interactive play style and his less immediate support in the face of frustration helps kids adapt to new situations or things, explore the world more vigorously, stick with difficult tasks longer before giving up, and become more competent problem solvers.
- He'll be smarter. Sons of nurturing fathers score higher on intelligence tests than boys whose fathers are less involved. And children of both sexes who grow up without involved fathers have more trouble solving complex math problems than kids whose dads are involved.
- It sets a good example. By being involved, you're demonstrating that both men and women can nurture. It shows young boys that being an involved father is something to aspire to when they grow up, and it shows young girls the kind of involvement they should expect from the father of their children.
- Your child will have fewer problems as a teen. The biggest predictor of whether a girl will take up sports or be physically active is having a father who plays with her (wrestling, playing ball, shooting hoops, whatever) when she's young. Adolescent girls who are involved in sports are less likely to drop out of school, get pregnant, develop eating disorders, put up with abusive relationships, smoke, drink, or develop breast cancer as adults. I know your child isn't even two yet, but hey, it's never too early to start thinking about these things.
- He'll be a more empathetic adult. Several long-term studies have found adult men's and women's levels of compassion and empathy depend more than anything else on how involved their fathers were during the toddler years.

IT'S GOOD FOR YOUR PARTNER AND YOUR RELATIONSHIP

- You'll be more committed to making your relationship work. Men think about marriage and family differently than women do. For men, "family" tends to mean a mother, a father, and some kids. As a result, once a man becomes a father, he also becomes very committed to keeping his family together. That way of thinking explains, to some extent, why after divorce men remarry sooner and more often than women. Women, however, can imagine themselves parenting without a man around and still consider themselves part of a family. That goes a long way toward explaining why about 75 percent of divorces are initiated by women.

Issues for Adoptive Fathers

Adopted children and their adoptive fathers develop in very much the same ways as biologically related fathers and kids.

Perhaps the biggest adoption-related issue at this stage is whether and how to tell a child that he's adopted. Your child won't be able to understand what adoption—let alone conception and birth—means until he's at least five or six. He may be able to tell you that babies come from mommies' tummies, but he doesn't really know how they get there in the first place. Adoption expert Gordon Finley tells a great story about a family with a three-and-a-half-year-old adopted child that went to the airport to pick up a newly adopted infant. "For a long period after," he writes, "whenever the family passed an airport, the oldest would point to the airport and talk about how that is where babies come from."

Many—but certainly not all—adoptive parents experience feelings of inadequacy at not having been able to produce their own children. By the time their children reach the toddler years, though, most adoptive parents have put aside their feelings about infertility, and they've shelved their fantasies of having a biological child. Instead, they're "coming to see themselves as they really are, the eminently entitled and very 'real' psychological parents of their adoptee," writes Finley.

But the thought of telling your child about the adoption can bring back any negative feelings about adoption—the infertility, self-doubt, conflicts with your spouse. Throw in a little fear that the birth parents might change their minds and you might lose the child, and you can see why this could be a very stressful time.

That said, many experts suggest talking about adoption and using the word *adoption* from the very beginning. There are lots of kids' books that deal with adoption, and you can even talk about the puppy or kitten you adopted. Again, your toddler is much too young to understand, but he's also too young to understand what love is and you've (hopefully) been telling him that you love him since day one. Adoption—like your love for your child—isn't a one-and-done conversational topic. The idea is that your child should grow up knowing that it's okay to talk about adoption and to ask questions.

IT'S GOOD FOR YOU

- You'll be less depressed. Constance Hardesty and her colleagues found that low levels of paternal involvement can lead to depression. In other words, higher levels of involvement may promote mental health in men.
- You'll have a longer, healthier life. Involved fathers suffer fewer accidental and premature deaths, less-than-average contact with the law, less substance abuse, fewer hospital admissions, less depression, and a greater sense of well-being overall, according to Joseph Pleck and other researchers. (For more on your health, see pages 154–55.)
- You'll be a more effective parent. Researcher Mary De Luccie did a fascinating study of 177 firstborn boys and girls in an attempt to figure out what made dads get involved and feel satisfied. She found that it was a kind of loop: fathers who were warm and firm with their kids felt they were doing a good job and thought they had good relationships with their kids. That, in turn, made them want to get even more involved. It just keeps getting better and better.

YOU AND YOUR TODDLER

Play

As your toddler gets closer to his second birthday, three major play-related developments occur, usually in rapid succession:
- He learns to play with others his own age.
- He learns to play alone.
- He learns to tell the difference between what's pretend and what's real.

PLAY WITH PEERS

If your child has been thinking of himself as the center of the solar system, he certainly considers you and your partner to be nearby planets, orbiting around him contentedly. But just recently he's realized that there are other objects floating around out there. And some of them seem to be stars—just like him.

A few months ago, your baby would have completely ignored a child playing nearby, unless the other child snatched one of his toys. But at the ripe old age of eighteen months or so, he's suddenly paying very close attention. He's not quite ready to actually play with other children, but he's extremely interested in everything they do. Researcher Kimberlee Whaley found that when a baby is in a room with his parent and another child, he pays more attention to the other child than to the parent. It's at about this age that toddlers start to realize that they may have more in common with one another than with their parents.

Benefits and Costs of Involved Fatherhood

I realize that it may sound like I'm telling you that being an involved dad is wonderful and fantastic and incredible every single minute. Well, it's not. The truth is that being a dad, just like anything else, has its ups and downs. It can be the greatest thing you'll ever do, and it can be the most frustrating. It creates opportunities for growth and fun but interferes with others. Below I've summarized many of the benefits and costs associated with being an involved dad. It's based in part on fatherhood researcher Rob Palkovitz's findings, as well as my own interviews with hundreds of fathers. We'll talk more about some of these themes in later chapters.

BENEFITS

- You're extending your family line, passing on your name and your genes; your children are your legacy.
- You gain satisfaction from watching your children grow and develop. You know that your teaching has made a difference in their lives, and you find joy in their accomplishments.
- You have a sense of pride. You feel that what you're doing is right, that you've achieved something meaningful by investing in your children's development. This feeling comes whether or not you get compliments from others on how great a dad you are or how great your kids are.
- You receive love. In a sense this is your compensation for being an involved dad. You get to be needed, loved, admired, and appreciated, and it feels great. This may explain why Finnish researcher Laura Pulkki-Råback and her colleagues found that dads are somewhat less likely to use antidepressants than men who aren't fathers.
- It's an opportunity for personal growth—in maturity, self-discipline, role modeling, and emotional expressiveness.
- You experience a shift in perception, an expansion of your sense of self. You're less goal-oriented, less driven, and more interested in the family.
- It's fun. Your kids give you all sorts of excuses to express joy, to experience life as a child again, to play and do things you'd probably never do without a child (go to a playground or the zoo, crawl around on the floor, collect baseball cards, go to G-rated movies).
- It's a chance for continued learning. You may develop skills and interests you never had before, just to keep up with your kids. You can also brush

continued on page 104

Benefits and Costs of Involved Fatherhood
continued

up on some of the subjects you'd forgotten long ago or learn some of the ones you never got around to in the first place.

- It gives life meaning. Having kids may give purpose and direction to an otherwise ordinary life.
- It may make you a better employee. Researcher Jamie J. Ladge and her colleagues found that "the more time fathers spend with their children on a typical day, the more satisfied they are with their jobs and the less likely they want to leave their organizations. Further, they experience less work-family conflict and greater work-family enrichment."
- It may enhance your marriage. Some men feel that having kids makes their marriage better, giving Mom and Dad a shared focus in life and in their children's accomplishments. Not surprisingly, a lot of women agree.
- It may make you healthier. Psychologist Rosalind Barnett has found that involved dads "are less likely to have chest pain, insomnia, fatigue, indigestion and dizziness." Being a dad may also inspire you to get more exercise and eat better.

COSTS

- Time. For some men, time is a metaphor for freedom or the opportunity to focus on themselves. Having kids requires giving up freedom to do what you want while you're with them. You may have to give up activities that brought you pleasure. (Although the opposite can be true: I rekindled an interest in martial arts when my middle daughter started taking karate.) You also may spend a lot of time thinking about your children when you're not with them. According to a report by the Pew Research Center, only 44 percent of working adults with children say they have enough free time to do the things they want to do, compared to 70 percent of those without children.
- Sacrifice. You may have to defer satisfying your own goals and dreams, putting off career advancement or continued education in order to be the good provider. This tends to be much more common among men who became fathers young.
- Lifestyle. You'll probably live in a different place, drive a different car, take different vacations, and maybe even have a different job than you would have if you hadn't had children.
- Finances. Again, a more common worry among younger dads. It costs a

lot—an average of about $250,000—to raise a child from birth through age eighteen. That includes food, childcare, transportation, medical expenses—including deductibles, toys, clothes, and so on.

- Marital closeness. You'll probably spend less private time with your partner. There'll be less time for physical and/or emotional intimacy, or even to talk over important issues.
- Energy. There's the sleep loss of early fatherhood, then the physical exhaustion of chasing a toddler around, then more sleep loss when you start worrying about a sick child, grades, friends, sex, drugs, and alcohol.
- Potential. All that time and energy you put into being a father is time and energy you could have devoted to writing a book, directing a movie, painting a masterpiece, finding a cure for cancer...
- Loneliness or isolation. This is especially common for stay-at-home dads, who don't usually have a support network or group of other guys they can get together with to discuss fatherhood, babies, or even the latest football scores.
- Lower self-esteem. Again, especially common among stay-at-home dads. Some of these men feel that because they aren't working outside the home, they aren't productive members of society anymore. And some worry that spending so much time with their children has made them less intellectual and might even have shaved a few points off their IQ.
- Health. Researcher Craig Garfield and his colleagues found that men who become fathers put on weight, increasing their body mass index (BMI) by an average of 2.6 percent (which works out to about four and a half pounds for a six-foot-tall guy) compared to non-dads. "The more weight the fathers gain and the higher their BMI the greater risk they have for developing heart disease as well as diabetes and cancer," says Garfield. Many dads go to the doctor even less than they did before they had kids, despite advancing age and all that goes with it.
- Kids grow up and don't need you as much. A lot of the meaning in your life will come from your relationship with your kids. If that relationship changes or gets strained, as it is likely to do as your child grows up and seeks independence, you may mourn the loss of meaning.
- You get spread out. All the demands on your time and energy leave you feeling like there isn't enough of you left.

It's going to be a while yet before your toddler has mastered the art of sharing. But there are a few things you can do to help him grasp the concept.

- **Show him how it's done**. If you're peeling an orange for yourself, give him half and tell him what you just did—something as simple as, "Daddy's sharing his orange with Bobby."
- **Talk to him about what belongs to whom**: Daddy's cell phone, Mommy's laptop, Aunt Ida's alligator purse.
- **Have duplicate toys**. If your toddler has regular playdates with another child, there'll be a lot less fighting if each one has the same toy.

PLAYING ALONE

Ordinarily, being ignored isn't considered a compliment. But if you and your toddler are together, and he wants to spend some time playing by himself, consider yourself praised. If he wasn't absolutely sure he could count on you to be there in an emergency, he'd never take his eyes off you.

The capacity to be alone is a critical sign of emotional maturity, says English pediatrician and psychoanalyst D. W. Winnicott. And when your child reaches this milestone, your role as a father, as usual, needs to be adjusted in response to his growth and development. "Toddler learning now depends in part on the

A Few Equipment-Buying Tips

- Make sure anything you buy for your child can be used easily. For example, if you have a mini basketball hoop, make sure the child—not just you—can hit a few jumpers. If it's too high, he'll get frustrated and quit.
- Chairs should be wider at the bottom than at the top to reduce the chance of their tipping over. They should also be low enough that a toddler can get up and sit down without having to ask for help.
- Tables should be high enough to fit comfortably above your child's knees while he's sitting on his chair.
- Be aware of your attitude about gender roles. Most toddlers will naturally gravitate toward gender-stereotypical toys, although the gravitation is helped along by parents, who generally discourage boys from playing with dolls and gently steer girls away from playing with trucks. Parents may also tend to furnish kids' rooms along gender lines: ballerina bedspreads and frilly curtains for girls, Spiderman bedspreads and dinosaur curtains for boys. In later chapters, we'll talk more about gender stereotyping and what you can do to avoid it.

freedom a child is given to explore the environment," says Kimberlee Whaley. "There is now a shift from adult as participant to adult as audience."

One very important thing you can do is minimize the amount of time your child spends cooped up in a playpen. The more time he's in it, the less time he'll be out exploring. Of course, safety should always be your top priority, and if your toddler is in the playpen to keep him from doing something dangerous, let him stay there.

Although your toddler may be playing alone, he'll often accompany himself by singing, humming, laughing, or squealing. The bottom line is that he's just begun to discover some of the wonderful things his spry young body can do, and it feels incredibly good. And anything that makes him feel good enough to squeal is certainly worth doing again.

PRETEND PLAY

Toddlers come prewired with a healthy imagination, and you should encourage your child's pretending any way you can: play imitation games, act out stories with your child and his toys, pretend to take a nap and use him as a pillow, or write a script and film your own movies. As it turns out, toddlers who do a lot of pretend play are more creative when they start school, have more advanced language skills, are less impulsive and better able to tolerate frustration, are better at sharing, and frequently become leaders in their peer groups, according to Yale psychologists Jerome and Dorothy Singer. So the next time your toddler starts talking into a carrot as though it were a telephone, grab a piece of broccoli and get in on the conversation.

Making Music

"In general, the more you and your child have become actively involved in music … the more your child's attention span and appetite for music will increase," writes music educator Edwin Gordon.

Even if you haven't done much more than sing a couple of lullabies or leave the radio on a few hours a day, you'll notice that your child has become a much more active music listener than he was in his first year. He clearly recognizes familiar songs and tries to sing along. At this age, he won't be able to get more than a note or two—usually the last one in the song or phrase, such as the O in "E-I-E-I-O," for example. But he's delighted to be able to do even that.

By the time he's about two and a half, he'll add the first few notes and an occasional short phrase in the middle of a song as well (all of "E-I-E-I-O," perhaps, or maybe even, "Yes, sir. Yes, sir. Three bags full"). And by his third birthday, he'll be putting all the pieces together and doing entire songs.

Here are a few things you can do to encourage your child's musical development:

- **Sing**. If you haven't done so already, make singing part of your everyday routine. Since your child is taking a more active role in singing, select songs that are short and repetitive, and change your focus from singing *to* your child to singing *with* him. If you can't think of any songs, set the words of a favorite book to music, making up a melody if you have to. Encourage him to make up his own songs and have him teach you the words or melody. Don't expect perfect

Thinking Music

Ever since you were just a few years old, you've been able to summon up images of objects or people, or imagine words and sentences or entire conversations without actually speaking a word. That's what thinking is. In music, the same basic process is called audiation. "To audiate is to hear and comprehend music that is not physically present, just as to think is to hear and give meaning to language, the sound of words not physically present," explain Richard Grunow, Edwin Gordon, and Christopher Azzara in *Jump Right In.* Just as you can't develop as a person without thinking, "without audiation, no musical growth can take place," they add.

Sound complicated? It really isn't. Think of all those times you haven't been able to get a particular melody out of your head, or the times you've taught someone else a song without looking at the music or listening to the CD. That's audiating.

One of the best things you can do to help your child build his audiating skills is to expose him to music without words. Because language development receives so much emphasis in our culture, the words of a song may distract your child from being aware of the music itself. In the case of kids with limited language skills, the words can actually slow down musical development. If a child's language "has not developed well enough to sing the words of the song," writes Gordon, "she may not attempt to sing the song at all."

Please remember that as important as it is to expose your child to music, having the stereo or your playlist going twenty-four hours a day isn't necessary or helpful. Learning to listen to and appreciate silence is important too. It's during periods of silence that your child has the opportunity to exercise his developing powers of audiation by remembering, thinking about, and experimenting with the music he's already heard.

pitch from your toddler. Although a few kids this age are able to sing in tune, most can't.

- **Go for variety**. Toddlers respond to the mood of the music they hear. Scary music will frighten them, happy music will get them onto the dance floor, and slow or sad music will slow them down. Look for music with dramatic changes—fast and slow, loud and soft, high and low, stop and start. The original *Fantasia* soundtrack is wonderful for this. If you'd like a little help selecting music, several companies produce sets of developmentally appropriate CDs or DVDs that are aimed at children but that you'll like too (and may even be able to put on your Spotify, or other, playlist). Two are listed in the Resources guide.
- **Let him make his own music**. He already knows plenty about percussion instruments, but if you have a guitar around the house, let him strum the strings while you finger the chords. Or get a few easy-to-blow whistles.
- **Forget the ulterior motives**. Despite what you might hear about the "Mozart effect," music isn't going to make your child any smarter. But it's a great way for the two of you to spend time together having fun.
- **Watch**. Just a few months ago, your child's arm and leg movements seemed almost random. But now, just before his second birthday, he has adopted his very own, unique rhythmic gestures—shaking, wiggling, half-crouching, or bouncing up and down—that are different from those of every other child his age. As before, your child's movements—which now come in groups of three to seven "pulses"—may not seem to have much to do with the music he's hearing. They are, however, definitely in response to the music and are internally very consistent, meaning that you can almost set your watch by the pulses.
- **Let him do what he wants**. The way your child moves to music is an expression of some primal part of his personality. So don't tell him how to move or show him new routines or move his arms or legs for him. That's the surest way to stifle his budding self-expression.

Keep on Reading

DEALING WITH BOREDOM

After reading the same book six times at a single sitting (or several hundred times over the course of a few months), you might find yourself less than completely enthusiastic about reading it again. If (when) this happens, spice things up by making some deliberate mistakes in the text, just to see whether your toddler is on the ball: switch characters' names, say "in" instead of "out," and so forth.

YOUR ATTENTION, PLEASE

The average almost-two-year-old's attention span is about three minutes, so try to get in at least three or four reading sessions every day. But be prepared: the range varies enormously. When my oldest and youngest daughters were this age, they could easily spend an hour listening to me read, but at the same age the middle one wouldn't sit still for more than thirty seconds at a stretch. Please also remember that attention span is not an indication of intelligence. Despite her seeming indifference, my middle daughter still ran around the house most of the day demanding to be read to and still managed to memorize at least as many books as her seemingly more attentive peers.

ADDING TO YOUR LIBRARY

If your child is still interested in the same books that you've been reading to him for the past year, don't worry. And don't push him to give up old favorites. This doesn't mean, though, that you can't slip in a few new titles every once in a while. Big hits for this age group include books that introduce numbers, sizes, shapes, colors, opposites, and special concepts (*up, down, in, out*), and discuss body parts. Below is a short list of some of my favorites that are developmentally appropriate for this age. As mentioned earlier, we'd love to hear your favorites too. Our contact info is on page 293.

FAVORITES

Across the Stream (and many others), Mirra Ginsburg
Can't You Sleep, Little Bear? Martin Waddell
Caps for Sale, Esphyr Slobodkina
Each Peach Pear Plum, Janet Ahlberg and Allan Ahlberg
The Family Book, Todd Parr
Fuzzy Yellow Ducklings, Matthew Van Fleet
Golden Bear, Ruth Young
A Good Day, a Good Night, Cindy Wheeler
Holes and Peeks (and many others), Ann Jonas
How Do I Put It On? Shigeo Watanabe
I Can, Helen Oxenbury
Jump, Frog, Jump, Robert Kalan
Little Gorilla, Ruth Borenstein
Lunch, Denise Fleming
Make a Wish, Midas, Joan Holub
Mouse Paint, Ellen Walsh
Owl Babies, Martin Waddell

Peekaboo Kisses, Barney Saltzberg

Planting a Rainbow (and many others), Lois Ehlert

Quiet Night, Marilyn Singer

Superhero Dad, Timothy Knapman

Ten, Nine, Eight, Molly Bang

Where Does the Brown Bear Go? Nicki Weiss

Who Hops? Katie Davis

Yummy Yucky, Leslie Patricelli

CONCEPTS

Becca Backward, Becca Frontward: A Book of Concept Pairs, Bruce McMillan

Cold Little Duck, Duck, Duck, Lisa Westberg Peters

Counting Kisses, Karen Katz

Duck and Goose, 1, 2, 3, Tad Hills

My Big Animal Book, Roger Priddy

On Market Street, Arnold Lobel

One Woolly Wombat, Rod Drinca and Kerry Argent

White on Black, Tana Hoban

Yellow Bird, Black Sun, Steve Light

(For more concept books, see pages 165 and 225.)

POETRY AND RHYME

A Child's Garden of Verses, Robert Louis Stevenson

Jamberry, Bruce Degen

Rainbow in the Sky, Louis Untermeyer, editor

Wake Up, Big Barn! Suzanne Tanner Chitwood

(For more poetry books, see pages 40, 166, and 226.)

FAMILY MATTERS

Tantrums

WHAT CAUSES THEM

Almost all kids of this age group begin having regular tantrums. They start in some cases as early as twelve months but most frequently between fifteen and eighteen months.

One of the major causes of tantrums is the frustration that results from the child's inability to use his limited verbal skills to express his specific needs and

A Few Fun, Educational Activities for Kids This Age

Of course, just because your child is starting to take an interest in other kids, enjoys being alone, and is developing an imagination, it doesn't mean that your days of playing together are over. Not even close. Your toddler still needs you, and you'll be his favorite toy for quite some time. Here are some fun activities you can do together:

- **Play games that emphasize letter, number, color, or size recognition**. Shape sorters are excellent for this. So are matching games. Cut postcards in half and have your child match the halves. Or, in a more advanced version, match playing cards.
- **Play games that involve digging, pouring, building, and destroying**. The more your child does these things, the more he's learning about how different materials respond or how the same material might respond in different situations. If he's playing at the beach, for example, he'll be able to make steeper mountains out of wet sand than dry.
- **Play games that emphasize abstract thinking**. Get a bunch of identical containers with tops (plastic yogurt containers work very well) and put in each one a different substance or item: sand, rice, Cheerios, water, and so on. Put on the lids and then shake the containers (or have your child do it himself) and ask him to guess what's inside.

wants. In other words, there is a disconnect between what he wants to say and what's he's actually capable of saying. Generally speaking, the more verbal the child (hence the better able to explain his needs), the less he'll be frustrated and the fewer tantrums he'll have. Many kids, however, are also frustrated by their body's inability to respond to their mind's rather sophisticated requests or desires.

Either way, frustrations build up over the course of a day or two until the child finally is no longer able to control himself and explodes. He may scream, cry, throw himself on the floor, kick, bite, or even hold his breath until he passes out. Just to put this into perspective, consider this: nearly 15 percent of twelve-month-olds and 20 percent of twenty-four-month-olds have two or more tantrums every single day.

Besides frustration, of course, a variety of other factors may account for tantrums:

- Your child is trying to assert himself. He may feel he's lost your attention and will do whatever it takes to get it back.

- **Take a nature walk**. Pick up things and discuss them. You'll be amazed at the variety of stuff that's just lying around and at the variety of educational opportunities. (Picking up a leaf, for example, can spark a great discussion about colors and shapes. And, if your child is interested, about how nutrients get from the root of the tree to the leaves and about the difference between deciduous and evergreen trees.) Activities like nature walks also encourage observation skills, and you'll probably find that your child is spotting a lot more interesting things than you are.
- **Cook**. Make simple edible recipes together, or just make some Oobleck—a kind of moldable dough: mix together 1 pound cornstarch, 1½ cups cold water, and some food coloring until smooth. Besides teaching all sorts of great things—measuring, textures, how things change shape and form when heated or cooled—cooking with your child will subtly teach him some valuable lessons about men's and women's roles in society. But best of all, it's a lot of fun. (See pages 238–44 for more on cooking with kids.)
- **Build a fort out of chairs and blankets**. Learn about structure, balance, privacy, light, and dark.
- **Relax**. Don't forget to build some downtime into your schedule. Read, draw, do puzzles, or even just watch your tropical fish swim around.

- Your toddler wants to explore and wander all over the place. You want to keep him safe and alive, which sometimes means restricting his movements.
- He may be frightened at how angry his frustrations make him and may be trying to attract your attention, hoping you'll help him regain control over his life and emotions.
- Illness, hunger, exhaustion, or overstimulation.
- Too much discipline. You may have set too many limits or laid down too many rigid or inconsistent rules.
- Not enough discipline. You may have imposed too few rules or established erratic or inconsistent limits. Tantrums may be, in a sense, a plea for more effective limit setting.
- Imitation. Do you get upset when you don't get what you want?
- They work. If a tantrum has been successful in the past, it might just work again…
- Temperament. Low-frustration-tolerance, slow-adaptability kids (see below,

pages 118–25, for a discussion of temperament) are much more susceptible to tantrums. This susceptibility can also result in parent-child personality clashes.

- Family stress. Divorce, separation, or even a major change in your or your partner's work schedule or lifestyle can be tough for kids to deal with.

WHAT TO DO ABOUT TANTRUMS

When your child is in the midst of a tantrum, he's no longer a member of the human race, and reasoning, shouting, hitting, or punishment will have little if any effect. Here are a few things that may work to minimize the tantrum and its effect on everyone:

- **Don't panic**. That's exactly what your child is trying to get you to do. If you get upset and rant, you'll only make things worse.
- **Use humor**. Say something completely silly. If that doesn't work, get down on the floor and thrash around in your own tantrum. This may help snap your toddler out of his own tantrum by showing him how ridiculous a tantrum looks.
- **Walk away** (assuming that your toddler is in a place where he can't hurt himself or anyone around him). In many circumstances, no audience equals no performance.
- **Stand firm**. If the tantrum is the result of some disciplinary measure, tell your child that the rule still stands and will continue to do so until he calms down.
- **Time-out**. If things are really getting out of hand, put the child by himself someplace safe and explain (privately) that he won't be able to be with other people until he calms down. Again, the no-audience-equals-no-performance theory applies here. Limit time-outs to one minute per year of age.
- **Explain**. Say things like, "I know you're upset because you really wanted to read that story."
- **Protect your child**. Kicking, swinging, and throwing things can hurt not only other people but your toddler as well. Holding him firmly but calmly often quiets an out-of-control kid.
- **After the tantrum, reassure the child that you're still there for him, that you still love him, and try to figure out what caused the problem**. But do not reward him for stopping.

WHAT NOT TO DO

- **Don't shout**. Any big reaction proves that the tantrum was the right approach.
- **Don't try to argue with a kid who's in the middle of a tantrum**. You'll be wasting your breath.
- **Don't impose physical punishment**. Another waste of time, since your child isn't usually in control of the tantrum anyway.

- **Don't give in**. Doing so offers kids conclusive evidence that tantrums do, indeed, work.

HOW TO PREVENT TANTRUMS

There's nothing you can do to prevent tantrums completely. But there are a few preemptive steps you can take that should greatly reduce the frequency and severity of these little outbursts:

- **Be a reliable source of help and support**.
- **Know—and pay close attention to—your child's temperament** (see pages 118–25). This is extremely important to do and will help you in every interaction with your toddler. Don't try to force an irregular child to be regular or a slow-to-warm child to warm quickly.

Public Tantrums

Sometimes I'm absolutely convinced that my children subscribed to some kind of special, underground podcast filled with super-secret techniques kids can use to drive adults nuts. And I'm sure one of the most popular features is, "Tantrums in the Produce Section and Twenty-Five Other Surefire Ways to Embarrass Your Parents into Giving You What You Want NOW!" In addition to the techniques described above, there are a few special methods for handling public tantrums:

- **Speak softly**. Bend over and whisper in your child's ear that if he doesn't stop right now, you and he are going to leave the area immediately. If that doesn't work, pick him up and do what you said you'd do.
- **Seek isolation**. Take the child to the bathroom, outside, to the car—anywhere you and he can be more or less alone.
- **Ignore the audience**. You'll be mortified at what your child is doing—and even more mortified at what spectators will think you're doing to him. If your child is particularly theatrical, he's liable to attract quite a crowd. Given that you're a dad, there's a good chance that everyone who walks past you and your screaming toddler will offer some absolutely brilliant piece of advice. A lot of these advice-dispensers don't even have children. If the peanut gallery gets overly aggressive or hostile, famed pediatrician T. Berry Brazelton suggests that you ask for volunteers to take over for you. You'll be amazed at how fast the crowd will disperse.
- **Impose consequences**. When you get home or to some other private place, tell your child that since he had a tantrum, he won't get dessert.

Breath-Holding, Passing Out, and Other Spectacular Variations

Starting at about eighteen months, toddlers who have finished in the top 10 percent of Tantrums 101 are invited to get advanced training, this time in how to scare the hell out of their parents by holding their breath and passing out.

The bad news about breath-holding is that it's incredibly frightening. (How could a child's turning blue and keeling over not be?) But the good news is that besides taking ten years off your life, it isn't all that dangerous. What usually happens is that the child starts to cry, takes a huge breath—and holds it. If he holds it long enough, he may lose consciousness, but the moment he does, he'll start breathing immediately and will usually recover within thirty to sixty seconds.

Somewhere between 1 and 20 percent of children have at least one breath-holding episode. The frequency peaks at around two years of age, and most kids will outgrow the behavior by age four or five. In a small number of cases—if, for example, your child seems drowsy for ten to fifteen minutes after coming to, or if he turns blue *while* unconscious instead of *before*—he could be having a true seizure. For that reason, the first time your child has a breath-holding episode, take him to see his pediatrician. Again, it's probably nothing to worry about, but it's worth letting the doctor know.

So why do kids really hold their breath? "When all else seems to fail in battling for control," temperament researcher Jim Cameron told me, "holding one's breath becomes the ultimate stronghold—no one can make you breathe."

Breath-holding is more common among active, intense, slow-adapting toddlers (see pages 118–25 for more on these temperament traits). According to Cameron, "The more energetic [children] are, the less they want to stop what

- **Give your child plenty of opportunities throughout the day to let off steam—** physical play, running around, and so forth—as well as some occasional periods without rules (or with as few as possible).
- **Encourage your child to talk about the things that make him angry**. And be supportive and empathetic when he does.
- **Make sure your child gets enough food and sleep**. Shortages of either can make kids cranky and more susceptible to having tantrums.
- **Think carefully before you say no**. Is what you're rejecting really that big a deal? Your giving in—perhaps partially, with some conditions or time limits— can give kids more control, thus reducing the "need" to throw a tantrum.

they're doing or to shift to things you want them to do." In addition, since active kids spend more time practicing large motor skills (running, crawling, and so on) than other kids, the joy of doing these things is greater. They also may be a little behind in verbal skills, which makes it harder for them to argue with you.

In some cases, advanced tantrum throwers may opt for banging their heads against something or screaming so intently that they make themselves vomit. Just about all you can do to keep these episodes from happening is to try to avoid the kinds of confrontations that precipitate them. But there's no guarantee that even that will work. If your child has started holding, or trying to hold, his breath, or has added head banging or vomiting to his repertoire, start with the dos and don'ts listed on pages 114–15 and add the following:

- **Give him extra time to adjust to change**. Instead of one ten-minute warning, give notice at ten, five, three, and one minute.
- **Don't react intensely to your child's reactions**. If your child has vomited, clean him up as matter-of-factly as possible. The bigger your reaction, the more likely your child will make breath-holding or vomiting a regular part of his routine. Also, don't become overly permissive out of fear of triggering another episode.
- **Talk, talk, talk**. Encourage your child to use words. As frightening as these fits are, they won't last forever. The more verbal your child becomes, the faster they'll fade.
- **Do not attempt to "shock" your child back to reality by slapping him or throwing water in his face**. Instead, hold your child.

- **Compromise as much as possible**. Offering a firm "two more minutes" gives the child a lot more control than insisting that he immediately do what you want him to do. If possible, set a timer and have your toddler start it. That way, when the buzzer goes off, you're not the bad guy, the timer is. But following your two-minute warning with a five-minute warning and then not going anywhere for fifteen minutes after that tells your child that you're an easy mark and that what you say is meaningless.
- **Avoid yes/no questions and open questions**, such as "Which pair of socks do you want to wear?" Give choices instead: "Do you want the red ones or the blue ones?"

- **Compliment good behavior regularly**. Tell your child you understand that doing some things is hard and frustrating, and that you appreciate his efforts.

Give clear, concise warnings. "Daddy and Mommy are going out later, and Grandpa will be babysitting. We'll be here when you wake up." Or, "Five more minutes, then we have to start cleaning up." Again, setting a timer helps a lot: "When the buzzer goes off, we'll have to . . ." Temperament

You've been watching your child grow and learn for more than a year now, and you've seen him develop a unique personality and his very own way of reacting to the world. Actually, *develop* may be the wrong word. If you think back to when your child was just a few months old, there's a good chance that you'll see that the way he is now—how loud, sensitive, curious, active, independent, emotional, and moody—is pretty much the way he's always been.

Way back in the 1950s, a husband-and-wife team of psychiatrists, Stella Chess and Alexander Thomas, developed a theory that children are born with a set of fundamental behavioral and emotional traits, which they called "temperament." Your child's temperamental characteristics determine whether he'll be "easy" or "challenging," and the way they blend together makes him different from every other child. You've got a unique temperament too. And what Chess and Thomas refer to as the "goodness of fit" between yours and your child's goes a long way toward setting the tone for your relationship with each other.

Over the decades, temperament theory has been expanded and refined by many researchers. Some even disagree completely with Chess and Thomas and suggest that what makes up a person is more "nurture" than "nature." Either way, it's important that you accept your child's (and your own) temperament. Immediately below, you'll find a brief overview of what each temperament trait is all about; on pages 120–21 is a quiz (based on the rating scale suggested by the Oregon-based Center for Human Development) that will help you determine the traits that best fit your child. Then, on pages 122–25, you'll find a thorough discussion of each characteristic.

1. **Approach/Withdrawal**. How your child reacts to new experiences: meeting new people, tasting new foods, going to sleep in a new place, and so on.
2. **Adaptability**. Similar to Approach/Withdrawal but deals with how well your child transitions as well as his longer-term reactions to changes in routines or expectations, new places, or new ideas.
3. **Intensity**. Your child's overall volume level, when both happy and unhappy.
4. **Mood**. Your child's general outlook—wildly excited, serious, or something in between—over the course of a typical day.

5. **Activity level**. Your child's overall preference for active or quiet play and his overall energy level throughout the day.
6. **Regularity**. The day-to-day predictability of your child's basic biological functions: hunger, sleep, and filling diapers. Each should be rated on its own scale.
7. **Emotional Sensitivity**. How your child responds emotionally to a situation. This trait has two subcategories (which often but not always go hand in hand): one for sensitivity to his own feelings and one for sensitivity to others' feelings.
8. **Sensory Awareness**. How sensitive your toddler is to pain, touch, taste, smell, hearing, and sight. Each category is rated on a separate scale. Note: It's quite possible for a child to be highly sensitive in some areas and insensitive in others.
9. **Distractibility**. The ease with which your toddler is distracted by all the sights, sounds, smells, and everything else happening around him.
10. **Persistence**. Similar to Distractibility, but goes beyond the initial reaction and concerns your child's ability to focus and the length of time he will stick with something—even when the task gets hard.

Now complete the quiz on pages 120–21. This brief evaluation should give you a pretty good sense of your child's temperament, how he'll react in different situations, and what you need to do to be the most effective parent. Chances are, he'll have one or two predominant traits, but most kids have a mix of more than one.

Now go through this evaluation again, this time rating yourself. How do the two of you compare? Where are you most similar? Where are you furthest apart? Areas where you and your child are very different are ripe for conflict.

For Readers of *The New Father: A Dad's Guide to the First Year*

If you read the previous book in this series, you already know a little about your child's temperament. But don't skip this section. The nine basic temperament traits we covered in that book are very similar to the ten presented here. The difference is that because your child's emotions are so much more sophisticated than they were a year ago, I've taken the advice of the folks at the Center for Human Development in Oregon and divided the Sensitivity category into two related but separate categories: Emotional Sensitivity and Sensory Awareness. So spend a few minutes going over the trait descriptions and taking the test on pages 120–21. Again, because your child is far more sophisticated than he was a year ago, the rating system is too.

Trait	Rating				
Approach/ Withdrawal	1	2	3	4	5
	Jumps right in			Slow to warm	
	What is your child's first and usual reaction to new people, situations, and places? Does he jump right in or hang back and observe for a while?				
Adaptability	1	2	3	4	5
	Easygoing			Strong-willed	
	How quickly does your toddler adapt to new ideas, new places, changes in routine or schedule, or even simple interruptions?				
Intensity	1	2	3	4	5
	Mild reactions			Dramatic reactions	
	How loud or physically dramatic is your child when expressing strong feelings?				
Mood	1	2	3	4	5
	Happy-go-lucky			Serious, displeased	
	Is your child primarily an optimist or a pessimist? Lighthearted or serious?				
Activity Level	1	2	3	4	5
	Calm and slow-moving			Wild and quick-moving	
	Is your child a "wiggler" or a watcher? Does he jump up and dance to music, or does he rock in place? At night, does he sleep like a rock or spin around like a propeller?				
Regularity Hunger	1	2	3	4	5
	Wants food at same time every day			Has irregular eating schedule	
Sleep	1	2	3	4	5
	Tired on schedule			No schedule	
Toileting	1	2	3	4	5
	BMs at same time every day			Try to guess	
	Does your child normally eat, go to bed, wake up, and have bowel movements at the same time every day?				

Trait	Rating				
Emotional Sensitivity Own feelings	1 Unaware of emotions	2	3	4 Feels emotions strongly	5
Others' feelings	1 Doesn't notice others' feelings	2	3	4 Highly sensitive to others' feelings	5
	Does your child often get upset over nothing, or does he rarely get upset, even when circumstances suggest that he could? Does your child feel sympathy or empathy for others?				
Sensory Awareness Pain	1 What nail in my foot?	2	3	4 *Eeeoowwwwhh!*	5
Touch	1 No reaction to contact	2	3	4 Easily irritated or pleased by contact	5
Taste	1 Can't make distinctions	2	3	4 Notices tiny variations	5
Smell	1 Doesn't notice odors	2	3	4 Human bloodhound	5
Hearing/Sound	1 Noise is no problem	2	3	4 Sensitive to sounds	5
Vision/Lights	1 Visually insensitive	2	3	4 Visually sensitive	5
Distractibility	1 Not easily diverted	2	3	4 Easily diverted	5
	Is your child very aware of and easily distracted by noises and people? Can you distract him from upset feelings by redirecting his attention?				
Persistence	1 Hard to stop	2	3	4 Gives up easily	5
	Does your child stick with things even when frustrated? Can he stop an activity when asked to?				

The Ten Temperament Traits of Toddlers

APPROACHING TODDLERS	WITHDRAWING TODDLERS
• are the opposite of shy	• are usually shy
• lack fear in potentially dangerous situations	• need time to get used to new situations
• may be friendly with strangers	• say they don't like things before even trying them
• separate easily from parents; may get lost in crowds or stores	• may be picky—eating only certain foods, playing only with certain toys
• may be impulsive	• usually have difficulty separating from parents
• approach new situations with great interest	• show fear in seemingly safe situations
	• hesitate before investigating strange sounds
	• stand back and watch when first entering a playground
FAST-ADAPTING TODDLERS	**SLOW-ADAPTING TODDLERS**
• are usually fairly compliant	• often refuse to go along with almost anything
• fall asleep easily and wake up happy	• need time to adjust to transitions and new ideas
• tend to go with the flow when faced with something new	• like to follow their own agendas, and can be bossy and stubborn
• may lack assertiveness	• may be quick to anger and slow to get over being angry
• like change and may get easily bored	• get "locked in" on what they are doing
• have little or no trouble getting used to new situations or people	• protest loudly against taking medicine
• may give into peer pressure later in life	• may have trouble getting to sleep in unfamiliar places

LOW-INTENSITY TODDLERS

- are hard to read—they have emotions, but they are difficult for others to notice
- may seem apathetic
- are sometimes mistakenly viewed as uninvolved, low in motivation or intelligence

HIGH-INTENSITY TODDLERS

- wear their hearts on their sleeves—you know exactly what they're feeling all the time
- shout instead of speaking and may scream so loudly it hurts your ears
- have intense reactions—good or bad—to new toys

POSITIVE-MOOD TODDLERS

- are rarely bothered by anything
- are often described as happy-go-lucky
- may lack seriousness
- tend to trust easily
- may be easily taken advantage of
- expect goodness/success

NEGATIVE-MOOD TODDLERS

- are often grumpy, cry often and easily, and frequently seem angry, depressed, or disappointed
- may be skeptical and expect the worst
- extend trust slowly
- complain when given a bath
- don't like traveling in a car or stroller

LOW-ACTIVITY TODDLERS

- may take a long time to complete tasks
- may avoid activities that require a lot of physical energy
- may dislike active games
- are attracted to low-key or quiet sports and activities
- may nag parents to entertain them
- absorb a lot of information by watching quietly

HIGH-ACTIVITY TODDLERS

- are often extremely active—running wildly, talking incessantly
- are usually *not* clinically hyperactive
- may be aggressive during play
- are often fidgety, squirmy, or restless
- may, however, be able to sit quietly in front of a video or TV for an extended period
- have to be watched carefully to prevent accidents
- are attracted to sports and activities that involve a lot of running around

continued on page 124

The Ten Temperament Traits of Toddlers

continued

HIGHLY REGULAR TODDLERS	IRREGULAR TODDLERS
• may be easy to potty train • love regular eating and bedtime schedules and resist changes to the routine • are so regular you can almost set your clock by them	• may be difficult to potty train • may not be hungry at meals, but want food at a different time every day • have highly irregular sleep/nap patterns • have bedtime struggles due to irregularity in sleep patterns
EMOTIONALLY LOW-SENSITIVITY TODDLERS • rarely display emotions • can be "instigators" who like to start a little trouble now and then • can be budding con artists who enjoy manipulating a situation to their advantage • can have what seems to be a mean or cruel streak • are often oblivious to others' feelings • don't seem bothered by others' insensitive behavior	**EMOTIONALLY SENSITIVE TODDLERS** • tend to be fearful • get upset when teased • are sensitive to how others are treated • seem particularly tuned in to others' feelings • may worry a lot • may cry easily • may be "people pleasers" • get their feelings hurt easily
LOW-SENSORY-AWARENESS TODDLERS • may have dull senses • may miss a lot of things going on around them—they just don't seem to notice • may have excellent concentration and aren't easily distracted • are able to fall asleep anywhere, anytime • are willing to try new foods	**HIGH-SENSORY-AWARENESS TODDLERS** • may have sharp senses • may be distracted by sensory input • can be picky, finicky, or particular about food, clothes, lighting, and everything else • sometimes complain about things others don't notice, such as temperature changes or itchy clothes

LOW-DISTRACTIBILITY TODDLERS	HIGH-DISTRACTIBILITY TODDLERS
• tend to stick with tasks until they are completed • often have terrific memories • may become caught up in their own world, not noticing things going on around them • can be excellent naggers who challenge their parents' ability to not give in • when upset, can be calmed by only one or two people	• have short attention spans • notice things easily • may have trouble concentrating on complex tasks • may leave belongings scattered everywhere • tend to be forgetful • when learning something new, will stop when hearing people or sounds
HIGH-PERSISTENCE TODDLERS	**LOW-PERSISTENCE TODDLERS**
• rarely give up on difficult tasks • take on challenges well beyond their skill level • sometimes persist at things that are unimportant • may tend to do things the hard way because they don't like to ask for help • may take things too seriously • may be perfectionists • may have long attention spans • may want to stick with a game long, long, long after you're ready to quit	• are frustrated easily, even by simple tasks • may throw tantrums in response to frustration • if interrupted, won't return to original task • may get angry and give up • may demand help from parents, grandparents, and other caregivers • may struggle to master self-care skills such as toilet training and dressing • tend to stick with things they're naturally good at and can look highly persistent when not frustrated • tend to "let go" easily • won't play in the playground for more than five minutes at a stretch

What Are Daddies Made Of?

WHAT'S GOING ON WITH YOUR TODDLER

Physically

- Now that your toddler has fairly good control over her legs, she's going to use them all the time. She runs (but still has some problems slowing down and turning corners), jumps forward with both feet, kicks a ball without stepping on it, rarely falls anymore, stands on her tiptoes, climbs and goes down stairs by herself (holding on to a railing), can push herself along in a toy car, and may even be able to pedal a small tricycle. Just about the only thing she can't do with her legs is use them to get herself started on a swing.

- She really wants to dress and undress herself but may not be quite able to do the job alone. Clothes that have larger head openings and looser pant legs will relieve some of her frustration.

- And she hasn't forgotten about her arms and hands: she draws nicely controlled straight lines, can fold paper if you show her how, throws a ball into a basket, makes beautiful mud pies, spends hours opening and closing screw-top containers, can turn doorknobs (so watch out), puts together more complex puzzles, and still has time to stack, pile, tear, and pour anything she can get her hands on. She can even unzip her pants (but can't zip them up) and put her shoes on (but can't lace them).

- She especially loves to pick up and examine tiny things, and her hand-eye coordination is good enough now that she can successfully maneuver a bobby pin or a fork into an electrical outlet. This is an excellent time to go through your house, yet again, to make sure it's properly childproofed (see pages 48–54).

Intellectually

- Although time still doesn't mean much to her, she's learned about sequences (*first* we'll put on our shoes, *then* we'll go for a walk), and can differentiate between *one* and *many* (although she'll probably say "two" for anything above one).
- She knows all about bigger and smaller now, and she's expanding her knowledge of spatial concepts—stuffing herself into boxes, climbing (or being held) as high as possible, pouring things back and forth. She also knows the difference between circles, squares, and triangles, and can even identify objects and people from upside-down pictures.
- She now thinks through possible solutions to problems instead of physically acting them out. For example, if an object is out of reach, she won't jump up to get it and probably won't try to knock it down with a stick. Instead, she'll bring a chair over, climb up, and grab what she wants.
- She's learning to tell the difference between animate and inanimate. She spends a lot of time staring at and comparing objects that move by themselves (dogs, people, fish) and those that need some outside intervention (blocks, bikes).
- She still has a tendency to regard everything—animate or not—as her personal property, but has a rudimentary understanding of *yours* and *mine*.
- She also deliberately imitates your every activity (sweeping, washing dishes, brushing teeth) but only while you're there with her.

Verbally

- Your child is using longer, more complex sentences and is beginning to use language in situations where she once used emotions. For example, she'll ask for desired objects by name and may say "Change my diaper" instead of crying.

Ownership Rights

Although it'll be a while longer before your child completely masters the concept of *yours* and *mine*, she's already able to understand the basic idea. In one study, researchers Hildy Ross, Ori Friedman, and Aimee Field gave toys to a number of two-year-olds and told them that they (the toddlers) were the owners. Those children were much more likely to claim ownership (by saying "mine" or by grabbing) of "their" toys than of the toys that were "owned" by another toddler. They were also much more likely to return a toy that had been labeled as the property of another child than one they believed was theirs.

- She also delights in the power that naming objects gives her and labels everything she possibly can. She's also discovering some of the *wh-* words—*where, what, who, why, when*—and may use them to jump-start conversations.
- She likes nursery rhymes, and if you pause for a few seconds, she'll fill in the last word of a familiar couplet ("Hickory, dickory, dock / The mouse ran up the ____"). And if you're reading a familiar book and make a mistake, she won't let you get away with it.
- She's tightening her grasp on pronouns, correctly using *I, me, his,* and *hers*. But she may get confused when trying to use two pronouns in the same sentence: "I want to do it yourself," for example.

Emotionally and Socially

- The contrary, negative temper-tantrum phase is passing, and your toddler is getting more cheerful and more cooperative. She'll come when you call her and may even put away some of her toys (if you ask really, really nicely and make it worth her while by turning it into a game).

Peer Pressure Starts Early

Most people think of peer pressure as an adolescent thing, but it actually starts in children as young as two. And, as it turns out, humans are more likely to give in to peer pressure than chimpanzees. Daniel Haun, a researcher at the Max Planck Institute for Evolutionary Anthropology, and his colleagues gave two-year-old humans, chimps, and orangutans a simple task: drop a ball into a box that was divided into three sections. Only one of those sections delivered a treat. It didn't take long for the participants of all three species to figure out how to get the treat again and again and again. Then Haun and his colleagues had the original subjects stop and watch several peers dropping balls into a box and getting treats—but the peers were dropping their balls into a different section. When it was the first group's turn again, the chimps and orangutans ignored the "peer pressure" and went right back to dropping their balls into the original section. The humans, however, changed the box they were selecting to the one their peers had been dropping the ball into—even though they stopped getting rewarded. "We were surprised to find that children as young as two change their behaviour to avoid the potential disadvantage of being different," wrote Haun.

- Nevertheless, she's still easily frustrated, often to tears, by the internal conflict between independence and dependence. She still walks away from you but comes flying back for reassurance that you're still there; she truly wants to please you by doing the "right" thing, but still needs to test your limits by disobeying.
- Perhaps as a result of this conflict, your toddler is also developing a lot of fears of things she may have loved before: night, dogs, bugs, vacuum cleaners. She may also be getting more fearful of things that she was only slightly afraid of before: loud noises, big trucks, and people (especially doctors). See pages 64–73 for more on fears.
- She's getting more and more curious about other people, especially fellow toddlers and babies, and may play with them for a few minutes. But you're still at the top of her A list.
- She may be getting a little bossy and likes ordering people around ("Go away!" "I don't like!" and so on).
- She's developing a wider range of emotions and is now quite affectionate with her friends, family, stuffed animals, and even pictures in books. She loves to "baby" her toys (and even parents), covering them with blankets and putting them to "bed." Her whole body lights up when you praise her, and her feelings are genuinely hurt when you criticize her.

WHAT YOU'RE GOING THROUGH

Your Changing Identity

There's an old saying in the Talmud that a man has three names: the one his parents gave him at birth, the one that others call him, and the one he calls himself. A person's identity, according to the rabbis, is a rather amorphous thing. What the rabbis don't talk about is that all three of those names are subject to change over time—especially the one you call yourself. The way you view yourself today may have nothing to do with how you'll see yourself tomorrow.

This point is nicely illustrated by a study conducted by family researchers Phil and Carolyn Cowan. Over a period of nearly two years, the Cowans asked a large number of men to create a pie chart and divide the circle up into sections that reflected how important each aspect of their life actually felt—not simply the amount of time they spent in the role.

Over the duration of the study, "Men who remained childless showed a significant increase in the 'partner/lover' aspect," the Cowans reported. "New fathers, however, were squeezing 'partner/lover' into a smaller space to accommodate the significant increase in the 'parent' piece of the pie."

As the parenting slice grows, other things happen too. Here are a number of ways that the men in my research (and several other studies as well) have said fatherhood changed them. (We'll talk about the emotional changes fatherhood brings on pages 187–88.)

- **Confidence and pride**. Having a close relationship with your child helps build her confidence and self-esteem. It also helps build yours. Being able to stop your child's tears, making her laugh, or knowing how much she idolizes you can make you feel incredibly competent, and the pride you feel when you see all the great things she can do becomes confirmation that you're doing pretty well at this whole dad thing. For a while, at least, your child is going to share all your tastes—in music, literature, movies, art, career, politics, and food (as long as it's not too spicy). A lot of these things will change as your child grows up. Still, I can hardly describe the feeling of pride I get when my kids start discussing Hitchcock movies with my adult friends, belt out a few Janis Joplin lyrics, or turn on Elgar's cello concerto while they're doing their homework. But beware. Confidence and pride are often made of a pretty thin veneer: any misbehavior—especially public—and you may suddenly feel as though you've failed as a father. (See pages 152–53 for more on this topic.)

- **Patience—and a better sense of humor**. Things are going to go wrong whether you like it or not, and you have two choices: take everything seriously and try to change the world, or roll with it and have fun. Learning to laugh at yourself can rub off in other areas and may also make you more understanding of the mistakes other people make.

- **Flexible thinking**. At this point, it's almost impossible to tell the difference between your child's needs, your needs, and your partner's needs. In a perfect world they'd mutually reinforce one another. But on this planet, the three often compete for your time and energy. As you get more experienced as a parent, you'll get better at preparing for the future and coming up with contingency plans. You'll also learn the incredibly valuable skill of being able to see a variety of different points of view at the same time. For example, most new parents say that having children brought them closer together. At the same time, though, they say that they devote so much time to their children that they hardly have any left for each other.

- **A return to childhood**. Having kids gives you a terrific opportunity to reread all those great books from when you were a kid and disappear back into the worlds of *King Arthur* and *The Hobbit*. It also gives you a rare chance to say words like *poop* and *pee* in public again. As film director Tim Burton put it after he became a father, "I'm rediscovering the joys of burping and farting, yes, and the humor therein."

- **Creativity**. A lot of parents suddenly get inspired to create. A. A. Milne (who wrote the *Winnie the Pooh* books) and J. K. Rowling (of *Harry Potter* fame) are just two who wrote for their kids. If you're giving your child music or art lessons, you might develop a talent you never thought you had or get hit with the urge to perform at school talent shows.
- **Reordered priorities**. Having kids contributes to a heightened awareness of others' perspectives, says Rob Palkovitz. A lot of guys admit that they were somewhat selfish and self-centered before becoming dads. This isn't necessarily a negative thing—it's simply an acknowledgment that having people depend on us, and putting their needs before our own, isn't something that comes naturally to most of us before we become parents. What's especially interesting is that, according to Palkovitz, getting married doesn't trigger this same realization.
- **Changed values**. Becoming a father will prompt you to take a long, hard look at your fundamental beliefs and values. Things you may have thought were harmless when you were younger, such as being careless with money or material possessions, having promiscuous sex, and even experimenting with drugs, look completely different now that you've got a family to support. You'll start seeing the world in different terms. You may have thought about issues like pollution, terrorism, energy policy, interest rates, AIDS, poverty, climate change, and even cloth vs. disposable diapers before, but now, instead of being abstract things that happen to other people, they're possible concerns or threats to your child and your family. Having children may also help you clarify many of your beliefs. Teaching your child to say that the candidate you didn't vote for in the last election is a jerk is one thing. But try explaining to your child—in terms she can understand—what war is, what the death penalty is, or why some people are rich while others live on the street. You might find yourself changing your mind about a few things, now that they affect your family. Fathers whose first child is a daughter are significantly more likely than dads of sons or of second-born daughters to support female candidates and gun control, according to University of Massachusetts, Amherst, researcher Elizabeth Sharrow and her colleagues.

In 1998, NPR radio host Terry Gross did an interview that beautifully illustrates the idea that fatherhood can change your values. Her guest, T. J. Leyden, works for the Simon Wiesenthal Center at the Museum of Tolerance, in Los Angeles, fighting racism and anti-Semitism. But what made the interview riveting was Leyden's past: he used to be a neo-Nazi and a white supremacist and had spent time recruiting teens to commit racist violence. What caused his dramatic turnaround? When his second son was four years old, Leyden heard him repeat some of the racist, anti-Semitic things he'd been spewing, and he was shocked. It was then that he decided to change.

Interestingly, older fathers report less of this kind of soul-searching than younger fathers. This is largely because older men come into fatherhood already feeling more mature and having had more of a chance to hone their philosophy of life.

The Ambivalent Father

Over the course of my writing career, I've written only a few things that I kept from my kids until they were old enough to understand them. Throughout this book (and the others in the series) we've talked a lot about the joys, anxieties, fears, and intense feelings of love that are all part of being a father. If you're like most men, the experience—despite the ups and downs—has been overwhelmingly positive, and you wouldn't trade it for anything. In fact, being a dad has become such an integral part of your life that you probably can't imagine not being one.

But one of these days, completely out of the blue, you may look at your child and realize that the intense love you felt just the day before has been replaced by a numb, hollow feeling. And the delight you took in raising her and being part of her life has been supplanted by complete and utter ambivalence. You're feeling overburdened and underappreciated, and you can hardly remember the last time you had a conversation with someone who knows more than forty words. You feel like chucking this whole dad thing and starting a new life somewhere else, as far away from your kid(s) as you can get.

Most of the time these feelings of ambivalence last only a few minutes or a few hours. Sometimes they go on for days or even weeks. But no matter how long they last, one thing is pretty much guaranteed: the instant after the ambivalence starts, you'll get hit by a wave of guilt for having felt the ambivalence in the first place. And that feeling will stick around long after you've fallen back in love with your child. After all, goes the internal monologue, if I'm not a completely committed father 100 percent of the time, I must not be cut out for the job at all.

Most mothers are quite familiar with this ambivalence/guilt pattern. But because they're generally more willing to discuss their worries and concerns with other mothers, they learn rather quickly that it's perfectly normal. They still feel bad about it, maybe even scared, but at least they know they're not alone.

We as fathers aren't alone either, but we rarely ever learn this lesson. If we have a few other fathers with whom we can talk things over, we're incredibly lucky. But it's still pretty unlikely that we'll actually talk to them about this ambivalence. It's already hard enough to ask for advice about diaper changing, discipline, or nutrition. Having ambivalent feelings is a serious weakness, perhaps a character flaw (or at least it sure seems like one). And we're certainly not going to expose any weaknesses or character flaws to another man, who would probably just laugh anyway.

Hopefully just reading this section has been enough to convince you—at least a little—that your changing feelings toward your children are completely normal. If you're still worried, though, or if you need more reassurance, force yourself to spend a few minutes talking to someone about what you're feeling—a close friend, your clergyperson, your therapist, even your partner (that may be a tough conversation to have, but at least she or he will know exactly what you're going through). And remember this: you're going to have these feelings dozens of times throughout the course of your fatherhood. So get used to dealing with them now.

YOU AND YOUR TODDLER

Identifying Your Parenting Style

You've been a dad for almost two years now, and you've probably noticed that the way you parent is quite a bit different from the way your parents managed. You may also do things much differently than your friends and perhaps even your partner. Sure, everyone has a unique parenting style. But according to Diana Baumrind, a sociologist at the University of California at Berkeley, almost all of us fall into one of three basic categories: authoritarian, permissive, or authoritative. The chart on page 134 describes these three styles as well as their relative advantages and disadvantages. (There is a fourth category, the neglectful parent, who rejects or ignores his or her child and sees her as an inconvenience. However, since neglectful parents aren't likely to be reading this book, I'm leaving them out of the discussion.)

Discipline and Your Parenting Style

As you might guess, authoritarian, permissive, and authoritative parents have different ways of disciplining (or trying to discipline) their children.

Naturally, we all slip in and out of each style from time to time, but almost everyone has a dominant mode. As you can see from the chart on pages 136–37, the authoritative approach is by far the most successful—in terms of discipline as well as family harmony. Moving away from either the authoritarian or permissive style isn't easy—there's a good chance that you parent the way you do because it's what you (and your parents, and theirs) grew up with. But here are a few tips that will help you start the process.

AUTHORITARIAN PARENTS ...	PERMISSIVE PARENTS ...	AUTHORITATIVE PARENTS ...
• Value obedience as a virtue and favor punishment whenever there's a difference between the parent's wants and the child's behavior. • Yell, command, order, blame, bribe, and threaten.	• Try not to exercise control and don't encourage the child to respect standards and rules. • Are tolerant and accepting of the child's impulses, and use as little punishment as possible. • Plead, hope things turn out okay, and often give up and do nothing.	• Exert firm control but don't overload the child with restrictions. • Use reason as well as power to achieve their goals. • Make requests, give incentives, negotiate, and establish consequences.

- **Divert**. This is far and away the most successful method of getting a child of age two or younger to stop misbehaving. And it'll keep on working fairly well for another year—especially when it's used in conjunction with the other approaches listed in this section. By diverting your child's attention early, you'll eliminate a lot of problems before they have a chance to develop. You won't feel the need to punish your child, and she won't feel that she's a failure or that you don't love her.
- **Be clear**. Let your child know exactly what kind of behavior you expect.
- **Set reasonable limits, explain them, and enforce them**.
- **Be consistent**. Your child will learn to adapt to inconsistencies between you and your partner. If you allow jumping on the bed, but she doesn't, for example, the child will do it when she's with you and won't when she's with your partner (see pages 90–94 for more on dealing with disagreements). But if *you* allow jumping one day and prohibit it the next, you'll only confuse your child and undermine your attempts to get her to listen when you ask her to do something.
- **Compromise**. Kids can't always tell the difference between big and little issues. So give in on a few small things once in a while (an extra piece of birthday cake at the end of a long day might avoid a tantrum, or you might extend your child's bedtime so she can spend some time with a relative who's in town for the day). That will give her a feeling of control and will make it easier for her to go along with the program on the bigger issues (holding hands while crossing the street, for example).
- **Be assertive and specific**. "Stop throwing your food now" is much better than "Cut that out!"
- **Think ahead**. If you find yourself butting heads with your child at certain times (such as when it's time to leave the park and go home) or places (grocery stores

are toddler favorites for meltdowns), give her plenty of warning and remind her of the behavior you expect.

- **Give choices.** Kathryn Kvols, author of *Redirecting Children's Behavior*, suggests that if your child is, for example, yanking all the books off a shelf in the living room, you say, "Would you like to stop knocking the books off the shelf or would you like to go to your room?" If she ignores you, gently but firmly lead the child to her room and tell her she can come back into the living room when she's ready to listen to you.
- **Cut down on the warnings.** If the child knows the rules (at this age, all you have to do is ask her if she does), impose the promised consequences immediately. If you make a habit of giving six preliminary warnings and three "last" warnings before doing anything, your child will learn to start responding only the eighth or ninth time you ask.
- **Link consequences directly to the problem behavior.** And don't forget to explain—clearly and simply—what you're doing and why: "I'm taking away your hammer because you hit me with it," or "I asked you not to throw that egg up in the air, and you didn't listen to me. Now you'll have to help me clean it up."
- **Don't bank consequences.** If you're imposing punishments or consequences, do it immediately. If you punish a child at the end of the day for something (or a bunch of things) she did earlier, she won't associate the undesirable action with its consequence.

GOOD DAD, BAD DAD

PARENTING STYLE	AUTHORITARIAN (THE BOSS)
The parents...	• Are frequently uncompromising, dictatorial, strict, and repressive. • Attempt to shape, control, and evaluate the behavior and attitudes of the child according to an absurdly high (and often theologically motivated) standard. • Rarely explain the rules.
As a result, the child...	• Learns to obey out of fear of punishment. • Learns to lie or hide misbehavior in order to avoid punishment. • Is less independent, takes on less responsibility, and does worse in school than her peers. • Is so used to being controlled that she does not develop self-control, and as a result can often be unruly and uncooperative when parents aren't present.
The power...	• Is with the parent.
Life at home can be...	• Tense • Rigid • Oppressive
The parent-child relationship is...	• Cold, rigid, and based on fear. • Verbal interchange between parent and child is discouraged. Instead, children are taught to blindly accept the parents' word as the way things ought to be.

PERMISSIVE (THE SERVANT, THE BYSTANDER)	AUTHORITATIVE (THE GUIDE, THE LEADER)
• Are often passive, weak, inconsistent, and yielding. • Consult with the child too much about family policies and give too many explanations for rules. • Don't ask the child to take on many household responsibilities. • Allow the child to regulate her own activities as much as possible. • May be under stress and don't have the energy to enforce rules.	• Are approachable, reasonable, and flexible. • Attempt "to direct the child's activities but in a rational, issue-oriented manner," says Diana Baumrind. • Don't regard themselves as infallible or divinely inspired.
• Is subtly encouraged to control others. • Is left to follow her own wants and instincts and can become self-centered and demanding. • Has less impulse control and is less responsible, less self-reliant, and less independent. • Doesn't do as well in school and has more social problems. • Doesn't learn to cooperate or to consider the needs of others or of the group.	• Is encouraged to think and to be a participant in the family. • Learns to take on more responsibility with age. • Becomes more independent. • Gets good grades in school. • Is able to focus on the needs of the group.
• Is firmly in the hands of the child.	• Is shared appropriately between parent and child.
• Chaotic • Uncontrollable • Wild	• Relaxed • Orderly • Consistent
• Distant and often marked by resentment and manipulation. • Parents make few demands for mature behavior, and without limits the child can feel unloved and uncared for.	• Close, respectful, and marked by sharing and communication. • Parents encourage "verbal give and take, and share with the child the reasoning behind the policy," writes Baumrind. • Encourages the child's independence and individuality. • Recognizes the rights of both parents and children.

- **Keep it short**. Once the punishment is over (and whatever it is, it shouldn't last any more than one minute per year of age), get back to your life. There's no need to review, summarize, or make sure the child got the point.
- **Stay calm**. Screaming, ranting, or raving can easily cross the line into verbal abuse, which can do long-term damage to your child's self-esteem.
- **Get down to your child's level**. When you're talking to your child—especially to criticize—kneel or sit. You'll still be big enough for her to have no doubt who the boss is.
- **Don't lecture**. Instead, ask questions to engage the child in a discussion of the problematic behavior: "Is smoking cigars okay for kids or not?" "Do you like it when someone pushes you down in the park?"
- **Criticize the behavior, not the child**. Even such seemingly innocuous comments as, "I've told you a thousand times," or "Every single time you . . . ," give the child the message that she's doomed to disappoint you no matter what she does.
- **Play games**. "Let's see who can put the most toys away" and "I bet I can put my shoes on before you can" are favorites. But be sure not to put away more toys or to put your shoes on first—kids under five have a tough time losing.
- **Avoid tantrums**. See pages 111–18 for some tips.
- **No spanking**. See pages 140–41.
- **No shaking**. It may seem like a less violent way of expressing your frustrations than spanking, but it really isn't. Shaking your toddler can make her little brain rattle around inside her skull, possibly resulting in brain damage.
- **No bribes**. It's tempting to pay a child off to get her to do or not do something, and once in a while you'll probably give in to the temptation in the interest of keeping the peace. But don't do it too often. The risk—and it's a big one—is that your child will demand some kind of payment before complying with just about anything.
- **Be a grown-up**. Biting your child or pulling her hair to demonstrate that biting or hitting is wrong or doesn't feel good will backfire—guaranteed.
- **Offer cheese with that whine**. Tell your child that you simply don't respond to whining and that you won't give her what she wants until she asks in a nice way—and stick with it.
- **Set a good example**. If your child sees you and your partner arguing without violence, she'll learn to do the same. If she sees you flouting authority by running red lights, she'll do the same.
- Finally—and perhaps, most importantly—**reinforce positive behavior**. We spend too much time criticizing negatives and not enough time complimenting the positives. So help your child understand that there are consequences

to good behavior. Heartfelt comments, like "I'm so proud of you when I see you cleaning up your toys," go a long way, as do small rewards (as opposed to bribes), such as, "You did a great job putting away all your toys, and that's why we're going to go get ice cream cones."

Discipline and Temperament

Not every approach to discipline works equally well with every child. And one of the best ways to improve your chances of finding the right one for your child is to take her temperament (pages 118–25) into consideration. As we discussed in the previous chapter, you can't change your child's temperament. But by understanding it, you'll see why certain things you're doing aren't working, and you'll be able to come up with some new ways of guiding your child's behavior that will work with her temperament instead of against it.

To start with, never punish your child for doing something that's probably rooted in her temperament. For example, if you have a very slow-to-warm child, don't criticize her for not cheerfully saying "Hi" and "Bye-bye" to everyone she sees. She'll only end up feeling that there's something wrong with her for being shy. Instead, encourage her to wave to people instead and compliment her when she does.

Here are some more temperament-specific discipline tips, some of which were suggested to me by Jim Cameron:

- Your **high-activity**, **slow-adapting** toddler needs to have some areas in which she can practice her assertiveness. She needs limits that are clear and consistent but reasonable and flexible (you may have to state the rule a few times, but she'll come around eventually). Too many limits will result in battles of will; too few will result in your being steamrollered or feeling that she's taking advantage of you. It's especially tough for your child to follow instructions in the evening, so as bedtime approaches, start getting her calmed down by reading or watching a video instead of wrestling.
- Your **highly active** toddler may seem as though she never stops moving, and asking her to slow down often makes her go even faster. Expecting her to sit still, with her hands crossed on her lap, will never work. But you'll have much better luck if you give her something to play with while she's sitting, such as some clay to knead, a book to read, or something to draw with.
- Your **slow-adapting** child is likely to argue with you about everything you ask for, and it's easy to interpret her dawdling as rebellion or an attack on your authority. If you respond immediately with anger, your child will resist even more. Instead, give her several firm warnings, starting well in advance. Parents of slow-adapting kids sometimes just give in out of frustration or lash out with

severe punishments, feel guilty, and become overly permissive again. "For slow adapting children, loss of control over their own world [e.g., by getting sent to their rooms] is the most effective punishment there is," says Cameron.

- Your **moderate-activity, low-frustration-tolerance** (see Persistence in the temperament chart, page 125) child has lots of tantrums. She wants something, you

Spanking

A recent national survey by ABC News found that while about two-thirds of parents think that spanking is an acceptable form of discipline, "only" about half admit that they sometimes resort to it. There are some interesting demographic differences. For example, 73 percent of parents in the South approve of spanking and 62 percent do it, while 60 percent of parents in the rest of the country approve and 41 percent do it. In addition, 38 percent of college-educated parents spank their kids vs. 55 percent of those with less education.

One big question, of course, is, does it do any good? If you want to attract your child's attention in a hurry, the answer is a definite yes. And a very small number of studies, including one by Robert McMahon and Rex Forehand (no, I didn't make that name up), have found that children who were spanked (or "smacked," "whupped," "popped," or whatever else you want to call it—as long as it's an open-handed hit on the bottom) as toddlers may be better behaved when they get older. But one could argue that the perceived improvement in a spanked child's behavior is less the result of the spanking and more the result of the child learning to be a better liar and to avoid the person who does the spanking.

The other big question is, of course, does it do harm? The evidence against spanking children conclusively shows that the long-term effects are quite negative. Trying to put any remaining controversies to rest, researchers Elizabeth T. Gershoff and Andrew Grogan-Kaylor recently analyzed data from dozens of studies on spanking and child outcomes. According to Grogan-Kaylor: "The upshot ... is that spanking increases the likelihood of a wide variety of undesired outcomes for children. Spanking thus does the opposite of what parents usually want it to do." Gershoff goes a step further, adding, "Spanking is linked with the same negative child outcomes as abuse, just to a slightly lesser degree."

Specifically, studies have found that adults who say they were slapped or spanked as children are more likely to suffer from anxiety disorders and alcoholism than those who were never slapped or spanked. In addition, children who get spanked are more likely to suffer from poor self-esteem and depression

hold your ground, and off she goes. Her goal, of course, is to get you to give in. Don't. (See pages 111–18 for more on handling and preventing tantrums.)

- Your **moderate-activity**, **fast-adapting** child needs to know exactly what the rules are and where the lines are drawn. Too many limits, and she'll be frustrated by the lack of freedom. Too few, and she'll run wild.

and have a greater chance of accepting lower-paying jobs as adults. While there may not be a direct cause-and-effect relationship—because people with poor self-esteem or depression and those who might be satisfied in low-paying jobs might, for example, be more likely to act out as kids and get their parents angry enough to spank them—there's clearly a correlation between being spanked and negative outcomes.

We know that our children imitate everything we do, good and bad. So it makes logical sense that spanking a child would teach her that violence and aggression are appropriate ways of solving her problems—not exactly the message most parents want to get across to their kids.

I still remember very clearly a scene that took place a few years ago at a bus stop not far from my house. A rather agitated woman was trying to keep her two kids—about five and seven years old—from fighting: "How many times," she said, smacking the older child, "do I have to [*smack*] tell you [*smack*] not to hit [*smack*] your brother [*smack*]?" Any guesses about where that little boy learned to hit his brother?

Author Doug Spangler suggests that fathers who spank their children are sending some very specific messages:

- It's okay to hit another person.
- It's okay to hit another person who is smaller than you.
- It's okay to hit someone you love.
- It's okay to hit someone when you feel angry and frustrated.
- Physical aggression is normal and acceptable under any circumstances.
- Daddy can't control himself or his temper.
- Fathers are to be feared.
- Children must always be quiet around their fathers.

When it comes to punishment—and just about everything else—parents treat boys and girls very differently. Parents of boys, for example, are more likely to report discipline problems than parents of girls. And boys are far more likely to be spanked, while girls are more likely to be sent to their rooms.

- Your **irregular, withdrawing** child can be, not surprisingly, a challenge, and your expectations are the key. Expecting your child to stay in her room at night is fine, but expecting her to stay in her bed or to go to sleep right away is a waste of time. And expecting her to eat dinner is reasonable, but expecting her to eat everything on her plate at every meal is not. The key here is to make repeated and firm requests for compliance. And try not to take your child's initial "deafness" as a personal affront.
- Your **highly distractible** child may also ignore you but for different reasons. Get down to her level and look her straight in the eye. Tell her in simple terms exactly what you want her to do and ask her to repeat it back to you.

One special note: whatever your child's temperament, don't use food as a behavior management tool—either by bribing her or by forcing her to eat when she's not hungry. Children two to five who throw regular tantrums over food are three times more likely to be overweight than kids who don't, according to a study of children in the San Francisco Bay Area.

FAMILY MATTERS

The Old College Try

We all know it's going to cost a ton of money to send a child to college. In 2019, a year a private college costs about $60,000 per year. Public college is about $27,000 for in-state students and about $46,000 or out-of-state students. Those numbers include room, board, and books, but not transportation home for the summer or winter break, or anything else. The US Department of Education estimates that college costs have gone up an average of 6.5 percent per year for the past decade. If they continue at that pace, eighteen years from now, a year at a private college will set you back $186,000; a year at an out-of-state college will be $143,000; and a year at an in-state college a relatively cheap $84,000.

Looking at all those zeros—and thinking you're going to have to write a check for the whole thing—is enough to make anyone panic. But take it easy. Most people would never consider paying cash for a house. So why should you consider paying cash for an education that costs about the same? Fortunately, there are a number of excellent ways to finance your child's education, none of which involve having to sell a kidney on the black market.

Traditionally, parents have opened savings accounts in their children's names as a way of putting money aside for the child's education. However, as counterintuitive as it sounds, start by putting as much money as you can into your own retirement accounts. Doesn't make sense? Consider the following:

If you were paying attention to the flight attendant before taking off on your last airplane trip, you know that if those oxygen masks drop from the ceiling, you're supposed to put yours on first, then your child's, right? The idea is that if you can't breathe, you certainly won't be able to help anyone else. Financial guru Eric Tyson once told me the same basic thing about money: take care of your finances first—especially your IRA, 401(k), 403(b), SEP, Keogh, or company-sponsored retirement account—and your whole family will be better off.

But that still doesn't explain how feathering your own personal retirement account instead of starting a college fund in your child's name will help put her through college. Well, here's how it works:

- Money you invest in your retirement accounts is often at least partially tax-deductible and always grows tax-free until you start withdrawing it. The dollars you invest in an account in your child's name are after-tax dollars, and interest and dividends may be taxable as income or capital gains.
- Plenty of financial-aid options are available: student loans (often available at below-market rates), grants, fellowships, work-study programs, and so on. But you'll need to qualify. College financial-aid departments assume that about 35 percent of assets held in your child's name will be used for educational

"Remember, son, these are your tax-free years.
Make the most of them."

expenses each year. However, they assume that only a max of 5.6 percent of your assets (which includes just about everything you own except your retirement accounts) will be available. It's pretty obvious that the less money you have in your child's name, the more financial aid you'll be able to get.

- If you'll be over fifty-nine and a half by the time your child starts college, you should be able to withdraw money from your IRA or other retirement account without incurring any penalties.
- Once you've maxed out your retirement opportunities, you can start earmarking money specifically for your child's education. There are two basic options:
  - Taxable savings, such as mutual funds, stocks, savings bonds, cash, and money market accounts.
  - Nontaxable (or tax-deferred) savings, such as Coverdell Education Savings Account (ESAs), trustee accounts, and, most commonly, 529 plans.

I'm not going to discuss the taxable options here because, generally speaking, you'll end up with less money after going that route. And within the nontaxable category, the 529s are by far the best option for most people, so I'm going to focus on them. The primary reasons are that there are no income restrictions, you can contribute a lot more money, and you have a lot of control over how your contributions are invested. There are two drawbacks to 529s: First, if you don't use

If You're Planning to Pay 100 Percent of Your Child's College Expenses

Despite all this sound financial wisdom, you may still be intent on paying cash for college. If you've got the money—and the desire—to do so, immediately disregard the above advice and start socking money away into an account in your child's name (with you as custodian). That way, you may be able to save at least a little on taxes: until she's eighteen, the first $2,100 or so of your child's interest and dividends won't be taxed at all. If her investment income is between $2,201 and $10,500, she'll have to file her own return but will probably be taxed at a lower rate than you will. If your child is in a higher tax bracket than you are, you can include her income on your return. Income over $10,500 will need to go on your return.

Whether you decide to include your child's income with yours or file a separate return for her will depend on your specific financial situation. Check with your accountant to make sure you're doing the right thing for your family.

the money for education, you'll get hit with a nice tax bill along with a penalty. Second, the money has to be spent on higher education only—not on high school.

If you anticipate needing money for high school expenses, consider a Coverdell ESA. Like 529s, ESAs (once known as Education IRAs) grow tax-free. However, there are very strict eligibility and contribution restrictions. They're also considered the child's asset, which will affect her ability to qualify for financial aid.

Every state offers its own 529 program, which is managed by a large financial services company, such as Vanguard, Fidelity, and the like. You can choose any program you wish, but there could be some advantages to going with the one in your own backyard: contributions may be deductible from your state taxes, and some states match contributions, while some penalize you for using another state's plan. You can find out more about your 529 options from the College Savings Plans Network at www.collegesavings.org.

Wills and Trusts

By this time, hopefully, you've got your life insurance situation under control. If not, put this book down right now and call your insurance agent. And while you're waiting for him or her to call you back, you might want to review the section on insurance in *The Expectant Father: The Ultimate Guide for Dads-to-Be* (fourth edition), page 111.

Knowing that your partner and kids will be financially secure in the event of your death should make you breathe a little easier. But don't relax completely—there are a few other things you have to worry about. For example, if, God forbid, you and your partner are killed tomorrow, who's going to take care of your kids? Who's going to make sure they get the kind of education and upbringing you want them to have? And who's going to get all your stuff?

The answers to these and other horrible but important-to-consider questions are up to you. They're outlined in a will or a trust or both. Unfortunately, about half of all parents with young children don't have either a will or a trust. If you die intestate (meaning without a will, trust, or other document that tells how you want your assets distributed), the details will be handled according to the laws of your state. In most cases, this means that a judge will appoint a guardian for your estate and another one for your children. Chances are, neither of these guardians will be the one you would have chosen.

So which is better? A will or a trust? Actually, the answer may be both. As a new parent, you absolutely, positively need a will to designate a guardian for your child. You can also use a will to distribute your assets, but many experts feel that setting up a revocable living trust is a better alternative. However, because of the time and expense involved, many parents decline to take advantage of the living trust alternative. Some of the advantages and disadvantages of wills and living trusts are listed below.

DOING IT YOURSELF

Without ever having gone to law school or earned a degree in accounting, you can probably write a will or set up a living trust by yourself. There are quite a few excellent books and software packages on the market that can take you through the whole process. U.S. Legal Forms has several packages of common legal forms

Wills

ADVANTAGES

- It's a lot cheaper to prepare a will than a trust.
- You can distribute your assets exactly as you want.
- There is an automatic limit on how long someone has to challenge the terms of your will (it varies from state to state). According to some estimates, one in three wills is contested, so this limit could be a very good thing.
- Creditors must make claims within a certain amount of time (again, it varies from state to state).
- The activities of your executors, guardians, and trustees are supervised by the court.

Living Trusts

ADVANTAGES

- The potential costs and time delays of probate are largely avoided. After your death, your survivors should have control over your assets within a few weeks, without involving the courts.
- The trust document is not public, so no one can see it unless you show it to them.
- A trust can be revoked or changed at any time.
- Assets are distributed as you wish—either directly to your heirs upon your death or gradually over time.
- A living trust allows you to directly manage your assets when you're able and ensures that they'll be managed according to your wishes if you become incapacitated or incompetent.

for dads available for readers of this book on its website, at https://www.uslegal-forms.com/mrdad.

If you have a lot of money or a complicated financial situation, or if you just feel more comfortable having a professional take care of things for you, your local or state bar association can give you referrals for attorneys in your area who specialize in wills and trusts. You should also talk to a good tax or probate lawyer if you aren't absolutely sure whether your needs would be best served with a will, a living trust, or some other instrument.

DISADVANTAGES
- Probate. This is the name for the process through which everything in a will must go before it is completely straightened out. Probate can easily last as long as eighteen months. And until it's over, your heirs won't have access to most of the assets of your estate.
- Court fees, attorneys' fees, executor fees, accounting fees, and so forth can eat up 3–7 percent (or more) of the estate.
- In most cases, probate files are public records. This means that anyone can go down to the courthouse and take a peek at your will.

DISADVANTAGES
- Trusts generally cost more and take longer to set up than wills. It will also probably cost you a few dollars to transfer ownership of your assets from you personally to the trust. However, all the probate-related expenses that wills require can come to about the same amount as the cost of setting up a trust.
- Improperly prepared, a living trust can cause some serious problems. If the IRS feels that your trust was not properly executed, your estate could wind up in probate—the very situation you were hoping to avoid.
- Since all your assets are transferred during your lifetime from your name into the name of the trust, you are giving up personal ownership in a lot of what you own. This can be tough psychologically.
- Trusts may not reduce your tax liability.

As Long as You're Thinking about Depressing Things . . .

- **Consider a durable power of attorney**. This document (which you may need an attorney to help you prepare) gives someone you designate the power to manage your affairs if you become incapacitated. You can include a health-care directive, which covers such topics as whether or not you want to be kept on life support, if things ever come to that.
- **Consider making some gifts**. You and your partner can each give away a cumulative total of $11.2 million during your lifetime without owing any gift tax (but you can't give any individual person more than $15,000 per year). This has the effect of reducing the size of your estate as well as the amount of estate taxes that your heirs will have to come up with later. (Estate taxes, by the way, are usually due and payable within nine months of death.) If you have a very large estate, there are a number of other ways to use gifts to reduce or eliminate estate taxes. But the IRS rules are a little complicated, so be sure to check with your accountant or financial adviser.

Off to School

WHAT'S GOING ON WITH YOUR TODDLER

Physically

- Your two-year-old is beginning a yearlong energy spurt and will spend a lot of time "thinking with his feet"—galloping around almost aimlessly, spending a few seconds engaged in some activity or other, then moving on to something else. Sometimes his desire to investigate outstrips his physical abilities, so make sure you keep an eye on him at all times.
- He's quite comfortable with his body and its capabilities; he can run without falling down, walk up and down stairs by himself, balance on one foot for a second or two, jump off a low step, and rock or march in time to music.
- He likes to walk by himself and may resist any attempt you make to carry him or put him in his stroller.
- His hand-eye coordination is getting much better, and he's now able to use his blocks to build structures that are more complex than towers: houses, forts, horse corrals, and long walls.
- He still loves piling and stacking and pouring, and he turns pages—and door-knobs—with ease. He can screw on the tops of jars and may even be able to open childproof containers.
- Nevertheless, he still has some problems using one hand independently of the other. "If he holds out an injured finger for bandaging, he tends also to hold out his matching uninjured finger," write child-development experts Louise Bates Ames and Frances Ilg.
- As recently as six months ago, your toddler could focus only on things pretty much right in front of his face. Now he's developing peripheral vision. He's also becoming aware of faraway objects such as planes, birds, and distant houses.

Intellectually

- At this stage of his development, he's not able to separate the goal of his actions from the process of achieving it. In other words, *how* he does something is just as important as *what* he does. For example, if he decides to make a painting, he's not just interested in being creative. He's equally interested in making a mess and exploring the feel of the paintbrush on the paper. And if he clambers to the top of a climbing structure, it's as much because he likes climbing as to conquer Everest.

- Your child may still push, yell, and grab, and may occasionally bite or hit. But as frustrating as aggressive behavior is to you, try to remember that he's not doing it to be mean or deliberately to cause harm.

- For at least the next year, your child's primary concern will be satisfying his own needs and wants. If he wants you to lift him into the air for the 327th time, the fact that your back is killing you and you need a break is of no concern to him. And he's outraged that you're tired of reading him the same book over and over.

- He's quickly mastering quantities—especially *more* and *all gone*—and has a good understanding of cause and effect ("I push the button that Daddy keeps telling me not to touch, and his computer screen suddenly goes black. Cool."). He's got some spatial relationships down too (*under, over, next to, front, back*), but he's still working on time. He understands *in a minute* and possibly *today*, but *tomorrow, next week, last year*, and even *yesterday* don't mean much.

- His feelings of power over his surroundings are reinforced by his burgeoning language skills. "He behaves as if the words give him control over the situation . . . as if he controls his own exits and entrances by means of the magic utterance," writes child psychologist Selma Fraiberg. Now that he can say "Bye-bye," he doesn't mind quite as much when you leave him alone. And he's more cooperative about going to bed when he's the one telling you, "Night-night."

Verbally

- Until now, your child learned about his world physically: he had to touch, feel, or taste things before he could truly understand them. But from here on out, language—questions, answers, explanations—begins to take over as his primary means of acquiring information.

- Your toddler uses twenty to one hundred words, his favorites being *again* and *no*. But he most likely understands two hundred to five hundred words, and that number is growing every day. This means that unless you want your toddler to understand your private talks with other adults, you'd better start s-p-e-l-l-i-n-g.

- He's now using adjectives ("I'm a good boy") and verbs ("I go to the store") but makes some adorable and completely logical mistakes when trying to use past tense ("I drinked milk" or "I runned fast").
- Ames and Ilg have found that despite your toddler's quickly increasing knowledge of the language, he talks mainly to himself, second most to you and other familiar adults, and little if any to other children. Most of what comes out of his mouth is self-initiated (as opposed to being in response to something you've said).
- *Note: Some two-year-olds speak in short, three- to five-word sentences. Others still speak one word at a time. Unless your child doesn't understand simple questions and requests, there's nothing to worry about.*

Emotionally and Socially

- The first few months of the third year are usually happy ones for both toddler and parents. He's having fewer tantrums and is generally more cooperative than even a few months ago.
- He's becoming much more aware of other people and will gleefully point out every child who walks by and announce, "Baby!" And although he's still not playing with other kids very much (you're still his favorite playmate), he's getting more content to play alongside them, often engaging in the same activity.
- He's getting good at identifying other people's emotions. He knows when you're happy and will laugh with you. He knows when you're sad and will try to cheer you up.
- He already had a rather short attention span, but thanks (in part, at least) to his widening peripheral vision, he's even more distracted than before—after all, there are so many interesting new things crossing his field of view.

Developmental Red Flags

As before, it's important to remember that the range of "normal" or "average" is a big one. That said, you should call your pediatrician if one or more of the following is true about your two-year-old. My child:
- Doesn't recognize himself in the mirror.
- Doesn't imitate.
- Isn't using two-word sentences.
- Doesn't seem interested in people or things he knows.
- Can't (as opposed to *won't*) understand basic directions, such as "Give me the book, please."
- Can't identify familiar objects in pictures or books.

- He's still learning a lot about life by imitating you, so be on your best behavior and don't even bother telling him to, "Do as I say, not as I do."
- After playing with their genitals for a while, boys and girls are now establishing a budding gender identity, typically identifying with (and becoming more attached to) the parent (or adult role model or other children) of the same sex.
- He may tell you in advance when his bowel movements are about to occur, indicating that he's finally ready to begin potty training (see pages 157–62 for more on this milestone).

WHAT YOU'RE GOING THROUGH

Taking Pride (and Dialing down Your Disappointment) in Your Child's Accomplishments

One of the best things about being a parent is that it gives you a chance to go back and do all the things you loved to do as a kid, all the things you missed out on, and all the things you did but want to do again. It's like having a second childhood.

The problem is, however, that some parents forget whose childhood it really is and act as though what the child does is somehow a reflection on them. This is especially true if we've fallen into the incredibly common trap of expecting our children to live our unfulfilled dreams and do as well as—or better than—we ever did. You might, for example, want your child to do or like or excel in the same things you did when you were his age. Or you might want your child to do or like or excel in some of the same things you weren't so successful at when you were a kid.

Part of the reason for this is a fear of failing, a fear that you haven't done a good enough job or that you haven't adequately prepared your child to be a good citizen. "The child acts as a mirror for his parents," according to the Group for the Advancement of Psychiatry. "If his behavior expresses positive aspects of the parents—if he is loving, happy, intelligent, creative—his parents feel that these qualities are reflections of themselves. They feel satisfied with what they have done thus far and more able to go on successfully." At the same time, though, if your child doesn't do well, doesn't live up to your expectations, or gets into trouble, you may feel that you've failed. Your little shot at immortality, at having the world recognize your true greatness, isn't working out quite the way you wanted.

Researchers Barbara and Philip Newman agree. "Parents may experience intense emotional reactions to their child's behavior," they write. "[Your children] can make you feel warm, joyful, and proud. They can make you feel furious, guilty, and disgusted.... It's one thing if someone else's child is rude or selfish. But if your own child is rude or selfish, intense feelings of anger, disgust, or embarrassment may be stimulated. You may feel pleased by the successes of a neighbor's child, but the success of your own child gives rise to the peculiar parental emotion called 'gloating.'"

Trying to live your life through your kids is a rotten idea for everyone. As with everything else in your life, your child is going to turn out differently than you'd planned. Taking his failures (including his failure to act like you want him to) too personally, setting your expectations too high, or pushing him to be someone he's not (you, for example) puts way too much pressure on him. Wanting to make your child into whomever you wish you could have been isn't a bad thing to do—it can expose him to all sorts of great opportunities you never had. The key is not to get upset if your child doesn't want to be you. He needs to know that being himself is okay, and he needs the freedom and encouragement to develop into the person he's supposed to develop into. Those are things only you can give him.

The bottom line is that the more realistic your expectations, the better off you'll be. So relax. No matter how well or badly your child does, his successes and failures are *not* a referendum on your parenting skills. You had your turn. Now move over and let someone else have a clear shot at being a child.

Gender Roles

A few months ago, we talked about how easy it is for parents to fall into the trap of treating boys and girls differently. Given that kids learn most of what they know from adults, it shouldn't come as much of a surprise to hear that the gender-based double standard works just as well in the other direction. In other words, kids treat men and women differently.

"Children learn the different roles that males and females play with children before the age of three," writes researcher Beverly Fagot. "And once this difference has been learned, the children will react to adults outside the home on the basis of this learned differentiation." Fagot found that in preschool classrooms, kids "elicited many kinds of play behavior from the male teachers; but when children needed materials or needed some caretaking, they approached female teachers."

So what can you do? First, just be a good role model. If you're a full participant in your home, and you love, nurture, and care for your children, they—boys and girls alike—will come to realize that men can be parents too. Studies have shown that the more responsibility dads take for household tasks and childcare, the less likely their kids will be to have rigid gender roles later in life. Second, make sure your children get the message that men and women and boys and girls are not locked into any particular roles or futures because of their sex. Your children should be free to dream of becoming whatever they want to be. This means that besides telling our daughters that they can grow up to be doctors, we need to tell our sons that they can grow up to be nurses (an idea one of my kids had a big problem with, even though the father of one of her best friends was, indeed, a nurse anesthetist).

A friend who has a particularly gentle, sweet little boy once confided that she was worried about her son's lack of physical aggressiveness and was concerned that he might be gay. First of all, it's way too early to tell whether a child is gay or transgender or anything else. For now, just let your child be whomever he or she wants to be. So if your daughter (like mine) demands Matchbox cars for her birthday, tears the heads off her Barbie dolls, and refuses to be in the same room with a tutu, let her alone. And if your son wants to play with dolls or wear your partner's nail polish or lipstick, let him alone.

Forcing your child into a particular type of behavior—either to conform with or buck gender stereotypes—can scar him for life. One fun way to dispel some of the myths about gender roles is to listen to the recording of *Free to Be, You and*

Go to the Doctor—Before It Kills You

One of the most damaging messages we send to our children is "big boys don't cry"—men don't complain when they're in pain. You can do your part to make sure that stupid idea doesn't creep into the next generation by starting to take better care of yourself now. Unfortunately, when it comes to health care, most men (myself included) are idiots. We don't get regular checkups, we don't do much in the way of preventive care, we ignore symptoms, and we don't get medical attention until the pain is unbearable (or, more likely, until a woman in our life insists). Overall, men are half as likely as women to visit a doctor or other health-care provider, and we make only about one-fourth the number of visits for diagnosis, screening, or test results. A recent poll by the Cleveland Clinic found that only 60 percent of men get an annual physical, and 40 percent go to a doctor or other provider only when they fear they have a serious medical condition (by which time it's often too late). When (if) we finally do seek medical attention, we frequently sabotage our providers' effectiveness by canceling follow-up appointments and not finishing prescriptions.

The results of all this negligence are startling: Men die at younger ages and in greater numbers from nine of the top ten causes of death. We're 40 percent more likely than women to die of cardiovascular disease, cancer, and diabetes; and twice as likely to die of liver disease. Overall, men's life expectancy is five years shorter than women's.

Me. It's more than forty years old but still widely available and has some very funny—and subtly educational—bits about gender.

YOU AND YOUR TODDLER

Sleeping Like a Baby?

On average, two-year-olds sleep eleven hours every night and take one two-hour nap during the day. Two-and-a-half-year-olds cut back to ten and a half hours at night and one and a half during the day. Of course, those are just averages; the range is from nine to thirteen hours total per day.

Starting at about two years of age, a lot of toddlers begin having sleep problems. Sometimes it's a question of separation anxiety: your child may not want to go to sleep because it means you'll be leaving him alone. In other cases, the issue is that there's so much cool stuff happening in his world that he resents

And once you get to the doctor, will he actually save you? Not necessarily. Almost 70 percent of men over forty who visit the doctor aren't even asked whether they have a family history of prostate cancer, despite the fact that prostate cancer kills about as many men every year as breast cancer kills women. In the past year, 40 percent of men over fifty—who should be getting a prostate exam every single year—weren't even screened by their doctors, 60 percent weren't screened for colon cancer, and 50 percent had neither a physical nor a blood cholesterol test.

Visiting a health-care provider also won't do much about the fact that four times as many men commit suicide as women, that the victims of violent crime are 75 percent male, that 98 percent of the people who work in the most dangerous jobs in this country are men, and that 94 percent of people who die in the workplace are men. And going to the doctor won't help men discuss private medical issues such as sexual dysfunction, which is often a symptom of a far more serious physical problem—clogged arteries, high blood pressure, or diabetes.

Bottom line? Go to the doctor or other provider. You should be having a complete physical at least every two years, and should be screened for prostate and colon cancer every year. It's important to get baseline screenings as soon as possible, because, while the numbers are important, often it's the change in the numbers over time that's even more important.

anything that interferes with his desire to explore. There's apparently a clause in the Toddler Code of Conduct that requires him to test every rule you make. He may come up with one clever excuse after another to put off bedtime: "One more story," "Tummy hurts," "Night-light on," and so on.

The problem here is that getting enough sleep is critical for toddlers—even more than it is for adults. Researchers used to think that the brain rested during sleep, but recent brain imaging shows that the brain is very active at this time, sometimes even more active than when awake. Not getting enough sleep can cause problems with memory, behavior, creativity, attention, and cognitive functioning.

Practicing good sleep hygiene and having regular routines are the best defenses against sleep problems. That means making sure that your child's bed is used only for sleeping—no playing, no games. His bedroom should be as quiet and as dark as possible (a night-light is okay if your toddler needs one).

Most people have bedtime routines, but they're also a good idea at nap time and first thing in the morning, especially if your toddler isn't a morning person. Sleep routines should involve some quiet time, reading, singing songs, or just cuddling and talking about your day. Whatever it is, the routine should be something the child looks forward to.

Keep in mind that it's perfectly normal for your toddler to wake up five or six times during the night. Usually he'll just take a look around, and if everything is where it's supposed to be, he'll go back to sleep. But if things have changed, he may be up all night. For that reason, it's best to put your child to bed when he's awake. Still, as a precaution, you should have a middle-of-the-night routine. (Nightmares require a different approach; see pages 72–73.)

When my oldest was about two, she started getting up in the middle of the night and wanting to play or chat. I'd take her down to her room, but she'd reappear a few minutes later. We went back and forth four or five times before she finally collapsed. After a week or so of this I told her that she could sleep anywhere she wanted, just as long as it wasn't in my room. As if to prove a point, she elected to sleep on the floor just outside my door. After a few nights of putting up with me stumbling over her on the way to the bathroom, she eventually gave up and went back to her own bed.

Is it possible for a child to get too much sleep? Generally speaking, the answer is no. Toddlers have a very zen approach, dropping off when they're tired. It is possible, though, for a toddler to sleep so much during the day that he's not tired enough to fall asleep at night. Combine that with an early wake-up time, and you end up back at square one, with not enough sleep.

Potty Training: The Real Thing

Looking at your toddler and thinking back at how much he's grown and developed over the past two years can be a bittersweet experience. On one hand, you love how big and independent he's become. On the other, you sometimes miss his younger, more dependent days. But no matter how fondly you recall your child's infancy, there's one part of his childhood that you probably can't wait to put behind you: changing diapers.

Is your child ready to be toilet trained? As basic as it seems to us adults, toilet training is actually a pretty complicated process that requires physical and intellectual maturity. How can you tell if he's ready? If most or all of the following statements are true for your toddler, he's good to go. My toddler...

- Seems interested in what my partner, I, and others do in the bathroom.
- Likes to do things "myself."
- Often wakes up dry from a nap or can at least stay dry for a few hours at a time.
- Doesn't have overnight bowel movements.
- Is curious about what's in his diapers.
- Knows the words our family uses for bowel movements and urination (limit the vocabulary to words you won't feel embarrassed to say in public).

But My Child Was Toilet Trained at Twelve (or Eight or Six) Months ...

If you haven't heard stories about people whose babies were toilet trained at incredibly young ages, you will soon—often by some superior-sounding parent just after your child has had an accident in a public place. But here's a reality check. Children under a year old generally aren't capable of understanding that they have a full bladder or bowel. If they are, they're usually not capable of understanding the connection between that feeling and the wet or squishy stuff that oozes out of their body. Parents who claim that their six- or eight- or twelve-month-old babies were potty trained were actually potty training themselves. They learned to recognize their child's involuntary pre-pee or pre-poop body language and rushed their child to the toilet.

This isn't to say that you can't start toilet training early. If you've read the signs (beginning above and continuing on the next page) and you think your child is ready, go right ahead. Some studies show that earlier training may reduce diaper rash as well as bladder and urinary tract infections.

- Gives indications that he's aware he's filling his diaper—grunting, grimacing, going off to a private corner, or actually coming right out and saying so.
- Indicates that he's uncomfortable in wet or dirty diapers.
- Can and will follow directions.
- Is physically able to pull his pants up and down by himself.
- Has bowel movements at about the same time every day.

If most of the above statements are not true of your child, check back in a few weeks. Trying to toilet train a child who's not ready can actually prolong the process. And there's absolutely zero connection between when a child is toilet trained and his intelligence. Some kids are ready sooner than others. That's it.

READY, SET, GO!

Typically, toilet training happens in this order: overnight bowel control, daytime bowel control, daytime bladder control, overnight bladder control. Here's how to get the process going:

Toilet Training Success Boosters

- **Get the right equipment**. Potty seats should be low enough to allow both the child's feet to rest firmly on the floor. Skip the urine deflectors (shields that attach to the front of the seat to keep boys' urine inside the toilet). They seem like a great idea but can sometimes hurt boys who don't sit down exactly right, and the last thing you want is to have your child associate going to the bathroom with pain. Some seats have multiple stages: they start out as a child-size seat that sits on the floor, then convert to an adapter that attaches to a regular toilet seat. Some even play music when there's butt-to-potty contact.
- **Don't flush in front of the child**. While some kids may be fascinated and want to flush over and over and over; others may be terrified, believing that a part of them is being sucked down the toilet. (See pages 64–73 for more on fears.)
- **Minimize or eliminate liquids within an hour of bedtime**. This will increase the chances that your child will wake up dry—something that will boost his confidence.
- **Learn to recognize the signs**. When you see that knees-together, bouncing-up-and-down dance, find a bathroom fast.
- **Be positive but not too positive**. Too much excitement about the contents

1. Leave a potty seat on the floor in the bathroom. Tell the child the little one is for him, the big one is for grown-ups. Put a stuffed animal on your child's seat, just to give him a preview. Twins (and greater multiples) often want to use the bathroom at the same time, so get each one his own seat. The seat should be low enough to allow your toddler's feet to rest on the floor.

2. After a few days, have the child sit on the potty seat in his clothes, while you sit on yours (clothed or otherwise). You might want to read a story to keep him sitting there.

3. After another few days, ask the child a few times a day if you can take his diapers off so he can sit on his special toilet. (Most toddlers will urinate or fill their diaper within an hour of eating or drinking, so those are good times for this.) You sit on your toilet as well, and tell him that you, Mommy, Grandpa, Grandma, and everyone else he knows does this every day. My younger daughter loved this stage and would sit on her potty seat for a few minutes shouting "Peeeeeeee!" (but without actually peeing).

4. After your child has a bowel movement in his diaper, take off the dirty diaper of a diaper (or potty or toilet) can give a toddler the idea that what he's produced is somehow valuable—a twisted notion that may result in him wanting to keep it for himself (inside his body if necessary).

- **Don't force it**. Children who feel pressured sometimes try to regain control of the situation by not going to the bathroom at all. This can lead to constipation or other conditions that will need to be treated by your pediatrician. If you think your child is ready but just needs a little encouragement, try a few of the books listed on page 166.

- **Be nice**. Toilet training can take a while (as in months, not days), and accidents are bound to happen. When they do, don't criticize, shame, punish, or yell at your child.

- **Be flexible**. Some regression is perfectly normal, especially if you've moved, changed babysitters, or had a death in the family, or the child has been sick.

- **Make it fun**. Teach your male toddler to pee sitting down first. Once he's got good bladder control, you can start to have him stand up. But be aware that boys in the early stages of toilet training are notoriously bad at aiming. Putting some Cheerios or other targets in the water, or adding some blue food coloring (which turns green when the yellow urine hits it), can make urinating more fun for your son and less messy for you.

and dump the contents into the toilet while he's watching. Emphasize that just as there's a special place for everything else, the toilet is the special place for urine and BM, and that it's where grown-ups put theirs. Do not flush in front of the child (see "Toilet Training Success Boosters," page 158).

5. If your child seems to be getting the hang of things, let him run around naked during the day for ten to twenty minutes (if you have expensive carpets or flooring, you may want to do this outside). Tell him he can go to the potty anytime he wants to. And give plenty of praise if he does.

6. Over the course of a few days, leave your toddler's diapers off longer and longer. Remind him every half hour or so to go to the bathroom. If he has an accident, don't make a big deal about it—it happens to everyone. Most daytime accidents are the result of the child being so caught up in another activity that he doesn't want to stop.

7. If at any point you notice that your child is giving those I-need-to-use-the-toilet signs, make sure you get him to his potty seat as quickly as possible. You want to make sure he learns to recognize the connection between those feelings and using the toilet.

8. Don't worry about night training for a while—at least until the child is regularly dry after waking from his naps and occasionally dry in the morning. Overnight bladder control doesn't usually come for a year or so after daytime control.

9. Teach girls to wipe from front to back to keep poop from making its way from the rectum to the vagina.

10. Teach your child how to wash his hands properly and to do so after he has used the toilet.

BOYS AND GIRLS DO IT DIFFERENTLY . . .
AND SO DO THEIR PARENTS

Ninety percent of girls are bowel-trained by two years, seven months, while 90 percent of boys aren't bowel-trained until three years, one month—a difference of six months. Ninety percent of girls are bladder-trained by three years, six months, while 90 percent of boys take until four years, ten months—a difference of sixteen months. (These numbers are up over twelve months from the 1950s, largely because disposable diapers are so great at keeping babies dry and comfortable that they have less motivation to want to get out of them.)

Although boys lag behind in toilet training, there is no significant biological reason for the delay. The real reason girls are "trained" sooner may have more to do with the trainer than the trainee. Women have traditionally done the training, and girls have an easier time imitating their mothers than boys do. In fact, a lot of boys resist even trying.

It's completely normal for boys this age to start developing a male gender identity and rebel against their mothers (the same way girls this age start developing a female gender identity and rebel against their fathers). So a little boy may balk at sitting down when urinating (it's no fun to sit when you can stand) and may resist Mom's instructions on how to grasp his penis—after all, she doesn't even have one!

Besides being done with potty training earlier, girls also have a much shorter lapse between bowel and bladder training (eleven months) than boys (twenty-one months). This difference may be the result of girls' not being taught to differentiate between the two functions. (Girls can't see either their urination or defecation, and they wipe after both, while boys can see their urine—and are encouraged to aim it—and wipe only after moving their bowels.)

Men and women traditionally have very different ways of teaching toilet training. "The female mode is compatible with and enhancing to the formation of a female gender identity," writes Moisy Shopper, a child psychologist who did an exhaustive study of toilet training (don't ask why). "The child is encouraged to be like mother; by seeing mother's eliminative functioning, they have an intimacy with each other's bodies that fosters the girl's gender and sexual identity." Using the female mode to train boys, "in no way enhances the boy's potential for

THE TRADITIONAL MALE MODEL	THE TRADITIONAL FEMALE MODEL
• Urinary control is taught as a stand-up procedure with emphasis on skill, mastery, and fun.	• Sitting down for all elimination, wiping.
• Wiping only after bowel movements.	• Wiping after both kinds.
• Active participation and modeling by the father and/or other males.	• Use of the mother herself on the toilet as a model for imitation.
• Encouragement to touch and control the penis so as to aim the urinary stream.	• Discouragement from touching self.
• Greater tolerance for absence of bathroom privacy.	• Greater need for bathroom privacy.
• Control, function, and naming of urine is sharply differentiated from control, function, and naming of feces (boys tend to talk about "making pee pee" as opposed to "pooping").	• Minimal distinction between bladder and bowel training in vocabulary, timing, or technique (girls tend to talk about "going to the bathroom").

further body differentiation or supports the sexual differences between him and his mother," continues Shopper. "In fact, in many ways it is antithetical to the boy's maturation."

FOR BOYS ONLY

Basically, the primary role in toilet training boys should be yours. This, of course, does not mean that your female partner isn't capable of training your son (except for not being able to provide a model for how to urinate standing up, there's no reason she can't) or that you can't train your daughter. Plenty of women support their sons' budding masculinity and encourage them to urinate standing up holding on to their own penises.

A small number of mothers, however, won't allow their sons any autonomy, according to Dr. Shopper, and feel "that they must hold their sons' penises as they pee." He concludes: "This is a rotten idea because your son may begin to question whether his penis belongs to him or to his mother, and that's just how serious sexual problems develop later in life."

When boys have a male model, they're much less conflicted about becoming toilet trained, since training no longer carries the connotations of gaining their mother's love, submitting to her, and becoming like her.

Reading

CREATING A READING ENVIRONMENT

Having books and other reading materials readily available to your child will help him make books part of his daily life. And one of the best ways to do this is to be sure there are plenty of books on shelves or in racks that he can reach without having to ask for help.

The goal here is to have your child view reading as something he can do whenever he wants, without fear of being punished. So give him free and open access to board books and any other inexpensive or easily replaceable books you won't mind getting torn up or stuck together with drool. Keep the books you had as a child (and any others that you want to keep in one piece) far, far away and take them out only for special occasions.

SOME ADVANCED READING CONCEPTS

By now you've probably gotten into a nice, regular routine with your child, reading together in a quiet place at times when you won't be interrupted. As you're reading (or planning your reading), make a conscious effort to keep the experience as interesting as possible for both of you. Here are some things to keep in mind:

- **Level**. It's better to read stories that are slightly advanced for your child (and explain a word or concept now and then) than to read ones that are too easy.
- **Variety**. Children's book illustrators use a huge variety of techniques: line drawings, photos, watercolors, charcoal, paint, collages, woodcut, needlepoint. Expose your child to as many approaches as possible and discuss what's unique about each of them.
- **Talk**. If your child interrupts the story to ask questions, follow his lead. Ask: "How do you think he's feeling?" "Why did the bunny do that?" or "What's going to happen when she opens the door?" This will help your child develop critical-thinking skills and encourage him to be an active participant.
- **Act out**. Instead of just reading "Little Red Riding Hood" for the 639th time, assign roles and switch off every once in a while—sometimes you're Little Red Riding Hood, sometimes you're the wolf.
- **Set an example**. Let him see you and your partner reading for pleasure.

HOME LIBRARY UPDATE

Here are more books to check out from your local library or add to your collection.

FAVORITES

Alfie Gets in First (and other Alfie books), Shirley Hughes and Bert Kitchen
Animals of the Night, Merry Banks
The Baby Blue Cat and the Smiley Worm Doll, Ainslie Pryor
Basket, Ella George Lyon
Bathwater's Hot (and others in the series), Shirley Hughes
Blue Hat, Green Hat (and others in the series), Sandra Boynton
Brown Bear, Brown Bear, What Do You See? (and others), Bill Martin Jr.
Carl (and the other Carl books), Alexandra Day
Corduroy (and others in the series), Don Freeman
Don't Let the Pigeon Drive the Bus! (and others), Mo Willems
Eat Up, Gemma, Sarah Hayes
Emma's Pet, David McPhail
Fantastic Flowers, Susan Stockdale
Follow Me (and many others), Nancy Tafuri
General Store, Rachel Field
The Great Big Enormous Turnip, Alexei Tolstoy
Guess How Much I Love You, Sam McBratney
Here, George, Sandra Boynton
How I Became a Pirate, Melinda Long
I Know a Rhino, Charles Fuge

In the Small, Small Pond, Denise Fleming

Kate's Car, Kay Chorao

Let's Make Rabbits, Leo Lionni

The Little Engine That Could, Watty Piper

Made for Me, Zack Bush

Millions of Cats, Wanda Gag

Miss Mary Mack (and others), Nadine Bernard Westcott

The Mitten (and many others), Jan Brett

Moonlight (and many others), Jan Ormerod

Mr. Gumpy's Motor Car (and others in the series), John Burningham

My Dad Is Amazing, Sabrina Moyle

My World, Margaret Wise Brown

Papa, Please Get the Moon for Me, Eric Carle

Peter Spier's Little Cats (and many others in the series), Peter Spier

Pretend You're a Cat, Jean Marzollo

Rosie's Walk, Pat Hutchins

The Runaway Bunny, Margaret Wise Brown

Shopping Trip (and others), Helen Oxenbury

Umbrella, Taor Yashima

A Very Busy Spider (and others), Eric Carle

A Very Special House, Ruth Krauss

Watching Foxes, Jim Arnosky

Wee Beasties, Ame Dyckman

We're Going on a Bear Hunt, Michael Rosen

What Are Stars, Katie Daynes

Where Do Diggers Sleep at Night? Brianna Caplan Sayres

Where's My Teddy? Jez Alborough

Who Said Red? Mary Serfozo

Yellow Ball, Molly Bang

ESPECIALLY FOR OLDER SIBLINGS

These books deal in a particularly sensitive way with the special concerns of kids who are suddenly (and usually against their will) displaced from the center of the universe by a baby sister or brother. See additional suggestions on page 226.

A Baby Sister for Frances, Russell Hoban

The Difference Between Babies and Cookies, Mary Hanson

101 Things to Do with a Baby, Jan Ormerod

And to Think That We Thought We'd Never Be Friends, Mary Ann Hoberman

What Shall We Do with the Boo-Hoo Baby? Jonathan Allen

CONCEPTS

A, You're Adorable, Martha Alexander

Alphabet under Construction, Denise Fleming

Anno's Counting House (and others), Mitsumasa Anno

Colors (and other concept books), Jan Pienkowski

Cookie Count, Robert Sabuda

Duck, David Lloyd

Fast Food, Saxton Freymann

Jump, Leap, Count Sheep, Geraldo Valerio

Of Colors and Things (and other photography books), Tana Hoban

26 Letters and 99 Cents, Tana Hoban

FOLK TALES

Fables, Arnold Lobel

Little Red Riding Hood, James Marshall

The Three Little Pigs, Joseph Jacobs

TRANSITIONS: GOING TO SCHOOL, BIG-KID BED, SLEEP, DAY CARE

Billy's Big-Boy Bed, Phyllis Limbacher Tildes

Going to Day Care, Fred Rogers

The Goodbye Book, Kay Chorao

Howard and the Sitter Surprise, Priscilla Paton

"And then Winnie the Pooh decided that it was time to check Daddy's e-mail again."

My New Bed, Stan and Jan Berenstain
My Nursery School, Harlow Rockwell
The Salamander Room, Anne Mazer
Time for Bed, Mem Fox

POETRY/RHYMES

Egg Thoughts and Other Frances Songs, Russell Hoban
Getting to Know You: Rogers and Hammerstein Favorites, Rosemary Wells
The Land of Nod and Other Poems for Children, Robert L. Stevenson
One Fish, Two Fish, Red Fish, Blue Fish (and anything else), Dr. Seuss
The Owl and the Pussycat, Jan Brett
Summer Evening, Walter de la Mare
Whiskers and Rhymes, Arnold Lobel
Whistle for Willie, Ezra Jack Keats

TOILET TRAINING

Everyone Poops, Taro Gomi
Koko Bear's New Potty, Vicki Lansky
Max's Potty, Harriet Ziefert
No More Diapers, J. G. Brooks
On Your Potty, Virginia Miller

FAMILY MATTERS

Family Planning

For a lot of couples, whether to have another child isn't really a question; it's a given. For others, though, it's more complicated. Quite often one spouse wants a second (or third) child, while the other isn't nearly as excited about the prospect—for a variety of reasons. Although I wanted a second child quite a bit, my memories of the incredibly long and painful labor my wife endured delivering our first baby made it almost impossible for me to consider putting her through another similar experience.

Besides the painful aspect of pregnancy and childbirth, plenty of other factors may affect your decision (or at least how you vote when you and your partner get around to discussing the issue):

- Do you really like being a parent? Is it as much fun as you thought it would be? Is it more—or less—work than you thought? Generally speaking, a second child is less stressful than the first; you'll feel like an old hand when the second baby does things that made you panic with the first one. As a result, you'll probably enjoy the second child's childhood more than the first one's. But since there's a lot of "been there, done that" associated with the second child, you'll probably be taking a lot fewer pictures and videos.

- Can you afford it? And if you can't, does it really make a difference? My parents, who were impoverished grad students when I was born, claim that I spent my first two years sleeping in a dresser drawer in their student housing unit.
- How are you and your partner going to divide the labor around the house? Are you both satisfied with the way things got handled the first time around? Two kids are going to be more than twice the work of one: each requires a certain amount of care and feeding, plus there's the additional job of keeping the two of them from killing each other.
- Do you have brothers or sisters, or were you an only child? How did you like growing up that way? Do you think your child would be better or worse off with a younger sibling?
- Your age and your partner's age. If she's close to (or over) forty, getting pregnant will be harder than it was the first time, and there's a greater chance (although still a small one) of conceiving a child with a birth defect. In addition, some research shows that children of older dads have slightly higher incidences of schizophrenia or autism than children of younger dads.
- Do you think you'll be able to love the second child as much as the first? This is one of the most common concerns of prospective second-time (and beyond) parents. The simple answer is that your capacity to love your children is infinite.
- The pregnancy is going to be different, especially for your partner. First, because the physical changes are familiar, she may not be as fascinated by what's going on inside her body. Second, many of the physical changes may happen sooner than they did the first time: she'll probably "show" sooner, she may gain more weight this time, and she may be more tired (being a parent is exhausting enough; trying to do it while you're pregnant is something altogether different).
- Try not to let your first baby's temperament influence your decision—it has absolutely no influence on how your next baby will turn out.

FILLING THE GAP

Once you make your decision to have another child, you'll probably need to decide on how far apart to space the children. The chart on the following two pages lists advantages and disadvantages of different age spreads.

Age Difference Between Children: 9 to 18 Months

ADVANTAGES	DISADVANTAGES
• Because they're close in age, there's a better chance the kids will be great playmates. • Your first child will adjust to the change more easily than if he were older; he won't really know what's going on and won't feel quite as displaced. • You're still in diaper-changing and baby-care mode. • You'll be able to immediately use your older child's clothes and toys as hand-me-downs instead of having to put them in storage.	• You may not like having two kids in diapers at the same time. • Your older child is still really a baby. He has plenty of baby needs and is going to have a tough time waiting for you to meet them. • "You can expect [the first child] to act very clingy at times, perhaps alternating with aggressive behavior towards you or others," warns nurse practitioner Meg Zweiback. • Because they're close in age, the two may compete with each other more. • Your partner is slightly more likely to develop the baby blues or postpartum depression if she had either after the first child. • Babies conceived less than six months after the birth of a previous child are 40 percent more likely to be born prematurely or underweight, according to a study in the *New England Journal of Medicine*. And a baby born less than two years after an older sibling may have an increased risk of developing autism, according to a study in the journal *Pediatrics*. • You'll probably need to buy a second crib.

Age Difference Between Children: 18 to 36 Months

ADVANTAGES	DISADVANTAGES
• This is the most common age difference in the United States, and some of your friends will probably have kids similarly spaced.	• The two kids are far enough apart to have very different schedules, activities, and interests. This means that when they're older, if you're doing the driving, you'll probably end up feeling like a taxi driver.
• This spacing leads to a lower incidence of low birth weight and other pregnancy-related complications.	• The older child is more likely to see the younger one as an invader. As a result, there's going to be more friction and rivalry between the two.
• Your older child is now more capable of waiting a bit before having his needs satisfied.	• It's hard to care for an irritable new baby and a challenging toddler at the same time.
• The older child is more articulate and can entertain himself for limited amounts of time.	• Your older child may regress, going back to thumb sucking or filling diapers or even crawling, as a way to reclaim his spot in the center of your universe.
• The older child is mature enough to enjoy the new baby and also to enjoy time away from you without seeing it as a threat.	

Age Difference Between Children: 36+ Months

ADVANTAGES	DISADVANTAGES
• The older child is even more articulate, more able to satisfy his own needs, and less likely to try to hurt the new child.	• A child who has been an only child for so long may have a very difficult time sharing you and your partner with anyone else.
• The older child can—and may very well want to—help out quite a bit.	• There may be a lot of sibling rivalry.
• A child whose sibling is more than four years younger may feel less sibling rivalry.	• There may be some regression in your firstborn.

Looking for Preschools

During the first eighteen months of your child's life, he should be the focus of his caregiver's attention. "Without this confirmation of self-importance, the child may experience insecurity that, in turn, will encumber the emergence of creative behavior," says psychologist John Rosemond. But over the second eighteen months, your child's needs change, and he needs to be taught—gradually—that he isn't the center of the universe.

At this point in your child's life, you've probably got him in some kind of day care, whether that's full-time or part-time, in a caregiver's home or at an organized childcare center. In *The New Father: A Dad's Guide to the First Year* (pages 178–188) we talked extensively about the various types of day-care options and how to select the one that's best for your child and your family. To keep this book to a manageable size, I won't repeat that information here. Instead, I'll focus on the childcare option many parents start thinking about in their child's third year: organized preschool programs.

But first, a point of clarification: A lot of people use the terms *preschool* and *day-care center* interchangeably. And while there can be some similarities, there are also some differences. For example, although both generally need to be licensed and/or accredited, day-care centers (including those run by employers and universities) typically have longer hours and operate year-round, while preschools follow a more traditional school schedule, meaning shorter hours and closures for holidays, winter break, spring break, and summer vacation. Preschools are usually designed to encourage children's cognitive, physical, social, and emotional development; often, quality day-care centers will have a similar focus. I mention this because, if you have your child in a good-quality day-care center, and you like the staff, you're happy with what he's learning and how he's developing, and he can stay there until he starts kindergarten, there's no need to disrupt his life by moving him to a preschool. However, if he's in an informal (for example, home-based) setting, you may want to consider making a change.

University of Virginia researcher Daphna Bassok and her colleagues found that in formal settings (preschools, day-care centers, and Head Start programs), caregivers are six times more likely to have a college degree in early childhood education than those in informal settings (56 percent vs. 9 percent). They're also more likely to take ongoing training and "provide a more developmentally stimulating environment." According to the researchers, "While formal caregivers read to children every day, caregivers in informal settings did so less frequently, and the same was true for math activities." In addition, in preschools and day-care centers, children watch an average of less than seven minutes of television per day. But in informal settings, kids spend nearly two hours per day watching TV.

Most preschools begin taking kids at around thirty-three months (two years, nine months). But in many major metropolitan areas, good preschools fill up months, sometimes even years, before the start of the fall semester. So get your applications together now. (It may seem kind of absurd to have to apply to get into a preschool, but if the author Robert Fulghum is right, and you really learn everything you'll ever need to know in kindergarten, then maybe it's not so crazy after all.)

THE CHOICES

There are likely dozens of preschool opportunities in your community, most of which fall into one of the following categories:

- **Cooperative.** The parents help out a lot, volunteering in the classroom, organizing activities, creating the curriculum.
- **Play-based.** Exactly what it sounds like.
- **Orthodox.** The teachers are trained in a specific method or philosophy of educating young children. This may involve using certain equipment or teaching methods. Montessori is the most common.

- **Free-form**. The school may include the best (or the worst) of a variety of educational philosophies.
- **Academic**. Structured classes in traditional subjects (math, language). Many early childhood development experts think this may be too much, too soon.
- **Head Start**. These programs are available only to low-income families. Head Start programs follow federally developed standards but usually include a mixture of play and learning activities designed to prepare kids for kindergarten. For more information, check out the National Head Start Association's website (https://www.nhsa.org) and the additional info under "Childcare" in Resources.

As with anything to do with education, preschools have lately become the subject of much controversy. One side cites research that "proves" that preschools are mediocre at best and that too many hours in preschool can lead to behavioral problems, jeopardize toddlers' attachment to their parents, and set them on a path toward a life of delinquency and crime. The other side cites research that reaches the opposite conclusions: kids who enter preschool as toddlers are more self-reliant and confident and do better in school. The contradictions are enough to drive you nuts.

Having looked at dozens of studies on the short- and long-term effects of preschool, I've reached a few conclusions of my own:

- Family problems such as stress and insufficient income cause at least as many problems as full-time day care does. In other words, if you and your partner really need to work full-time, reducing your (or her) hours at work so one of you can take on more childcare could cause financial strain and tension at home that in turn may have a negative impact on your child.
- Conversely, the quality of the child's home environment has a bigger influence than the type of childcare arrangement on child development and outcomes, according to a study by the National Institute of Child Health and Human Development. Specifically, the study found that children showed "more cognitive, language, and social competence and more harmonious relationships with parents," when their parents "provided home environments that were emotionally supportive and cognitively enriched."

  Your child will do best in a preschool that's safe and stimulating, where child-adult ratios are low, and the staff is experienced and educated. Yes, some preschools out there are bad. But you don't have to send your child to one of them. If you know what to look for and what questions to ask, you can ensure a loving, caring learning environment for your child.
- Compared to other childcare options, preschools have some distinct advantages and disadvantages. A few are listed on page 174.

WHAT TO CONSIDER WHEN CONSIDERING PRESCHOOLS

Perhaps the most important factor is your child's temperament and how it meshes with what the school has to offer (see the chart on pages 178–79). Another important factor is stability—particularly that of the children. "In child-care settings, the availability of a stable group of age-mates results in more complex, coordinated play," say the Newmans. "Children who have had many changes in their child-care arrangements are less likely to engage in complex social pretend play." Finally, you'll need to consider the financial cost. Unless you're eligible for Head Start or some other subsidized program, the sad fact is that preschools (and licensed day-care centers) are pretty expensive.

GENERAL GUIDELINES

Because finding the right preschool is the first big decision you'll have to make about your child's education, it'll probably take a while, and you shouldn't give up until you've got exactly what you were looking for or have come as close as you possibly can. At a minimum, the preschool you choose for your child should comply with your state's rules and regulations. But standards vary wildly from state to state, so licensing and accreditation are not necessarily the guarantees of quality that they ought to be. On the national level, however, the National Association for the Education of Young Children (NAEYC) accredits programs that meet its extremely high standards, and you can get referrals to accredited providers in your area at the association's website (www.naeyc.org). Another great source of high-quality referrals is Child Care Aware (www.childcareaware.org).

A Few Preschool Red Flags

As far as I'm concerned, any school that doesn't satisfy all the qualifications listed on these pages should be viewed with suspicion. Beyond that, though, here are a few things that should make you take a prospective preschool off your list completely and run the other way.

- Parents are not allowed to drop in unannounced. You need to call before visiting or coming to pick up your child.
- Your child is unhappy or scared after more than a few months.
- The staff seems to change every day.
- The staff ignores any of your concerns.
- You child reports being hit or mistreated, or you hear similar reports from other parents. Check this one out thoroughly, though. Kids have been known to fabricate stories.

But accreditation and assurances of quality aren't all there is. You should also keep the following general guidelines in mind (some of which were suggested by the NAEYC, Child Care Aware, and the American Academy of Pediatrics).

CHILD-TEACHER RATIOS

The younger the kids allowed in the preschool, the lower the child-teacher ratio should be. In a typical preschool, kids' ages range from two and a half to five. Overall, there should be no more than seven kids to each adult caregiver, and the

ADVANTAGES OF PRESCHOOL	DISADVANTAGES
• Most teachers have some experience in early childhood education and development.	• Your child may have to be potty-trained before being accepted.
• Children learn to socialize and get along with people who aren't in their family.	• Your child may be sent home if he's sick.
• State or local licensing ensures that the school will meet at least minimum health and safety standards.	• You may need to make a year-long commitment to a minimum number of days per week.
• Preschool may be less expensive than a nanny or other in-home care option.	• The child-teacher ratio may be higher than you'd like. This may mean that your child could get less individual attention than with a nanny or other caregiver.
• Schools probably have more equipment and a larger play area than you do. They also have a structured program that should expose your child to a wide variety of activities.	• Schools may be closed on holidays or for training days, which could leave you scrambling to find a caregiver.
• You might meet some other parents who have similarly aged children.	• The school's scheduled operating hours may not work well for you, or there could be extra charges for early drop-off or late pickup.
• You don't have to worry about a nanny or sitter getting sick and leaving you without care.	• Your child will come home with almost every possible childhood illness. However, this might be an advantage, since studies indicate that exposure to all those germs builds a healthier immune system.

total size of the group (not including the teachers) shouldn't exceed twenty. But check with your state's licensing department to get the most up-to-date numbers.

NUTRITION AND HEALTH
- There should be no smoking on the premises.
- Proof of immunization should be required of each child.
- If the school provides meals and/or snacks, they should be varied, wholesome, and nutritious. Menus should be available in advance.
- Rest and nap times should be scheduled, and each child should have a clean, individual place to sleep. There should also be special quiet activities for kids who don't nap.
- Teachers should wear disposable gloves whenever changing diapers and clean their hands with soap and water or, better, alcohol gel before and after. They should also wash their hands after helping a child go to the bathroom, and before touching food.
- Parents should be notified immediately of any accident or contagious illness, and there should be a clear policy for what is done with kids who get sick while at school (isolation, for starters).
- Teachers should give medication to children only with a parent's written permission.
- Emergency numbers should be clearly posted near a phone.
- At least one teacher (but all would be better) should have up-to-date first-aid and CPR certifications.

GENERAL CLEANLINESS
- Alcohol-gel hand sanitizer and paper towels should be available—at kid level— and children should use them after going to the bathroom and before all meals and snacks. A recent study of children under three in day-care centers in Spain found that compared to children who washed with soap and water, kids using hand sanitizer were 23 percent less likely to develop respiratory infections. That said, if hand sanitizer isn't available, hot (but not too hot) running water and soap is much better than nothing.
- The entire area—kitchen, tabletops, floors, sleep areas—should be clean. All garbage cans, diaper pails, and bathrooms should be cleaned thoroughly and regularly disinfected, as should toys that tend to end up in toddlers' mouths.

SAFETY
- The facility should be licensed by your state.
- Outlets, heaters, and radiators should be covered.

- Equipment should be up-to-date and meet current safety codes.
- Cleaning fluids, medicines, and any other potentially dangerous substances should be kept in places inaccessible to the children.
- There should be an emergency plan, including regular fire drills. Fire extinguishers should be available as required.
- The school should have a plan for dealing with violent children. While some hitting, pushing, and biting is pretty normal for very young kids, anything more serious (stabbing, hitting with large objects, or repeated, unprovoked attacks) is not.
- Children should not be allowed to ride in any moving vehicle without a properly installed car seat.
- Children should be adequately supervised on all field trips—even if it's only a nature walk around the block.
- Children should not be released to any adult whose name is not on a written list provided by you and your partner.
- Outdoor play areas should be carefully supervised and meet basic safety guidelines, such as having cushioned flooring underneath playground equipment, plenty of room around swings to prevent collisions, no access to bodies of water, proper fencing to prevent kids wandering off, no opportunities for kids to get their head stuck between bars, and so on. Unfortunately, there don't seem to be universal safety standards for playgrounds. However, several organizations have voluntarily come up with best practices, and the US Consumer Product Safety Commission has a checklist that you can download from its website (https://www.cpsc.gov); the full URL is under "Safety" in the Resources section.
- Outdoor areas should be safe from animal contamination (for example, the sandbox should be tightly covered).

PROGRAM

- The school's program and philosophy should be a good match to what you want and what your child needs. If you have a child with special needs that can't be accommodated at a mainstream preschool, visit the Center for Parent Information and Resources (parentcenterhub.org/resourcelibrary) for a wonderful source of referrals and resources.
- To the extent possible, substitute teachers should be familiar to the kids.
- Children should have daily opportunities to participate in a variety of active and quiet activities, including free play, age-appropriate academics, art, music, and group and individual play.
- Children should have adequate time to play outside every day, weather

permitting. There should be plenty of space for active, physical play, such as climbing, running, and jumping.

- Indoor areas must be large enough to accommodate all the kids at one time. The area should be well organized, so kids know where things go and what happens where. There should be a wide variety of age-appropriate toys, books, and materials. And there should be more than one of each toy, so that the kids don't have to wait in long lines to play.

- Parents should be welcome at any time, without advance notice. When you visit, pay attention to how your child behaves. If he basically ignores you, that's good news: it means that he's involved and interested in what he's doing. If he comes running over, that could mean that he's not being given activities that are stimulating enough.

- Overall, the preschool should be a place you wish you could have gone when you were a kid.

STAFF
- Should have completed some college level work in early childhood education and child development.
- Should seem to genuinely care for the children.
- Should be available to answer the children's questions and get down to their level when speaking with them.
- Should give you regular reports on how and what your child is doing.

EASING THE TRANSITION

Several months before our older daughter's first day of preschool, my wife and I started trying to get her ready. We'd visited the school a number of times; the principal had sent us a five-page handout on how tough this first big separation can be for kids; and my wife and I spent hours with our daughter reading books about other kids' first days, talking about who else would be at school, telling her about our own school experiences, and describing the fun things she'd get to do. We bought her new clothes in her favorite colors and a Little Mermaid lunch box and reassured her over and over that we'd pick her up every day right after lunch and that, of course, we still loved her.

Even the school itself tried to help ease the transition. A few weeks before school started, one of the teachers came over to the house and spent hours playing with our daughter and getting to know her. She also brought along a Polaroid camera and left our daughter a snapshot of her with her new teacher. On the morning of the fateful first day, we gave her cookies shaped like her favorite

Temperament and Preschool

TRAIT	SPECIAL CONSIDERATIONS
Activity Level	
• High	• Your child will need lots of room to run around, plenty of indoor activities for rainy days, lots of ways to burn off excess energy. He will also, however, need some moderately structured activities. Look for a program that has many kids his age or older: he'll admire the others' skills and want to emulate them. And make sure the teachers' energy level is at least as high as your child's.
• Low	• This child needs a quieter, smaller setting, and small groups.
• Moderate (especially those who are also a bit slow to warm)	• Your child will probably stick to the sidelines for a few days, watching and learning. He'll jump in after about a week. He likes more structure and predictability, and doesn't do well in large preschools, especially if there are a lot of more active kids his age—they can be frightening.
Sensory Awareness	
• High	• Look for a fairly calm, subdued, relaxed environment. Lots of noise, colors, and activity may frighten your child.

alphabet letters and drizzled with honey, to remind her that learning should be a sweet experience. By the time we got in the car for the drive to school on the first day, I felt pretty confident that we had prepared her both psychologically and emotionally for this milestone.

As soon as we got inside the building, I knew I was right. My daughter caught sight of a few of her friends and the teacher who had come to our house, and promptly disappeared, laughing and giggling. I shouted a goodbye (which she barely acknowledged), reminded her when I'd be back to pick her up, and walked out to the car.

Some kids won't even notice when you've gone on the first day of school. Others will freak out completely. Either way, here are some absolute musts (and must nots) for the first days:

TRAIT	SPECIAL CONSIDERATIONS
Distractibility	
• High	• This child will need a constantly changing array of things to do and play with. Look for a staff that is large enough to have a teacher that can spend extra time with your child to expose him to new things.
Regularity	
• High	• This child will need a regular schedule, regular meal and nap times, and so forth.
• Low	• This child doesn't need much in the way of scheduling but should have some anyway.
Adaptability	
• Slow to adapt	• Avoid schools with rigid schedules and highly structured activities. Also avoid unstructured schools. Look for teachers who will make a special effort to involve your child and introduce him to new materials slowly. Make sure you can stay with your child for a few minutes each morning (for at least the first week or so) to help ease his transition.
• Moderately low to adapt, intense	• This child may occasionally bite or hit other children. This will fade as he becomes more articulate. He may be upset when you drop him off at school and just as upset when you come to pick him up.

- **Prepare yourself**. Don't forget you're undergoing a difficult transition too. For more on this, see pages 259–61.
- **Never just drop your child off on the first day**, no matter how well-adjusted he seems. Go inside and get him settled.
- **Never sneak out**, even if he's deeply involved in some activity.
- **Create a goodbye routine**: kiss, do a quick drawing together, wave bye-bye through the window.
- **Don't chastise your child for crying**. Reassure him that you love him, and that you'll be back.
- **Don't be upset if your child comes home a mess**: covered with dirt, paint, glue, sparkles, or even an occasional bruise. It means he's interacting with other people and having fun.

PASSING THE BUCK

Coincidentally, the same week that my older daughter was admitted to preschool, a friend of mine was admitted to the University of San Francisco's medical school. My friend was griping about how much her tuition cost and was surprised that I wasn't more sympathetic. But when I told her that my daughter's preschool was more expensive than med school, she stopped. Naturally, not all preschools cost as much as medical school, but preschool is not going to be cheap. If you have the money, great. But most of us could use (or wouldn't turn down) a little financial assistance. And asking your employer to help out a little may be your best bet. Here are a few alternative ways that might happen:

- Direct financial assistance. Your employer pays for all or part of your expenses at the preschool of your choice.
- Negotiated discounts. Your employer—maybe in conjunction with other local employers—can negotiate group rates or discounts with a nearby preschool.
- Employee salary reductions or set-asides. If you're married and filing a joint tax return or you're a single parent, you can have your employer put up to $5,000 of your pretax salary into a Dependent Care Assistance Program (DCAP). These plans also go by other names, such as Flexible (or Flex) Spending Accounts (FSAs). Using one will enable you to reduce your preschool expenses by paying for them with pretax dollars instead of after-tax ones. Your employer will save money too, since he or she won't have to pay Social Security tax or unemployment insurance on your DCAP money.

Of course, asking your boss—or anyone else, for that matter—for help isn't easy. In fact, the reason employees most often give for not asking their bosses to get involved in employee day-care problems is fear of losing their jobs.

Nevertheless, it's worth a try. The first thing to do is to remind your boss that some assistance programs won't cost the company a cent (see above). Then read your employer this quote from the Child Care Action Campaign (CCAC): "Studies have shown that working parents' anxiety about their child care arrangements erodes their productivity—and directly affects employers' profit lines." And if you need a little more ammo, tell them about the recent study that found that employees of companies offering dependent-care services were more productive in at least one of the following ways: they were late to work less often because of family issues, they left work early less often, or they were able to concentrate better on their work.

If those approaches don't work, follow the CCAC's advice and:

- **Talk to other employees**. Do any of them have trouble finding or paying for a good preschool? How do their worries affect their productivity?
- **Find out what other employers in your field are doing about preschool**. Some prospective employees are making decisions on which companies to work for based on benefits, and if the competition offers a more family-friendly environment, your company will have to follow suit.
- **If you're in a union, speak to your union rep**. Have other employers bargained for family-friendly benefits? You may be able to include some in the next contract negotiation.
- **Encourage other employees to let management know about their childcare issues and challenges**.

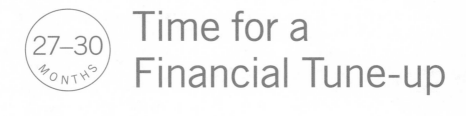

27–30 MONTHS

Time for a Financial Tune-up

WHAT'S GOING ON WITH YOUR TODDLER

Physically

- You may have noticed that your child looks different lately—less like a baby and more like a little kid. Her arms and legs are growing much faster than the rest of her body, which makes her head seem less out of proportion. Her face isn't as round, she's lost most of her baby potbelly, and those adorable little fat pads on the bottoms of her feet are almost gone.
- She's got a very busy schedule—lots of things to do and places to go. And you'll be busy too, chasing around after her to make sure she's safe.
- She can kick a ball in the direction she wants it to go and may be able to pedal a tricycle.
- She's getting much better at dressing herself and is especially interested in shoes (although she's still more than a year away from being able to lace them up). She can, however, manipulate Velcro fasteners, which she'll do over and over and over.
- Your child's emotions are more frequently expressed physically than verbally. When she's happy, she may jump up and down with glee; when angry, she may throw something down.

Intellectually

- In a toddler of this age, "self-control is still dependent upon factors outside himself, namely the approval or disapproval of his parents," writes child psychologist Selma Fraiberg. Your child is still a long way away from developing a conscience or a true ability to regulate her own negative impulses. But as her memory improves, and she can recall the things you've told her to do or not to do when you're not there to remind her in person, you'll see occasional glimpses of self-control.

- Another by-product of her improving memory is her new ability to imitate you when you aren't there with her. Welcome to the true beginning of fantasy play.
- She continues to choose less physical and more intellectual ways of solving problems. She does a lot less by trial and error and a lot more by thinking things through. For example, rather than pull you over to the bookshelf and point to the book she wants you to get down, she may simply tell you, "Bring me book."
- Your toddler is able to focus on incredibly tiny details—ones you probably would never notice. In the middle of the 417th reading of *Goldilocks and the Three Bears*, my older daughter suddenly stopped me and pointed out that the artist had made an error in a picture of the bears' breakfast table: both the daddy bear's porridge (which is supposedly too hot) and the mommy bear's porridge (supposedly too cold) were steaming. What an outrage!
- She's now able to count all the way up to two—and maybe even to three. Anything more than that, however, falls into the broad category of *many* or *lots*. She may also be able to use the word *more* to distinguish a group of three or more objects from a group of two.
- She can now follow a series of unrelated instructions, such as "Put your book back on the shelf and go wash your hands before dinner."

Verbally

- Your toddler is probably increasing her vocabulary by two to five words per day. She's so thrilled with the sound of her own voice that she'll repeat her new words over and over, including quite a few you had no idea she knew.
- She runs around naming every object she knows, and will accompany just about everything she does with a steady stream of chatter, which is directed mainly at herself. If she's looking for a conversation partner, she'll still choose you over another child almost every time.
- She's making some major advances in mastering the language. Her first two-word sentences probably consisted of one noun and one verb ("Kitty meow"), a noun and an adjective ("Pizza hot"), or a declarative statement ("All gone"). But over the next few months, she'll start creating possessives ("Daddy's hat"), plurals ("Daddy's fingers"), and using small but important words like *on*, *in*, and *the*.
- She still makes a lot of really cute (but extremely logical) grammatical errors with pronouns, though ("I went to he's house," "Give the cup to she"). And she's a little unclear on past and future tenses: "I go to store" can mean, "I am going now," "I went," or "I will go."

- Perhaps the most interesting language-related development is that at this age, according to Selma Fraiberg, "language makes it possible for a child to incorporate his parents' verbal prohibitions, to make them part of himself." This isn't always 100 percent successful, though. You may find her sitting on the floor, eating sugar out of the box and saying, "No, baby not eat sugar," between mouthfuls.
- In addition to "Whazzat?" your toddler now asks such questions as "Why?" and "Where is _____?" According to child-development experts Louise Bates Ames and Frances Ilg, your child will master more space words (*in*, *out*, *up*, *down*, *in front of*, *behind*, and so on) in the six-month period from two to two and a half than in any other six-month period of her life.

Emotionally and Socially

- Your toddler shows incredible pride in the things she's able to do and actively seeks your approval. "Look at me!" she will implore you, a hundred times a day, as she climbs up the stairs to the slide, fills up her bucket with sand, draws a straight line, or rides her trike.
- You might not be able to tell yet, but she's slowly becoming more interested in other kids. You'll realize it for yourself when, out of the blue, she starts making a strange noise or using a word she never used before—the same noise or word used a few days before by that two-year-old at the park, the one your child seemed to be ignoring completely.
- Another way she shows her interest in other kids is by physically exploring them. Unfortunately, this may involve some hitting, pushing, shoving, and hair pulling. But remember, your child isn't intentionally being mean; she's still learning about the difference between animate and inanimate objects and is fascinated by cause and effect. As Ames and Ilg write, "A child may begin stroking another child's hair because he likes the way it looks, then may pull it to see how it feels."
- Marked by near-instant 180-degree mood swings and arbitrary mind changes, this can be an exceedingly demanding time for you and your child.

WHAT YOU'RE GOING THROUGH

Taking a Long, Hard Look at . . . Yourself

I always felt proud when someone told me how much my daughters look like me (although it embarrassed them to no end). And I felt tickled inside when my parents or other relatives told me how much the girls acted like I did as a kid. But

I was a little less enchanted when one of them spit out one of my "goddamnits" (or worse) when she couldn't tie her shoes or I told her it was time for bed.

When this kind of thing happens (and if it hasn't yet, it will very soon), you may suddenly find yourself imagining your child imitating some of your less savory

Responding to "Look at Me!"

As mentioned above, you'll be hearing the phrase, "Look at me!" quite a bit for the next few years. Most of the time, your toddler just wants to get your approval for something she's doing or to get you to look at something she finds interesting. In those situations, it's important that you respond quickly and positively. The more you do, the more cooperative your child will be when you want her to do something later, according to researcher Marie-Pierre Gosselin. The way you respond will also influence the way your child tries to get your attention in the first place.

You've probably noticed that the fastest way to get your toddler to want to interact with you is to ignore her, either deliberately or simply by turning your attention to something else, whether that's a phone call, a crossword puzzle, a football game, or any other activity. Toddlers whose parents have responded positively to their child's requests to "Look at me!" tend to employ what Gosselin calls "high-quality attention-seeking behaviors," such as laughing, smiling, and saying "excuse me." Toddlers whose parents have been slower to respond or less attentive use "negative attention-seeking behaviors," like crying, screaming, or grabbing the remote out of Dad's hands and throwing it across the room.

Now is the time to start giving your toddler some strategies for attracting your attention when you're occupied. For example, she's old enough now to learn that if she wants to talk to you or show you something, she should politely say, "Excuse me." If that doesn't work, she should add a few gentle hand squeezes. Whenever she does either of these things, you must respond quickly and positively.

If you're in the middle of something that can't be interrupted, respond to your child's attempts to break through by gently squeezing her hand (unless you smell smoke, in which case, all bets are off). That tells her that you know she wants to say something but that you need a bit more time. Avoid responding verbally, however, because in her mind, the fact that you stopped whatever you were doing to tell her that she shouldn't interrupt you is proof that interrupting works.

and less cute behaviors. And you'll be horrified. "The honest and direct response of children to some 'bad habits' forces men to confront these behaviors and consider the consequences, not only for themselves but also for their children," says parenting educator Glen Palm. If, for example, you eat a lot of candy bars and potato chips, you may find yourself questioning the kind of example you're setting and decide to cut back on trans fats (partially hydrogenated oils). If you're a smoker, seeing your child sitting in her high chair "smoking" her spoon could be just the incentive you need to quit.

Bottom line? Your child is looking at everything you do, and she'll model her behavior on yours. She's still too young to care about whether you cheat on your taxes or under-tip the waitstaff—but she hasn't yet learned to lie. I remember taking my thirty-month-old to a movie. When we got to the front of the ticket line, the clerk asked how old my child was. Seeing a sign that read "Two and under free," I didn't miss a beat. "Almost two," I lied. Unfortunately, my excessively verbal daughter didn't miss a beat either, and yelled out, "No, Daddy, I'm two and half!" In that incredibly long moment of embarrassment, I wondered whether saving the price of a movie matinee ticket was worth teaching my daughter that lying is okay.

Your child will also be paying special attention to your relationship with your partner. If you have a son, he'll use you as an example of how to treat (or not treat) the women in his life. If you treat your partner with respect and love, share the workload at home, and take an interest in her and her life, he'll probably do the

"You're right—this is way better than a standing desk."

same with his own partner and children when he gets older. If you get stuck in the role of disciplinarian or leave all the parenting or housework up to your partner, he'll do that instead.

If you have a daughter, she's learning how she should expect to be treated in her future relationships and how important it is to have an involved, loving co-parent around. If she sees you taking an active role, she'll expect her future partner to do the same. If she sees you on the periphery, that's where she'll expect the father of her children to be.

Throughout all of this, make sure your child sees you and your partner having some fun—as individuals and as a couple. There's no question that parenting is an incredibly demanding job. But it can be incredibly fun too. So laugh a little.

Emotional Changes

One of the most commonly heard complaints about men is that we're out of touch with our emotions or that we suppress them. Before I became a dad, I think I might have agreed. But since then, I strongly disagree. Fathers—especially those who are actively involved with their children—feel tremendous joy, anger, affection, fear, and anxiety. The problem is that men in our society don't have places where we can safely express our feelings. We're supposed to be the tough guy, the stoic provider-protector. It's hard for most men to talk about their deepest emotions with their male friends. And it's even harder to talk about them—especially the so-called negative ones—with the women in our lives.

As a result, we learn to regulate our emotions. But please remember: regulating is not the same as suppressing. "The ability to control one's own impulses in the service of caring for one's children and emotionally supporting one's spouse would seem to be an important marker of maturity," write family researchers Phil and Carolyn Cowan. Nevertheless, don't forget that you provide a crucial model for how your child learns to express her own emotions—fear, anger, disappointment, sadness, happiness, and excitement.

Besides regulating our emotions, fathers undergo a variety of other changes in how we experience and react to the world around us. Here are some of the many ways men say that being a dad has broadened their emotional range (see pages 129–33 for some of the other changes fatherhood brings). It's drawn from research done independently by Glen Palm, Barbara and Philip Newman, Phil and Carolyn Cowan, and me.

- **Empathy**. Learning to see the world from another person's perspective (in this case, your child's) is what empathy is all about. Very young children don't disguise their emotions, and the more time you spend getting to know your toddler, the more aware you'll be of her feelings and how she sees the world.

- **Expressiveness**. Seeing how emotionally expressive your child can be and helping her express and accept her feelings (from "I love you" to "I'm sad because my feelings are hurt") may allow you to accept and express your own more readily.
- **Selflessness**. Another major marker of maturity is the ability to take pleasure in doing something for someone else—without any expectation of repayment.
- **Sensitivity**. Try to equate your child's bruised and unhappy feelings with physical bruises. This is exactly the approach taken by one father interviewed by parent-child communication experts Adele Faber and Elaine Mazlish. "Somehow the image of a cut or laceration helped him realize that his son required as prompt and serious attention for his hurt feelings as he would for a hurt knee," they write.
- **Outrage**. I know that before I was a father, I had seen plenty of parents hit or even abuse their children. I'm sure it bothered me—but not the way it bothers me now. And I'm more bothered by reading or watching reports of kidnapped or murdered children than I ever was before I had children of my own. (See pages 252–55 for information on what to do when you witness abuse.)
- **Expansion**. Before becoming fathers, men are generally limited in the ways they express affection: kissing, hugging, holding hands, and having sex. But having children frequently allows men to expand their repertoire. Kissing, hugging, and holding hands are still appropriate affectionate gestures, but so are tickling, rocking, tumbling, snuggling, and stroking.
- **Emotional control**. Although being a dad will expand your emotional range, it also requires learning when and how it's appropriate to express emotions such as anger and frustration. You won't suppress them entirely, but you'll simply be more aware of how your emotions affect the people around you.

YOU AND YOUR TODDLER

Deployed Dads: Staying Involved When You Can't Be There

For about half a million toddlers, Dad or Mom (sometimes both) is in the military. It used to be that most military families could stay together—on base or off—no matter where the service member was stationed. But these days, there's a good chance that you could find yourself deployed overseas and away from your family for a year or longer.

Being separated from the people you love most in the world is never easy. But it's especially hard—on everyone—during times of war. For that reason, it's important to prepare yourself and your family as far in advance as you can. If you think you're in any danger of getting deployed, start by making contact with your built-in support network. A number of organizations offer resources and services to military personnel. You can get help preparing a will, find checklists of things to take care of before you go, learn about how you and your family can stay in touch, get your partner plugged into a spouses' support group, and much more. Two great resources are the National Military Family Association (https://www.militaryfamily.org) and my book *The Military Father: A Hands-on Guide for Deployed Dads*.

Once you get your orders, here are a few tips that can make the incredibly stressful time before you ship out a little more bearable:

- **Spend as much time as you can with your child**. Talk with her about your upcoming trip. She won't be able to understand many of the details, but tell her you're going away for a while and that you'll be thinking of her and that you'll send her kisses every night. If your child cries or seems sad, don't try to talk her out of her feelings. Encourage her to express as much as she can. Offer to draw a picture for her of what she's feeling. (For more on how to talk to your child, see pages 195–98.)

- **Take care of business**. If you're the one who's managed the family finances, paid the bills, or done all the online banking, start handing off those duties to your partner. Make sure she has access to all your accounts, has a schedule of which bills need to be paid and when, and knows where all your important papers are. Since you probably won't need much money while you're overseas, arrange to have most or all of your paycheck automatically deposited into an account your partner can access.

- **Write a bunch of notes to your child and give them to your partner**. Ask her to "find" one every few days and read it to your child.

- **Take a picture of you and your child** and get it framed so she can look at it whenever she wants to and so your partner can show it to her to keep your image firmly implanted in her memory.

- **Try not to change your family routines and rituals before you go, and ask your partner to maintain them after you've left**. Whether or not your child is fully aware of the consequences of your deployment, her life will be very different without you. Her routines will be something she can count on. If you don't have any routines or rituals, start some now.

- **Make audio and/or video recordings of yourself reading books**. Include some of her favorites and some brand-new ones she hasn't heard. Ask your partner to make "reading" a story with Daddy part of her nighttime routine. And don't forget to tell your child and your partner at the end of every recording that you love them.

- **Make sure important people (day-care providers, grandparents, parents of playmates, and so on) in your child's life know what's going on**, and let them know that your child's behavior could change suddenly.
- **When it's time for you to leave, say goodbye**—don't just disappear.
- **After you leave, communicate as frequently as possible**. Depending on where you are, you may be able to send e-mail or snail mail, or post audio or video to a website or blog. Tell your partner and your child everything you're allowed to—even the most mundane details. Include drawings or small keepsakes if possible. Ask your partner to send you as much as she can—recordings of your toddler saying, "Hi, Daddy!" finger paintings, and anything else that's practical for her to send and for you to receive.
- **Take this book or *The Military Father* with you (both are available as e-books) and read up on your toddler's development while you are away**. She is going to look and sound very different when you get back. Knowing what to expect and where she is developmentally will help you stay up-to-date.
- **Don't forget about your partner**. She's going to miss you a lot too, and she's going to have a lot more responsibilities and stress in her life when you aren't there. And because she's the one who reads the papers and watches the news and knows the risks service members face, she's going to be worried and frightened. She needs plenty of reminders that you're okay and that you're thinking about—and missing—her.
- **If your partner is the stepmother of one or more of your children, be sure to take advantage of the military's free legal services to draft documents that will give her the legal authority she'll need to make decisions that affect the children**. (This is assuming the children's biological mother is out of the picture for some reason. If she isn't, try to draft an agreement that will allow your partner to have regular contact with the children while you're gone. She and they need to maintain their relationship.)

Technology for Toddlers, Part II

In the first chapter we talked about introducing your child to technology, preferably not until she's two (see pages 31–36). As she gets older, it gets increasingly important to monitor her screen time. But what, exactly, does that mean? And what counts as screen time?

The place to start is by thinking of technology, especially apps, as pretty much like all those other toys you have around the house, except that they should be used, in the words of University of Michigan pediatrician and researcher Jenny Radesky, as tools "to support family connection." Here's how to make that happen:

- **Watch the clock**. At this age, unless your child has already become a tech addict, she probably won't be interested in spending any more than a few minutes at a time playing on your phone, tablet, or computer, but those short sessions can really add up. So limit your child's screen time to an absolute maximum of one hour, in total, per day. Much more than that can interfere with sleep, physical playtime, her ability to handle emotions, and the possibility of building relationships with others, and it may contribute to obesity later in life, says Radesky.

- **Allow for tech use that promotes family bonding and communication**. Video chatting with a parent who's stationed overseas or away on a business trip, or with the grandparents who live several states away, doesn't count toward that hour. Neither does watching a video together and talking about it.
- **Do not install devices in bedrooms**. And don't leave the TV or video games on in the background, even at mealtimes.
- **Don't allow your toddler to use a device solo** (except in rare circumstances). Ideally, you should sit with your child while she's playing on a device. Talk together about what she's doing and why, what's happening on the screen, and whether she's having fun.
- **Don't forget about physical play**. No matter how much your child likes mobile devices or how convenient and engaging they are, remember: your child needs at least a few hours of physical play every single day. University of California at Santa Cruz researchers Nick Antrilli and Su-hua Wang wanted to see how touchscreen play affected the cognitive flexibility (that's the ability to switch our thinking between concepts or to think about more than one thing at a

"It's very important that you try very, very hard to remember where you electronically transferred Mommy and Daddy's assets."

Picking Good Apps

There are literally hundreds of thousands of educational smartphone- or tablet-based apps aimed at kids. Product sellers in the various app stores will assure you that their app will make you rich and your child smarter, taller, and more beautiful. However, just because an app is being sold by a big-name company, like Apple, Google, or Amazon, is hardly a guarantee that it's (a) educational, (b) high quality, and/or (c) appropriate for your child. Here are some guidelines to keep in mind, some of which were suggested by Stamatios Papadakis and Michail Kalogiannakis, from the University of Crete; Heather Kirkorian, from the University of Wisconsin; and Kathy Hirsh-Pasek, from Temple University, and her colleagues.

- The app should have a clearly stated objective and purpose. Will it help your child learn letters? Shapes? Colors? Numbers? Animals? AP calculus?
- Information and lessons must be meaningful and relevant to the child (otherwise, honestly, what's the point?). For example, if a game is teaching about shapes, it should go beyond simply identifying a triangle among a bunch of circles and squares. Instead, it should point out how various shapes show up in the real world (square and rectangular windows and books, round balls, holes in toilet-paper tubes and wheels, triangular trees, and so on).
- The app should require active involvement. I'm not talking about physical involvement, such as swiping or poking, but mental involvement: thinking through how to solve a puzzle, figuring out what steps to take to help a character navigate its way out of a maze, or moving objects around on the screen to make two groups of the same number of items.
- The app should be intuitive. (Your toddler isn't going to sit down and read a manual.)
- Your child should be in control of what happens in the app. For example, your child—as opposed to you or some other adult—should be the one to help the bunny find the carrot.
- The app and the environment must be engaging and distraction-free. A lot of apps start with a story, and that's great, because it's easier to remember what happens in a story than a collection of random facts. Too many apps, however, interrupt the story with games, ads, pop-ups, music, animation,

and other stuff that diverts the child's attention. "You don't want to have a lot of distracting things that pull away from the key lesson. But if there are interactive features that help move the story forward, that can be helpful," says researcher Heather Kirkorian. Studies suggest that lots of distraction at this age may be associated with attention problems by age nine. At the same time, having TV or music on in the background is also a distraction that may draw the child's attention away.

- The app needs to be in the Goldilocks Challenge Zone. If it's too easy, your child will be bored; too hard, and she'll be frustrated. In either case, she looks away. In addition to looking for apps with the right combination of age appropriateness and challenge, you should also choose those that will grow with your child and continue to challenge her as she gets older.

- Apps should provide feedback and appropriate rewards. Emphasis should be on hard work, not on how smart the child is. Carol Dweck and other researchers have repeatedly shown that praising children for their intelligence steers them away from taking on challenges and risks by stimulating their fear of appearing stupid.

- Apps must provide opportunities for social interaction. Some will allow several children to work together to solve problems. Others encourage conversations or cooperative play between parent and child. As mentioned on page 191, solo device play should be rare.

- Avoid fast-paced graphics, violence, and stereotyping.

It'll be pretty hard to find an app or a program that satisfies all these conditions. But the more boxes you can check off, the better. Still, unless you're a specialist in early childhood education, you probably won't be able to make a very informed decision about the appropriateness of whatever app you're considering. The number of reviews or stars an app has can be helpful, but they're often suspect. Fortunately, you can get reliable reviews from Common Sense Media (https://www.commonsensemedia.org), for free; or from CTREX, or Children's Technology Review (http://reviews.childrenstech.com), as a paid subscriber. You may also want to check out the unbiased ratings from ESRB, the Entertainment Software Rating Board (https://www.esrb.org).

time) of two-and-a-half-year-olds. Two groups of toddlers spent nine minutes playing with either a touchscreen or playing physically, while a control group colored. The researchers then gave all three groups a task designed to measure cognitive flexibility. Compared to the control group, the kids in the physical play group showed a gain in cognitive flexibility. Those in the touchscreen group did no better than the control group. Antrilli and Wang noted, though, that "toddlers who played the touchscreen game in a socially interactive way outperformed those who treated gaming as solitary play."

- **Don't use media to calm your child** (except in rare cases). You don't want to create a situation where your child becomes dependent on technology.
- **Don't allow use of any device within at least an hour of bedtime**. Using smartphones or tablets or watching television before bedtime is associated with delayed bedtime, shorter total sleep time, and poor sleep quality, according to Stony Brook University researcher Lauren Hale and her colleagues. Many experts believe that the culprit is the blue light that's emitted from so many of our screens. Swedish researchers C. Martyn Beaven and Johan Ekström have found that as little as a few minutes of exposure to blue light has the same effect as 240 milligrams of caffeine (about the same as three cups of coffee). For adults, the extra alertness and focus that blue light provides might be a good thing. But for a toddler, who needs a lot of sleep, it's quite the opposite. If, for some reason, you're not able to limit your child's (and your own) exposure to devices close to bedtime, at least get blue-light filters for your devices.
- **Preview smart toys**. A friend got my youngest daughter a toy oven that "talked" whenever certain buttons were pushed or doors were opened. At first it seemed fairly harmless, and my daughter loved it. But then I got to thinking about the mixed messages she was getting: while I always told her that our oven is hot and that she shouldn't open the doors or touch it at all, the talking oven gleefully encouraged her to do exactly the opposite.
- **Limit your own screen time, especially when you're with your child**. First of all, if your nose is buried in your phone or you're glued to your tablet, you're setting a rotten example for your child—one she'll immediately imitate. Second, it'll interfere with your relationship with your child. "Heavy parent use of mobile devices is associated with fewer verbal and nonverbal interactions between parents and children and may be associated with more parent-child conflict," says Radesky.

CHILDREN'S APPS AND PROGRAMS

Back in the early days of computers, researchers Susan Haugland and Daniel Shade found that there were two basic types of software programs for children:

nondevelopmental (also called "drill-and-practice"), which, according to Shade, is the "computer equivalent of flashcards and is not good for preschoolers," and *developmental* (or "open-ended"), which provides children with "the opportunity to explore an environment, make choices, and then find out the impact of these decisions." Haugland tested four groups of children: the first used nondevelopmental software programs; the second used developmental; the third also used developmental but supplemented it with additional activities; and the fourth group used no computers at all.

After eight months, the kids in the three computer groups all showed huge gains in self-esteem over the kids in the fourth group. However, children who used the drill-and-practice software experienced an amazing 50 percent drop-off in their creativity—a drop not experienced by either the kids who used open-ended software or those who had no computer exposure. "Clearly," concluded Haugland and Shade, "nondevelopmental software may have a detrimental effect on children's creativity."

Kids who worked with the developmental (open-ended) software had "significant gains on measures of intelligence, nonverbal skills, structural knowledge, long-term memory, and complex manual dexterity." About thirty years later, Haugland and Shade's findings still hold true.

For tips on selecting apps and software, see "Picking Good Apps," pages 192–93.

Listening So Your Child Will Talk

Generally speaking, there's not a lot of sense in talking if no one's listening. And the only way your child will ever learn how to be a good listener is if you show her the way. Here's how to do it:

- **Pay attention**. When your child wants to talk, face her and look her in the eye. Turn off the TV, radio, and your music playlist; don't answer the phone; and disregard any other distractions. You may not even need to speak; sometimes all your child wants is for you to look at her.
- **Get your child involved**. Asking your child for her vote on the dinner menu or weekend plans (and taking her advice once in a while) or asking for her opinion of a movie you saw together or on how to rearrange the furniture shows her you respect her and that what she says is important.
- **Allow your child to have her feelings**. Don't tell a kid who says she's angry (or sad or hungry or sick or sleepy) that she's not.
- **Keep things moving**. Asking yes or no questions is the quickest way to end a conversation. Instead, pick up on something your child said and ask a question that restates it or uses some of the same words your child used. Doing this has two purposes. First, you're sending a strong signal that she's important and that

you value what she has to say. Second, by repeating some of her words, you're reinforcing her budding language skills.

- **Don't interrupt**. If you're having a discussion with your child, listen respectfully to her ideas—from beginning to end—before jumping in. You want her to do the same for you, right?
- **Be patient**. No matter how verbal she may be, your toddler still has a limited vocabulary, and there may be occasional delays between what she's thinking and what actually comes out of her mouth. Let her struggle for a few seconds before you start filling in the missing words.
- **Show that you're listening**. According to parent-child communication experts Adele Faber and Elaine Mazlish, short, simple phrases that indicate you're listening, like "Oh, I see" and "Hmmm," are much better for stimulating your child to talk than jumping in with advice.
- **Give your child's feelings a name**. If your child tells you she wants to smash a friend's face in, telling her, "I can see that you're really angry," is far better than telling her that she shouldn't talk that way about her friends. "Parents don't usually give this kind of response," say Faber and Mazlish, "because they fear that by giving a name to the feeling, they'll make it worse. Just the opposite is true. The child who hears the words for what he is experiencing is deeply comforted. Someone has acknowledged his inner experience." But watch out: children usually hate it when you blindly repeat their exact words back to them ("Daddy, I hate Bobby!" "It sounds like you really hate Bobby." *Duh*.)
- **Help her fantasize**. Rather than give a logical, rational response to your child's irrational request ("No, we can't go to Grandma and Grandpa's house for dinner—they live in Paris, and it's too far to go right now"), jump in and fantasize ("I wish I could just snap my fingers and take us there right away. Would you please drive the magic carpet? I want to take a nap").
- **Watch for nonverbal cues**. Your child's mood, tone of voice, and energy level may tell you more about what she's feeling than what she actually says. Encourage her to talk about how she is feeling.
- **Don't ask why**. Kids don't always know why they feel a particular way (do you?). "It's easier to talk to a grown-up who accepts what you're feeling," say Faber and Mazlish, "rather than one who presses you for explanations."

Talking so Your Child Will Pay Attention to You

Once you and your child are able to communicate with each other verbally, you'll find that a lot of what you say to her is, in one form or another, an attempt to gain her cooperation. Here's how to improve the chances that your child will (a) hear what you say, and (b) respond the way you want her to:

- **Describe what you see, not what you think**. Instead of "You always take off your socks in the living room and dump sand on the rug. Do you have any idea how long it takes me to clean up after you every day?" try something like, "There's sand on the rug. Where do you think it came from?"
- **Give information**. Instead of "What on earth is the matter with you? I've told you seven hundred times to stop jumping on that couch!" try "Couches are not for jumping on."
- **Say it with a word**. Instead of "I've been telling you for the past hour and a half to put your crayons away, get your clothes off, and get ready for bed," you'll probably have better luck with, "Pajamas!" This approach, by the way, works equally well with teenagers, who also don't like long-winded sermons.
- **Talk about your feelings**. Rather than criticize the child in a personal way ("You're really annoying me with your constant shouting and screaming" or "You're such a pain"), keep the focus on you ("I get frustrated when you yell at me like that. I do much better when people speak to me in a nice way").
- **Make specific—not general—requests**. "I want you to help me put your cars back in the box" is much better than "Clean up your stuff."
- **Be consistent**. Don't mumble "no" a few times about a behavior and then forget about it. That only encourages your child to ignore you.
- **Give choices**. "Do you want an apple or an orange?" is far more likely to get a response than "What do you want to eat?" Offering choices in this way is just about guaranteed to reduce the number of adult-toddler power struggles.
- **Don't ask questions if you don't want answers**. "Can you help clean up your room, please?" only gives the child the (incorrect) impression that she has a choice in the matter.
- **Don't repeat yourself**. If she didn't listen the first six times, why would you think she would the seventh?
- **Don't make idle threats**. Kids often take a threat as a challenge. Will you really carry through? If you don't, you've lost credibility. If you do, you might have to raise the ante every time you want your child to do something.
- **Admit your mistakes**. Your child will learn that it's okay to be wrong every once in a while.
- **Keep your promises**. Your child may not have a very developed sense of time, but she'll never forget that you promised her a trip to the zoo or a candy bar. And if *you* forget, you've lost a ton of credibility.
- **Whisper**. Kids hate to miss anything that might have anything to do with them. Speaking softly has been known to stop even the loudest child in her tracks.
- **Do your scolding in private**. If your child misbehaves in public or in a social setting, take her into a separate room or space—it'll be less embarrassing for

both of you. It will also reduce your child's instinctive need to try to save face by flouting your authority in public.

- **Praise effectively**. Statements like "Great job!" can become so automatic that they lose their meaning. Try to be more specific: "Wow! Did you ride your trike all the way around the block?" Besides being more satisfying, this type of praise encourages conversation.

- **Make a big deal out of good behavior**. As we've discussed elsewhere, your child craves your attention—any way she can get it. And if the only time you pay attention to her is when she's misbehaving, she'll misbehave as often as she can, feeling that behaving well is a waste of time, since no one seems to notice.

- **Say *yes* more often and give your child lots of opportunities to succeed**. Children hear the word *no* (or "You can't" or "You shouldn't" or "Stop that" or "Don't") about ten times more often than *yes*. That explains why *no* is the first word many children learn to say. It also explains why kids frequently ignore the word. You can decrease the number of negatives your child hears by keeping your rules reasonable, keeping her out of situations (such as stores with lots of breakables on low shelves) where you'll likely need to stop her, and analyzing situations where your child repeatedly ignores you to find out why she's doing what she's doing.

FAMILY MATTERS

More about Nutrition

Just a few months ago you may have been worried that your toddler was eating only one food for days at a time. Well, at least she was eating. But now she may seem to be giving up food altogether. And in a way, that's true. For the first two years of life your baby was storing body fat, and her weight was increasing by about 9 percent every month. But now that she doesn't need all that fat, she's slowed way down, gaining only about 1 percent a month.

The good news is that your child isn't starving to death. When it comes to eating, toddlers are notoriously unpredictable and picky. She may go a day or two without eating much, but then over the next few days she'll put away more food than you would have thought possible. During those odd moments when your toddler does eat, she'll probably limit herself to only two or three foods. The solution to handling this? You decide what your child eats and when; she decides whether to eat it and how much.

I know, I know, that sounds like the nutritional equivalent of giving your toddler the keys to your car, but it really works. Expecting her to eat three balanced

Dealing with Dessert

Promising your child a cookie if she stops crying may seem like a good idea at the time, but in the long run it's not. Using dessert as a bribe is sending the message that whatever it is you're offering (which will probably be packed with fat and sugar and empty calories) is extremely desirable. The same thinking happens when you tell your child that she can't have dessert until she eats everything on her plate. She interprets that as an admission on your part that the food she doesn't want to eat is disgusting and the dessert that you're dangling in front of her is wonderful.

A nutritionist friend suggests that the way to avoid these problems is to put all the food you'd like your child to eat on the plate at the same time—including dessert. Her theory is that when dessert is no longer forbidden, it becomes less desirable, and your child won't be any more attracted to a brownie than to a carrot. (Of course, you can have fresh fruit or low-fat ice cream for dessert, and brownies don't have to be an option at all.)

meals and two healthy snacks every day is completely unrealistic. But if you keep offering a wide variety of options, she'll balance things out on her own over the course of a week or so. Giving your child some control over her own food intake may have the additional side effect of making her braver and more willing to try new things.

MINIMIZING FOOD FIGHTS

Mealtimes are a great opportunity for the whole family to spend time together. They're also a great opportunity for your toddler to test some limits. Here are some suggestions that can make family meals a little more enjoyable for everyone:

- **Relax**. If your child doesn't want to try a new food, leave her alone; the bigger the deal you make of it, the more fights there will be. You may have to introduce a new food as many as twenty times before she takes her first bite. In the meantime, let her sniff it, play with it, and even spit it out a few times. And does she really have to eat in a high chair at this point? Just put her someplace where she can't make a huge mess (or at least where her mess will be fairly easy to clean up).
- **Keep serving sizes reasonable**. A toddler's serving size is about one-quarter of an adult's, so limit servings of each food to one or two tablespoons—an amount roughly as big as your toddler's fist. Much more than that could intimidate her.
- **Be a good role model**. If your diet consists mostly of peanut butter and jelly sandwiches, you can't really expect your toddler to be very adventurous.

The Dream Diet

Just in case you're wondering what an ideal toddler diet would look like, your child should have the following every day:

- Five to six servings of grains, cereal, bread, rice, pasta (one serving is one-half slice of bread or bagel, one-quarter cup of rice or cooked pasta, or one-half cup of dry cereal).
- Two to three servings of veggies, particularly broccoli, cauliflower, brussels sprouts, cabbage, spinach, carrots, yams/sweet potatoes, tomatoes, or beans (one serving is one-half cup of cooked vegetables or one-third cup of raw vegetables).
- Two to three servings of fruit, such as apples, apricots, cantaloupe, oranges, grapefruit, berries, and so on (one serving is one-quarter cup or one-quarter of a piece of fruit).
- Three servings of low-fat dairy (one serving is one-half cup of milk or yogurt or one ounce of cheese).
- Two servings of poultry, fish, meat, or high-protein vegetarian equivalent (one serving is one or two ounces of lean meat or tofu, one tablespoon of peanut butter, or half an egg).
- Two healthy snacks, which can be a serving of fruit, cheese, or vegetables.

Sounds great, doesn't it? Unfortunately, getting a toddler to eat anything that remotely resembles the ideal diet is going to be a struggle. But here are a few things you can do to improve your chances:

- **Stay away from products labeled "drinks."** Anything that has the word *drink* in its name is probably more sugar than juice.
- **Limit juice**. Toddlers should get no more than one-half cup (four ounces) of 100 percent juice per day. The problem is that while juice is an excellent source of a number of vitamins and other nutrients, it usually has little or no fiber and a lot of calories. Whole fruit has the same nutritional benefits plus the fiber, so go for that instead.
- **Limit chocolate milk**. In an attempt to boost their children's milk intake, some parents give their kids chocolate milk. While it has the same nutritional benefits as unflavored milk, an eight-ounce serving of chocolate milk has twenty-seven grams of sugar and 190 calories. Eight ounces of Coke has twenty-six grams of sugar and 199 calories. No, I'm not suggesting switching to Coke. Neither one has any place in a child's diet.

- **Limit caffeine**. A single can of Coke has the same effect on a toddler that drinking four cups of coffee does on you.
- **Limit processed and fast foods**. Lunch meats, hot dogs, and many other processed and fast foods contain sodium nitrates, which the American Cancer Society believes may cause cancer in children.
- **Limit candy and other junk food**. Kids between two and three consume about 1,300 calories a day, and a candy bar has about 200 calories—a pretty big chunk of the day's intake.
- **Limit fat**. Starting at about two years of age, no more than 30 percent of your child's calories should come from fat. You can reduce fat by using less butter, switching to low-fat milk and cheese, serving less meat and more fish and poultry, and using lower-fat cooking methods such as grilling and broiling rather than frying.
- **Limit dairy**. Unless your pediatrician says otherwise, your child should probably not have more than one or two eight-ounce cups of low-fat or nonfat milk a day. Any more than that could interfere with absorption of iron.
- **Limit protein**. According to studies, toddlers get two to three times more protein than they need.
- **Increase fiber**. Your child needs about nineteen grams of fiber every day, but most get only about half that, eleven grams. Good sources include whole-grain breads, beans, peas, and others legumes, brown rice, apples, bananas, nuts, figs, plums, pears, berries, potatoes, and spinach.
- **Set a good example**. Don't eat junk food in front of your child. If you stop at a convenience store for a candy bar, when you finish it, brush your teeth—and don't leave the wrapper lying around. If your child doesn't smell the chocolate on your breath, she'll certainly recognize the empty packaging and know she's been left out.
- **Take things out of their original packages**. What's often most attractive about certain foods is the box they come in. Transferring cereals and other sugary things into a large jar or plastic container can make them a lot less attractive.
- **Eat a rainbow**. Naturally colorful fruits and vegetables—the more colorful the better—tend to be high in vitamins and other important nutrients.
- **Talk to your pediatrician about vitamins and supplements**. If your child is getting a balanced diet, she probably won't need any. But if she's especially picky or absolutely refuses to eat, get the doctor's advice.

Food and Your Child's Temperament

Researcher Jim Cameron has found that your child's eating habits—like just about everything else in her life—are greatly influenced by her temperament (you can revisit temperament types on pages 118–25):

- The **slow-adapting toddler** may consider your efforts to feed her intrusive and may try to get out of her high chair as if it were a straitjacket. She often rejects new foods, not because they taste bad but because they taste new or because she doesn't like the texture. And old foods prepared in new ways may be rejected on principle.
- The **high-intensity toddler** may seem to exist on only five or six foods. Don't bother introducing a new food when your toddler is really hungry—she's probably tired and not in the mood for new things. Her first reaction to new foods will be one of suspicion, so if you really want her to try something new, wait until she's a little hungry and not too tired. The more intense your child, the more problems you'll have trying to get her to stick to a strict eating schedule. The more you insist, the more likely your efforts will result in a tantrum.
- The **high-activity toddler** wants to be in complete control of her meals. She may refuse to be fed by anyone but herself, and may not eat if she can't hold the food (or at least the utensil it's supposed to be on). It's impossible even to guess how much she'll eat or when. If she's tired, she won't eat much, but you might get her to try an old favorite. If she's well rested, she'll eat even less (she'll want to run around instead). Have lots of snacks available for quick refueling, and don't waste your time trying to get her into a high chair.
- The **irregular, slow-to-adapt toddler** may be the toughest of all. You can expect her to sit at the dinner table for a while, but don't expect her to actually eat anything. Instead, she'll want to eat on her own schedule. Again, have lots of healthy snacks around for her swings through the kitchen.

- **Spy**. When your child is at someone else's house—especially one where there are older kids to imitate—find out what she ate. She may try something at a friend's that she wouldn't have touched if you had given it to her.
- **Peel foods with skins (apples, pears, plums)**. Some kids are looking for any excuse not to eat something, and a tough-to-chew peel is a perfect pretext.
- **Plant a produce garden**. Even kids who don't like vegetables may be willing to eat something they planted, watered, and picked.

- **Keep foods far away from each other on the plate**. Kids this age like to keep everything in its own special place (just another way to exercise control), and mixing two foods—even if they're both favorites—could end up causing a tantrum. In a similar vein, kids like to have certain quantities of things and may ask for more milk in their glass even though there's already plenty there.
- **Get your child involved**. Have her set the table, decide on pizza toppings, and make shopping decisions.
- **Have fun**. Even liver can look more appetizing if you cut it into the shape of a friendly animal or familiar cartoon character.
- **Encourage snacking**. Your child is burning tons of calories. Make sure she gets plenty to eat throughout the day, and if she wants some apple slices or a piece of cheese between meals, let her.
- **Encourage exercise**. Active children tend to be hungrier than less active ones.
- **Pay attention**. Your child isn't going to starve herself to death just to show you up, but if you're truly worried about her eating habits, check with your pediatrician. Early signs of malnutrition include uncharacteristic, constant crankiness, frequent illness, listless behavior, and little or no weight gain over a long period of time.

Giving Yourself a Financial Tune-up

Whether you're rich or poor, when it comes to money, there are only three kinds of people:
- Those who spend less than they bring in and save the difference.
- Those who spend exactly what they earn and have nothing left over.
- Those who spend more than they earn and get deeper and deeper in debt.

If you're in the first category, congratulations! Only about 46 percent of Americans say they earn more than they spend, which means that more half are either living hand to mouth or going into debt. To make matters worse, at least one in four American families has experienced a change in their income of 25 percent or more from one year to the next, according to a recent Pew Research Center study. That goes a long way toward explaining why 42 percent of Americans have less than $10,000 saved for retirement and almost 60 percent have less than $1,000 saved for emergencies.

If you're in any of these situations (or things are generally okay but you'd like to make them better), you're going to have to get under your financial hood and do a little tinkering. It's a simple process, really, with only two steps:
- Reduce your expenses (and your debts)
- Increase your savings

REDUCING EXPENSES AND GETTING
OUT OF DEBT AT THE SAME TIME

Although starting a savings or investment plan sounds like a lot more fun than going on a financial diet, the truth is that you can't save money until you've got a good handle on your expenses. The first step is to take a hard look at your current spending. It may be a little scary, but trust me, it's important.

Gather together every money-related scrap of paper that's crossed your hands in the past four or five months. Categorize each by type of expense (housing, insurance, medical, food, and so on). Using several months' worth of data will help you average variable expenses, such as gas and clothes, and include irregular expenses, such as auto repairs or major appliance purchases. Be sure to include the money—especially cash—you spend on lunch, dry cleaning, gifts, and the like.

Once you've got this done, go over each of the expense categories to see where you can do some cutting. Here are a few suggestions. You may be able to produce almost immediate, and often painless, returns.

- **Cut food costs**. Buy in bulk from Costco, Sam's Club, Smart & Final, or other discount outlets; use coupons and watch sales; and eat out less.
- **Comparison shop**. Prices vary widely on everything from refrigerators to cellphone providers, so check three or four places before you buy anything.
- **Carpool or try to telecommute or use alternative transportation a day or more per week**. Using your car less can help you reduce many auto-related expenses, such as gas and oil, repairs, and insurance rates.
- **Review your auto insurance**. If your car is more than five years old, you can probably save some money by getting rid of collision and comprehensive coverage. Check with your insurance agent.
- **Rethink your health insurance**. If you and your partner are both on employer-paid plans, your employers might be willing to refund some of the money they pay for you if you can prove that you're covered under your partner's plan. If you're self-employed and paying for your own plan, consider increasing your deductible or putting your child(ren) on a separate plan. Sometimes family coverage is much more than two separate policies—one for the adults, one for the kids.
- **Use savings to pay off your debts**. If you have $1,000 invested at 2 percent, you're earning $20 a year, which becomes $15.20 if you're in the 24 percent tax bracket. If you owe $1,000 on a 20 percent credit card, your interest payment is $200 a year, which, since you're using after-tax dollars, is really $263 if you're in the 24 percent tax bracket. Get the point? In this scenario, taking the money out of savings would save you about $249 a year. That may not sound like a lot, but it's enough to pay for most of the clothes your child will go through in a

year, or a good chunk of your annual health-club membership, or a few sessions with your therapist. You'd have to earn more than 30 percent (before taxes) on your investment to justify not using your savings to pay off your debt. And if some emergency comes up, and you really, really need the money again, you can always get a cash advance on your credit card.

- **Stop charging**, especially for things that lose their value, such as gas, clothing, cars, furniture, and meals out. If you can't afford to pay cash for these things, maybe you can't afford them at all. (One study found that people who use credit cards to charge fast-food meals spend as much as 100 percent more than when they pay cash.) If you make a 2 percent minimum payment on that $1,000 card balance, it will take you more than nine years to pay it off and cost you a total of $2,168. And if you keep buying stuff, you'll never get clear.

The Best Investment

After paying off your credit cards, one of the most important—and safest—investments you can make is in yourself. If you never finished high school or college or grad school, get it done now. The US Department of Labor's Bureau of Labor Statistics estimates that those with an associate (two-year) degree earn an average of $6,000 more per year than those with only a high school diploma. Having a bachelor's degree adds another $18,000 per year; a master's adds another $10,000 to that, and a professional degree (MD, MBA, or JD, for example) adds yet another $22,000. Oddly, people with a PhD earn about $5,000 less than those with professional degrees.

In addition to the financial benefits of education, there are a number of other reasons to finish or go back to school. According to the Department of Labor, those with only a high school diploma are about twice as likely to be unemployed as those with a bachelor's and two and a half times as likely as those with a professional degree. And, generally speaking, the more education you have, the more likely you are to have health insurance. That, in turn, probably affects life expectancy, which is a decade longer for people with a bachelor's than for those who didn't finish high school, according to researchers Robert A. Hummer and Elaine M. Hernandez.

Extra education is a sound investment: over the course of your life, the higher salary you'll command, those extra years of life, and your increased self-esteem, confidence, and general level of happiness will more than pay for the cost of tuition.

- **If you still insist on charging, at least try to pay off your balance in full every month**. Some 62 percent of Americans don't, and on average, every American family owes about $9,000 ($4,500 per borrower) in credit card debt.
- **Use a debit card instead**. These cards look just like credit cards but take the money directly out of your checking account. Keeping that in mind might just scare you out of using the card altogether.
- **Take charge of your credit cards**. You probably get a few offers a week for credit cards that offer zero or low interest on balance transfers. The hitch is that there's almost always a fee of 3–5 percent of the amount you're transferring. Alternatively, you may be able to get a zero-fee transfer, but the interest rate won't be zero. If you're extremely disciplined, you can keep rolling your balances from card to card and save a lot on interest payments. But if you're not, you could end up in worse trouble than when you started (those zero balances on the cards you just paid off with the transfer can look awfully tempting…).
- **Take out a consolidation loan or home-equity line of credit**. Chances are your bank or credit union offers loans at lower interest rates than those you're paying now on your credit card balance. In many cases, the lender may want you to cancel your credit cards (or at least turn the cards over to them). The interest you pay on these loans may be tax deductible. Either way, you'll be able to pay off your bills faster and at a far lower cost.

BOOSTING YOUR SAVINGS

Now that you've done everything you can to cut your expenses, you're ready for the fun stuff. For most people, the first big questions are: "How much should I try to save?" and "When should I start?" The short answer is, "As much as you possibly can, and as soon as possible." A more accurate answer depends on a number of factors, including:

- How old you are now.
- How old you think you'll be when you retire, and how old your partner will be when she retires.
- How long you expect to live (people are generally retiring later and living longer).
- Where you'll live when you retire (for example, will you sell your house and move to a smaller place?).
- What you expect your expenses to be while you're retired (for example, will your house be paid off by then?).
- Whether you think you and/or your partner will work while you're retired.
- How much you and your partner have already invested for retirement, and how much income you expect those assets to generate for you.

- Your best guess about how much you'll be able to earn on your investments, and what the inflation rate will be from now until you retire.
- Your other assets.
- How big an estate you want to leave to your heirs.

When Your Finances Get Really, Really Out of Control

Of course, you want to pay your debts. Just about everyone does. But sometimes, despite your best intentions, things just get to the point where they're no longer manageable. Fortunately, debtors' prisons went out with the nineteenth century. But that probably won't keep you from feeling helpless, humiliated, infuriated, frustrated, and, often, somehow less than a man. Men are supposed to know how to handle money, after all. If you've gotten to the point where you're feeling completely overwhelmed by your debts, and you're being hounded by creditors and collection agencies, you have three basic options:

- **Continue doing what you've been doing**. But since that hasn't worked up to this point, why keep making yourself miserable?
- **Get some professional help—a far more sensible approach**. Credit.org (www.credit.org) is a nonprofit group that helps people avoid bankruptcy and restructure their debts. The group also offers free online counseling. You might also want to look into Debtors Anonymous. You can find local chapters or even attend an online meeting via the organization's website, www.debtorsanonymous.org. But whatever you do, *do not* get involved with one of those companies that promises to cancel your credit card debts and restore your credit. As the old saying goes, if it sounds too good to be true, it probably is.
- **File for bankruptcy—truly the option of last resort**. Bankruptcy can essentially wipe out all debts from credit cards, auto loans, medical bills, utilities, and a few others. And if you choose this option, you certainly won't be alone: About one million US households file for bankruptcy every year. On the downside, though, doing so will screw up your credit report for at least seven years, depending on the type of bankruptcy you choose. And even after you're done, you'll still owe any debts related to alimony and child support, taxes (in most cases), and student loans. Bankruptcy isn't for everyone. So if you're even considering it, get some sound advice first. Nolo (www.nolo.com), a network of legal-services websites and publisher of legal guides, is a good place to start.

Since the answers to these questions are different for everyone, it's impossible to tell you exactly how much you'll need to save. But working backward, the conventional wisdom is that most people will need about 70–80 percent of their current income to meet their retirement expenses.

Again, the most important things are to save as much as possible and to start as soon as possible. Here are a few points to keep in mind as you're getting started:

- **Put together a plan**. Your answers to the questions above will help you get a handle on how much you'll need to have on hand at retirement and how much you'll need to save between now and then to meet your goal.
- **Pay yourself first**. Let's say you've decided to sock away 10 percent of your income. Do that first: the theory is, if you force yourself to live on the remaining 90 percent, you'll adjust your spending accordingly.
- **Start an emergency fund**. Ideally, you should have enough cash on hand to pay for three to six months of your current expenses, just in case you get laid off or the economy goes belly up. In addition, it's a good idea to have some extra money to pay for big expenses you know are coming up, such as braces, school tuition, bar mitzvahs, the down payment on a house, or major renovations of your current home; or on such future items as weddings, the vacation of a lifetime, that gull-wing Lamborghini, and so on.
- **Out of sight, out of mind**. Have money for your savings taken out of your paycheck automatically—that way you'll miss it less than if you had to write a

"Just what exactly is your generation going to do about my generation's social security?"

208

DRIP a Little Savings into This

If you're going the do-it-yourself route and you're thinking about investing in stocks, here's a way to save yourself some real money. Hundreds of companies now offer current shareholders dividend reinvestment plans (DRIPs) that allow them to buy stock directly from the company without having to pay a broker. Some make this service available to new investors as well. These plans almost always allow investors to reinvest dividends without commission. Many allow for automatic electronic purchases direct from your checking account, and several dozen actually allow DRIP participants to buy stock at a below-market rate. Finally, most plans will also let you sell your stock at rates far under what even a discount broker would charge.

So how can you find out about DRIPs? The hard way is to contact individual companies directly to find out whether they offer such programs. A much easier way is to check out one of the online companies that specialize in DRIPs.

check out every month, and you'll be more inclined to contribute regularly. Most employers have direct deposit, and many can set up automatic contributions to retirement plans. Most financial institutions are more than glad to help you set up regular electronic withdrawals to a savings account of some kind.

- **Invest**. You definitely want to keep some of your savings in cash (or the equivalent) for easy access in case of emergency. But for longer-term savings, you may want to consider investing in the stock market. Over time, the major market indices (the Dow, S&P, and NASDAQ) generally do a lot better than whatever interest you'd earn on money sitting in a bank or money market account. However, unlike cash, stocks and other investments can lose value, so don't invest any money you might need right away. One easy way to start investing is to purchase the same amount each month—an approach called "dollar cost averaging." When prices are up, you're buying a smaller number of shares. When prices are down, you're buying more. On average, then, you'll be fine. This strategy also keeps you from falling into the trap of buying high (just to get on the bandwagon) and selling low (when the bottom has already fallen out of the market).
- **Reinvest any interest and dividends**. It's free money, so why take it out? Leaving earnings in the account also helps your balance grow faster. Along the same lines, immediately invest any bonuses or raises. If you're able to live on what you're currently making, all that extra money can go directly into savings.

Picking a Financial Planner

Although you may be tempted to do your retirement planning and investing on your own, think long and hard before you make your final decision. Sure, it's fun to buy a stock you read about in the paper or that a friend tells you about. You might do fairly well for a while, but the long-term odds are against you. Even professional traders have trouble outperforming the market. These are people who do nothing all day long but follow individual stocks or sectors. If they can't beat the market with their armies of researchers and fancy computer models, what makes you think you can? Still, your odds are better with a professional. So, unless the financial markets are your passion, or you've decided to quit your job and manage your money, have someone else handle things.

Many financial planners are paid on a commission basis, based on your insurance purchases, stock trades, and/or the total value of your portfolio. So whether or not your investments do well, the financial planner gets his commission. Commissions typically range from as low as a few dollars per trade on some mutual funds to the entire first year's premium on a cash-value life insurance policy. Other planners are paid on a fee basis and typically charge from $50 to $250 per hour, often depending on how much money they're helping you manage. In most cases, they make recommendations and have you execute the actual transactions yourself, usually through low-fee companies such as Schwab, Vanguard, or Fidelity.

This doesn't mean, of course, that fee-based planners are inherently better than their commission-based colleagues (although many experts believe that you'll be happier, and possibly richer, with someone who charges an hourly fee). Your goal is to find someone you like and who you believe will have your best interests at heart. Here are a few things you can do to help weed out the losers:

- **Get references** from friends, business associates, and so forth. Alternatively, the Financial Planning Association (http://www.plannersearch.org) can refer you to certified planners in your area, and the National Association of Personal Financial Advisors (www.napfa.org) makes referrals only to fee-based (as opposed to commission-based) planners.
- **Select at least three potential candidates** and set up initial consultations

- **Get an ESOP**. No, it's not a fable, it's an Employee Stock Ownership Plan, and it's offered by more than ten thousand employers across the country. Basically, these plans allow employees to purchase stock in their company without paying commission fees. Sometimes you can make your purchases with pretax

(which shouldn't cost you anything). Then conduct tough interviews. Here's what you want to know:

- Educational background. Not to be snobby here, but the more formal the education—especially in financial management—the better. Certified Financial Planners (CFPs) go through a rigorous training program, and the CFP certification can help you differentiate between someone who's really a planner from someone who just sells stocks and insurance.
- Licenses. Is it important to you that the planner is legally able to buy or sell financial products such as stocks, bonds, mutual funds, and insurance?
- Level of experience. Unless you've got money to burn, let your niece break in her MBA on someone else. Stick to experienced professionals with at least three years in the business.
- Profile of the typical client. What you're looking for is a planner who has experience working with people whose income level and family situation are similar to yours.
- Compensation. If fee-based, how is the fee calculated (hourly or as a percentage of assets)? If commission-based, what are the percentages on each product offered? Any hesitation to show you a commission schedule is a red flag.
- Sample financial plan. You want to see what you're going to be getting for your money. Be careful, though: fancy graphics, incomprehensible boilerplate language, and expensive leather binders are often used to distract you from the report's lack of substance.
- References. How long have customers been with the planner? Are they happy? Better off? Any complaints or weaknesses?

- **Check your prospective planner's record** with state and federal regulators. The North American Securities Administrators Association (http://www.nasaa.org) has a list of each state's security regulators. On a national level, you can also contact the Financial Industry Regulatory Authority (www.finra.org) to check on disciplinary action and to see whether your candidates have ever been sued.

dollars, sometimes with after-tax dollars. Some employers let you buy at below-market prices, and some even match your contributions or contribute extra money to your account, which vests (becomes yours) over time, usually five to seven years.

- **Avoid temptation**. Don't put your long-term savings money in any kind of account that has check-writing privileges. Making your money hard to get may increase your chances of having it for a while.
- **Max out all of your retirement options**—especially the ones that your employer matches or contributes to, which typically include 401(k)s and 403(b)s.
- **Think about Uncle Sam**. Before (or at least at the same time as) you make any real changes to any part of your financial picture, you should be sure to talk to someone knowledgeable about the tax consequences. Your financial planner may be able to offer some help, but a good accountant would be a lot better.

The next big question is, "So what do I do with all the money I'm going to be saving?" Again, there's no magic formula. Whether you put your money in government bonds or short the pork-belly futures market will depend on your individual and family goals and how much risk you're willing to tolerate.

Correctly analyzing all these factors is a process that's far too complicated to cover here in a way that would be at all helpful. So unless you're already sophisticated financially, get yourself some help. Full-service financial managers typically charge 1–1.5 percent of your assets per year. There are a number of "robo-advisers" out there that use highly technical algorithms and formulas to allocate and manage your money. They generally don't offer anything less than full service, and their rates range from 0.25 to 1 percent of assets.

Bottom line: be very careful. Start by getting recommendations from people you trust. Research your options thoroughly, check references, and stay far, far away from people who promise you consistent, above-market returns. If you don't know who Bernie Madoff is, Google him.

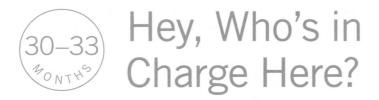

Hey, Who's in Charge Here?

30–33 MONTHS

WHAT'S GOING ON WITH YOUR TODDLER

Physically

- There's almost nothing your two-and-a-half-year-old can't do on his feet. He walks short distances on tiptoe, broad-jumps with both feet, makes sudden starts and stops while running, turns sharp corners on the move, and even steps over obstacles. He'll charge up stairs, alternating feet, but he's not quite as confident on the way down and may put both feet on each step.
- His fine motor skills are coming along nicely too. He can now differentiate between the two sides of his body (in other words, when pointing with one finger, he doesn't extend the same finger on the other hand).
- He can draw an *X* on purpose and a circle if you draw one first, and can consistently catch a large ball.
- He uses a cup and spoon like a pro, can build incredibly high block towers, likes making shapes—especially snakes—with Play-Doh, and is able to button up his clothes.
- He loves puzzles and has graduated from the one-piece-per-hole kind to simple jigsaws. He'll have an easier time of it, though, if each piece has a handle.

Intellectually

- Kids this age are still quite egotistical and have trouble controlling their impulses. Your toddler may have to pull all the books off the shelf 275 times before he's able to forgo his own pleasure in favor of parental approval.
- Symmetry, order, and patterns are especially important to your two-and-a-half-year-old. Half an apple (or a cookie with a bite taken out of it) is completely

unacceptable. He won't appreciate any deviations from his rituals, such as you being too tired to read him a bedtime story. And if you forget to fasten your seatbelt before starting the car, you're likely to get a stern talking-to.

- He's also beginning to recognize a double standard when he sees one, and might ask why you get to snack before dinner and he doesn't.
- Band-Aids are your child's best friend, so you'd better stock up. Every single bump, scrape, or bruise—whether you can actually see it or not—can be "cured" instantly with a Band-Aid. As child psychologist Selma Fraiberg put it, "It's as if a leak in the container, the body, is sealed up and his completeness as a personality is reestablished by this magic act."
- Although he's just as physically active as before, he seems to be a bit more focused. Instead of doing things and going places for the simple pleasure of doing or going, he now has a specific goal in mind for each action.
- He's getting more and more aware of the people around him. If you pay attention, you'll notice that he uses different words and intonation when he's talking to you than he does when talking to a playmate, an older sibling, or your dog.

Verbally

- Your toddler is not much of a conversationalist. He still initiates a lot of verbal interactions but doesn't always respond when you speak to him. When you do, he understands just about everything you say. But he gets extremely frustrated if you don't understand what *he's* trying to say.
- He's the absolute master of the word *no*. And his negative reactions to you (or refusals to cooperate) are more likely to be verbal than physical.
- He still hasn't completely grasped the concept of large chunks of time (*yesterday*, *today*, *tomorrow*), but he can express small pieces and sequences: "I get dressed now, then I have my cereal."
- Feeling pretty confident about his budding language skills (and why not?—he probably knows a thousand words and is adding a few more every day), your toddler is now starting to play with language, in almost the same way that he plays with objects. He knows what words are "supposed" to sound like and laughs hysterically when you replace a few words of a familiar nursery rhyme with nonsense syllables. Soon he'll begin to imitate these language games and will start giving silly-sounding names to objects he doesn't know.

Emotionally and Socially

- He's rebellious, defiant, negativistic, and exasperating; he doesn't always know what he wants, but he knows that he doesn't want to do most of the things you want him to do. Sound like a teenager? Could be, but it's also a description of the average child between the ages of two and three. It's no wonder that psychologist Fitzhugh Dodson calls this period "first adolescence."

- He may drive you nuts with his seeming inability to make a decision and stick to it. This can make something as simple as getting dressed frustrating. You: "Do you want the red pants or the blue?" Toddler: "Red." You: "Red it is." Toddler (screaming): "No, I want blue!" You: "Okay, let's put the blue ones on." Toddler: "No!" You get the point. If you're taking care of him, he'll demand his mother. If she's with him, he'll demand you. And if you're both with him, he may demand to do it "myself."

- Being contrary and disobedient is an exhausting job for so young a child, and your toddler is likely to be tired a lot. Unfortunately, tiredness usually makes tantrums worse.

- For most toddlers, this is a fairly aggressive time, and minor violence is common. Fortunately, most aggressive behavior is still experimental and not intended to cause real harm. As Louise Bates Ames and Frances Ilg explain: "[It's] as if the child wonders what kind of response he will get. Thus, a child may hit, grab at, or push another child, then look closely to see what is going to happen."

- Despite all these struggles, when he's in a good mood, he's delightful, cooperative, happy, and affectionate. Don't miss a second of it.

WHAT YOU'RE GOING THROUGH

Power Struggles

Here are perhaps the three most important words you will ever hear as a parent: *choose your battles*. Basically, this means that you should think carefully about whether it really matters that your child wants to wear one blue sock and one orange sock instead of a matched pair. As your child gets older, he becomes more independent. And the more independent he becomes, the more he tends to resist the limits you set. It's all part of growing up: your child needs to know how serious the rules are and how you'll react when they're broken.

I used to spend huge amounts of time arguing with my middle daughter, trying to get her to put on her shoes before she got in the car. I'd threaten, cajole, plead, and bribe, and gradually I'd wear her down and she'd put them on. But the moment she was strapped into her car seat and I was behind the wheel, she'd yank off her shoes and smirk at me in the rearview mirror. Finally, I gave up, and we've both been a lot happier ever since.

A friend who lives in Chicago told me that his son suddenly began refusing to get into the family car unless he was stark naked. My friend and his wife made themselves and their son miserable for a few days before shrugging their shoulders and giving up. The three of them enjoyed several peaceful months, and when winter came their son rather sheepishly asked for some clothes.

Young Dads and Old Dads

It may seem obvious that at the same time as we're developing as fathers, we're also developing as men. What's a little less obvious, though, is that the two developmental paths aren't always parallel. This means that two fathers of three-year-olds—one in his twenties or thirties, the other in his forties or fifties—are probably going to parent very differently.

If you're in the young category, you may be just out of college, not yet solidly established in your career, and trying to carve out your place in the world. You may also still be doing some experimenting—trying lots of new things, taking risks, having a great time. You're also probably spending a lot of time rolling around on the floor or playing other physical games with your child.

If you're in your forties or fifties, you're less likely to be wrestling with your child and more likely to be doing something intellectually stimulating. Overall, older dads tend to be more relaxed, caring, flexible, supportive, interested in parenting, involved in daily childcare, and likely to have a positive experience as fathers, according to Ross Parke. They also feel more appreciated by their children than younger fathers do.

Earlier we talked about the small health risks to children born to older fathers, such as increased risk of their children having schizophrenia or autism (page 167). However, children of older dads also enjoy some fascinating benefits:

- Magdalena Janecka, a researcher at King's College London, found that sons of older fathers tend to be more intelligent, do better in school (especially in STEM—science, technology, engineering, and math—subjects), and are less concerned about fitting in socially.
- Your children and grandchildren may also live longer. Dan Eisenberg and his colleagues at Northwestern University found that sons born to older fathers have longer telomeres—structures that protect the ends of our chromosomes from damage—than children born to younger fathers. Short telomeres are generally associated with shorter life spans, while longer ones are associated with longer life spans. And the benefit may extend to two generations.

Earlier we discussed the importance of setting firm, consistent limits for your child. But believe me, if you're prepared to go to the mat to enforce compliance with every request you make, you'll spend a lot of unnecessary time butting heads with your child. And you won't have the energy to enforce the rules that really matter, such as, "Don't go into the street unless you're holding hands with a grown-up." More important, you'll waste a lot of perfectly good quality time fighting.

Regaining Control

During your child's first year, you had to get used to the idea that your baby was pretty much running the show. It was the baby, not you or your partner, who decided when to eat, when to sleep, when he wanted to be changed, and when he wanted to play. Everyone else around him simply adjusted to his desires. Not being in control is hard, especially for men. After all, we're bigger and smarter and older, and we should be in charge, damnit. But it doesn't work that way.

Fortunately, as your child gets older, things will change. There's an old saying that we spend the first two years of our children's lives teaching them to walk and talk, and the next sixteen years trying to get them to sit down and shut up. All that walking and talking requires a shift in the balance of power from your child to you. You're setting basic boundaries for health and safety. And you're gradually establishing other rules—say, for how to speak to and behave with other people, how to treat animals, when to go to bed, and so on. You're also getting close to selecting your child's school and taking your first steps toward overbooking him: soccer, piano, ballet, chess club, polo lessons . . .

Don't expect much cooperation from your child, for two reasons. First, while you're trying to be the boss, your child is continuing his never-ending quest for independence, which involves rejecting you and your rules. Second, intellectually, your child is still pretty attached to the idea that he's the center of the universe.

There will be plenty of times when you won't be in control at all, or at least not as much as you'd like to be. If your child has a disability or a chronic illness, for example, his needs will still dictate your schedule. And ill or not, when your toddler throws himself down next to the banana display in the grocery store and has a huge tantrum, you'll remember the incredible frustration of not being in control.

Stepping into a Prefab Family

About half of all marriages are remarriages for at least one of the partners, a lot of whom have children. It's quite possible, then, that you're starting your fatherhood experience with someone else's child. Or your new partner might be the incoming stepparent. (We'll talk about stepmothers on pages 244–45.) Either way, the most important thing to remember is to have reasonable expectations and be patient.

The Mouth That Roars

Has your child asked you (loudly, of course) why that senior citizen looks like she's dead or whether that obese man has eaten an elephant? Or has he let loose with a string of four-letter words that sounds eerily like one that came out of your mouth when you stepped on a Lego he left on the living room carpet? He will.

Way back in 1977, Art Linkletter wrote a book called *Kids Say the Darndest Things*. And boy, was he right. Every parent has dozens of stories about the shocking, embarrassing, horrifying, and hilarious things their innocent toddlers have said. I remember taking two of my kids to a matinee a while back. The theater was crowded, so my older daughter had her own seat and the younger one, who had just turned two, sat on my lap. A few minutes into the movie, I felt something wet on my leg and instinctively put my hand on the baby's bottom to feel whether her diaper had leaked. Suddenly, at the top of her lungs, she screamed, "Get your hands out of my pants!" It was one of the more discomfiting (and funny) moments of my life. We'll talk more about the crazy things toddlers say a little later in the chapter.

Fortunately, not everything your child says will make you want to disappear down the nearest hole. But in many ways the non-embarrassing statements and the ordinary "Why?" questions are harder to deal with than the embarrassing ones. They'll make you think about the world in a way you never have before, and jar you into realizing just how little thought most of us give to what's going on around us and how much basic information we just take for granted. How, for example, do you explain homelessness, terrorism, AIDS, natural disasters, and violent crime? And the Internet? Well, that's just magic.

When faced with tough questions, the best thing to do is turn them into learning experiences (even questions about old people who are still very much alive can lead to a discussion about what it means to have your feelings hurt). One of the greatest sources of these "teachable moments" is the newspaper (it's got enough pictures to spark the child's interest and is a lot easier to censor than the television). My two oldest used to "read" the paper with me over breakfast in the mornings and often asked me to explain the articles that accompanied interesting photos.

It's not easy being a stepfather, and there isn't a lot of social support out there. Fortunately, though, you're not alone. In fact, more than half of Americans have been, are now, or will be in one or more blended families during their lifetime. And there are over 1.3 million families (including nearly 3 million kids) made up of a biological mother and a stepfather.

A lot of stepfathers erroneously think that they're going to ease into their new situation right away and that their new, blended family will behave just as a regular biological family would. In reality, this hardly ever happens. It's not always clear what the stepfather's role is in the new family or how he's going to fit into the new family structure. And it's not easy trying to mold relationships with children who already have a father somewhere else. Stepfathers also rarely have any kind of legally established authority—that stays with the biological father. Still, even if their places were clearly prescribed and protected by law, most men, even if they're fathers themselves, don't have much practice or training in parenting other people's kids.

Many stepdads are also surprised when the love they expected to feel for and from their stepchildren doesn't materialize—either as soon as they'd hoped or at all. In one important study, researcher Kay Pasley found that fewer than half of stepfathers said that they felt "mutual love" between themselves and their stepchildren. Lawrence Ganong and his colleagues found that stepparents (male and female) often feel like outsiders in their new family. And Danielle Shapiro and Abigail Stewart found that stepparenting is linked with depression and increased stress levels.

In general, marriages that include children are twice as likely to end in divorce as those without. But given all the additional challenges that stepparents face, it's no surprise that about two-thirds of second marriages and nearly three-quarters of third marriages end in divorce, according to the website Divorce Statistics (divorcestatistics.info).

Major problems include conflicts over child-rearing, the children's behavior, and the relationship between the stepparent and the stepchildren. So if you're already a stepfather or are about to become one, there are a number of important issues that you need to prepare yourself to deal with. Ignored, they can get out of control and interfere with your new partner, her kids, and even your own kids, if you have any.

Tips for Successful Stepfathering

According to researchers Kari Lee Adamsons, Marion O'Brien, and Kay Pasley, three factors can accurately predict whether a stepfather will be satisfied with his role.

1. The amount of communication with his stepchildren—the more, the better.
2. The amount of time he spends with his stepchildren. Again, the more, the better.
3. The support he gets from his new partner for his involvement in the discipline of the stepchildren. What a surprise: the more, the better.

Besides communicating well, spending lots of time with your stepchildren, and getting plenty of support from their mother, here are some other very important steps you can take to make stepfathering a more enjoyable experience for everyone:

- **Have realistic expectations**. The idea that her children and you are going to fall instantly in love with one another is a complete fantasy. Relying on it too much will only set you up for failure. Taking a stepparenting class may help you keep your expectations reasonable.

Stepdad vs. Biological Dad

A lot of kids, regardless of their age, fantasize that their parents will get back together. Your marriage to a child's mother dashes that hope. Expect to hear, often, "You're not my father, so I don't have to listen to you."

Don't be offended if your stepchildren want to spend lots of time with their biological dad. There's going to be some natural competitiveness between the two of you, especially if your partner tells you he isn't a particularly nice guy. But you absolutely must support the kids' relationship with their father. (If the situation is reversed, try to help your new wife to understand that your kids are going to want to spend a lot of time with their mother and that she should try as hard as she can to support that relationship.)

One of the most important factors in a child's adjustment to a stepparent is his desire to maintain the one-on-one relationships he had with his natural parents. Kids often feel that they're losing their biological parent to the new stepparent. And in a way, they're right. Before, it was just them and their parents, but now they have to share their mother with some interloper—you. This brings up all sorts of loyalty issues for a lot of stepkids. They may feel that if they love you, they're somehow being disloyal to or betraying their father. As a result, they may lash out at you for what seems like no reason at all. Even stranger, these explosions often happen just when you think your relationship with your stepchild is getting better. If (when) they happen, try to take them as a compliment.

- **Don't try to get attached too quickly**. Doing so makes you vulnerable to rejection, which you're probably going to get a lot of for quite a while anyway.
- **Don't let the stepkids get to you**. Or at least don't let them see that they did. It'll encourage them use the same hurtful tactics over and over.
- **Be a grown-up**. If they hurt your feelings, don't try to get even by rejecting them or responding in kind.
- **Establish some new family traditions**. Rituals and customs help families bond. You have some from your family; your partner has some from hers. Neither is better or worse, they're just different. Coming up with something new can make all of you feel that you're working together to create something special.
- **Devote a lot of time to keeping your relationship with your new partner healthy**. And be sure to discuss the role she expects you to take in her children's life, or that you expect her to take in your kids' life. Don't be naive and think that everything will work itself out—it won't. So don't be afraid to get some couples therapy if you need it. The more support you get from your partner, the less likely you'll be to experience any of the negative consequences we discussed earlier (feeling unloved, isolated, depressed, or stressed).
- **If you and your new partner both have kids from previous relationships, pay special attention to how the kids react**. Moreover, don't underestimate the magnitude of the changes they're going to experience: new routines, a new house, new customs, new bedrooms—they may even have to share a room— and even a new birth order. A child who was once the oldest, with all the privileges that went along with that, might resent being bumped by an older child. The opposite might happen to a child who gets displaced as baby of the family. Give the kids plenty of time to get used to each other and to their new stepparents. It's not going to be easy on any of you.

YOU AND YOUR TODDLER

Wacky Things Toddlers Do

As you've no doubt discovered, toddlers are marvelous little creatures who have the amazing capacity to charm, captivate, shock, humiliate, and make us laugh or cry—sometimes all in the span of three minutes. Part of what makes toddlers who they are is that they're impulsive, emotional, innocent, and most of all, unfiltered. Over the next few years, your child will gradually lose that impulsivity, get a better handle on his emotions, develop a sense of modesty, and learn that it's not always okay to say the first thing that pops into his head. In the meantime, though, if you pay attention, you'll get to witness a dazzling display of heartwarming, infuriating, hilarious—and sometimes just plain scary—behavior. For example, your toddler:

- May prefer to spend his time completely naked. Or he may decide to strip down to his birthday suit in the middle of dinner—in a restaurant.
- May pick his nose or explore his genitals, or play with the contents of his diaper or the potty, in front of your friends.
- May suddenly decide to behave like an animal, barking or growling at people— or licking them, following them around, and eating his food from a bowl on the floor, just as your pet does.
- May escape through your pet door.
- May say absolutely outrageous things that will make you want to disappear. At the ripe old age of two, my middle daughter asked me—rather loudly—whether the African American woman in front of us in the grocery store checkout line was made of chocolate.
- May make absolutely adorable speaking mistakes that you'll never want to correct. My oldest had trouble pronouncing the letter *L*, and I loved it when she used to say, "Yook at my yegs!" She also used to summon me over to the couch, pat the seat alongside her, and tell me to "sit be-next to me."
- May give you a big, sloppy kiss, a long hug, and announce, "I love you, Daddy." That will turn you to Jell-O.
- May scream, "I hate you, Daddy." That will turn you to Jell-O too, but a very different flavor.

- May offer to put a Band-Aid on your boo-boos to make them feel better.
- May adopt a new identity—for a long, long time. When my oldest was eighteen months old, I showed her the movie musical *Oliver!* For the next year and half, she insisted that she was Oliver Twist, answered only to Oliver, demanded that we buy her a little suit like the one Oliver wore, and refused to call me anything but Mr. Bumble (if you know the story, you know that's not a compliment.)
- May line up his toys and stuffed animals in a specific order and flip out if you move anything around.
- May cry hysterically if you cut his sandwich into squares instead of triangles; or if you cut the crusts off—even if he just asked you to; or if you flushed the toilet before he had a chance to say goodbye to the poop.
- May mispronounce common words and phrases, asking for a "penis butter sandwich" or for you to "pass the porn" (corn), or pointing out a "dumb f–ck" (dump truck), wondering how many humps a "cannibal" has, or refusing to get into the "alligator" to go up a few flights in a tall building, because, well, we all know how alligators can be.
- May ask horrifying questions like, "What happens to Daddy's phone if you drop it in the toilet?"

Early Readers

According to reading expert Jim Trelease, studies of children who learned to read early have identified four characteristics of their homes. The first two are fairly obvious, and you're probably doing them already: the child is read to on a regular basis, and a wide variety of printed materials—books, magazines, newspapers, comics—is available in the home at all times.

The other two are a little less obvious but may be even easier to implement than the first two:
- Paper and pencil are available to the child. Most kids are made curious about written language by watching their parents write things.
- People in the home stimulate the child's interest in reading and writing by answering questions, praising the child's efforts at reading and writing, taking the child to the library frequently, buying books, writing down stories that the child dictates, and displaying the child's creations in a prominent place in the home.

At this point, your child is still at least a year away from reading—and there's no need to rush him. But if he seems to be taking an interest in letters and what they symbolize, don't hold him back. He may, for example, point to various words and ask you to tell him what they say. Or he may imitate you by "reading" a book to his stuffed animals. If he's got one of his favorite books memorized, he might even want to "read" it to you, turning the pages in all the right places.

This is a good age to subtly introduce letters. Sing the alphabet song a few times a day, just so he can get the sounds down. And point out the letters you see as you're out and about—on stop signs, exit signs, store awnings, and so on—especially the ones that are in your child's name. If your child is especially interested, you might want to point out "unintentional" letters—a bent straw making an L shape, for example, or an X pattern in a fence.

HOME LIBRARY UPDATE

Here are suggestions for adding to your child's ever-growing home library—or to the list you take together to your local library.

FAVORITES

Beautiful Birds, Jean Roussen

Big Words for Little People, Jamie Lee Curtis

Blueberries for Sal (and others), Robert McCloskey

Bread and Jam for Frances (and the other Frances books), Russell Hoban

Carl Goes to Daycare (and others), Alexandra Day

The Cat in the Hat (and many others), Dr. Seuss

Curious George (and others), H. A. Rey

Diary of a Worm, Doreen Cronin

Dragons Love Tacos, Adam Rubin

Frog and Toad Are Friends (and others), Arnold Lobel

The Gingerbread Man, Paul Galdone

Gossie, Olivier Dunrea

The Gruffalo, Julia Donaldson

Happy Birthday, Moon, Frank Asch

Harry the Dirty Dog (and others), Gene Zion and Margaret B. Graham

Here We Are: Notes for Living on Planet Earth, Oliver Jeffers

How Do Dinosaurs Say Good Night? Jane Yolen

I Hope You Dance, Mark D. Sanders and Tia Sillers

I Need All of It, Petra Postert

Just Like Daddy, Ovi Nedelcu

Louella Mae, She's Run Away! Karen Beaumont Alarcón

Madeline (and others), Ludwig Bemelmans

Mike Mulligan and His Steam Shovel (and others), Virginia Burton

The Monster at the End of This Book, Jon Stone

Moo Who? Margie Palatini

Napping House, Audrey Wood

Olivia (and its sequels), Ian Falconer

Pet Dad, Elanna Allen

The Rabbit Listened, Cori Doerrfeld

Rolie Polie Olie (and others), William Joyce

Say Zoop, Hervé Tullet

Sheep in a Jeep, Nancy Shaw

The Snowman, Raymond Briggs

The Snowy Day, Ezra Jack Keats

The Story of Babar, Jean de Brunhoff

The Story of Ferdinand, Munro Leaf

Strega Nona (and others), Tomie dePaola

Use Your Words, Sophie, Rosemary Wells

Vehicles, Xavier Deneux

Walter the Farting Dog, William Kotzwinkle

When I Am Old with You, Angela Johnson

Where the Wild Things Are, Maurice Sendak

Wibbly Pig Likes Bananas, Mick Inkpen

With My Daddy, Jo Witek

CONCEPTS

Cats (and many others in the series), Seymour Simon

Hello, Hello, Brendan Wenzel

How Many Snails, Paul Giganti

If You Look around You, Testa Fulvio

Let's Eat! Beatrice Hollyer

Numbers (and others), John J. Reiss

Rufus, Tomi Ungerer

Trucks You Can Count On, Doug Magee

Wheels on the Bus, Jerry Smath

FOLK TALES

Goldilocks and the Three Bears, Jan Brett

Jack and the Beanstalk, Joseph Jacobs

Stone Soup, Marcia Brown

Teeny Tiny, Jill Bennett

The Three Billygoats Gruff, Marcia Brown

POETRY

All Small, David McCord

Blackberry Ink, Eve Merrian

I'll Be You and You Be Me, Ruth Krauss

Miss Spider's Wedding (and others), David Kirk

Where the Sidewalk Ends, Shel Silverstein

GOING TO SCHOOL/DAY CARE

Molly, Ruth Shaw Radlauer

School, Emily McCully

GOING TO THE DENTIST

Curious George Goes to the Dentist, H. A. Rey

Doctor De Soto, William Steig

Just Going to the Dentist, Mercer Mayer

ESPECIALLY FOR OLDER SIBLINGS

Babies! Dorothy Hinshaw Patent

Baby's Catalog, Janet Ahlberg and Allan Ahlberg

Happy Birth Day! (and others), Robie H. Harris

Hello Baby, Jenni Overend

I'm a Big Sister / I'm a Big Brother, Joanna Coles

I'm Going to Be a Big Sister / I'm Going to Be a Big Brother, Brenda Bercun

Julius, the Baby of the World, Kevin Henkes

Let Me Tell You about My Baby, Roslyn Banish

Oonga Boonga, Frieda Wishinsky

Peter's Chair, Ezra Jack Keats

Shadow's Baby, Margery Cuyler

There's a House Inside My Mummy, Giles Andreae and Vanessa Cabban

The Very Worst Monster, Pat Hutchins

Waiting for Baby (and others in the series), Rachel Fuller

We Have a Baby, Cathryn Falwell

What Baby Needs, Dr. William and Martha Sears

When You Were a Baby, Ann Jonas

Za-Za's Baby Brother, Lucy Cousins

Screening Your Child's Entertainment

Throughout this book I've talked about the fantastic benefits of reading to your child. But as your toddler gets older, he'll get more and more of his information from other sources, in particular, television and videos. (We've discussed computers and mobile devices elsewhere in this book, on pages 31–36 and 190–95, so I'll leave them out of this discussion.) In principle, there's nothing wrong with TV and videos. There are several great options out there for very young children, including *Sesame Street*, *Doc McStuffins*, *Beat Bugs*, and *Word Party* (the latter two from Netflix). Moderation is key (try to keep screen time to no more than an hour a day) and so is selecting age-appropriate programming. Still, there are a number of problems:

- Children watch entirely too much television. A study done by Common Sense Media found that on average, kids two to four spend nearly three hours per day on various types of screens, including TV. Children eight to twenty-four months are exposed to five and a half hours of background TV per day (meaning that it's on even if no one is watching), while kids two to four are exposed to four hours and twenty minutes per day, according to researcher Matthew Lapierre and his colleagues. Furthermore, Ellen Wartella and her colleagues at Northwestern University found that, in more than a third of households with children under eight, a TV is on all or most of the day.

- Most of the programming those kids are exposed to is completely inappropriate for them, according to researcher Suzy Tomopoulos and her colleagues. A significant amount of recent research has shown that even babies as young as ten to twelve months are influenced by the behavior of the characters they see on television.

- Children under eight can't tell the difference between reality and fantasy. As a result, they may believe that they can do all the amazing things that TV characters can do. They may also get frightened by violence or bad behavior they see in all that inappropriate programming they're exposed to.

- TV is passive and deprives the child of one of his most important ways of learning: asking and answering questions. There's no one to ask, and no one to answer.

- TV discourages thinking. It's nearly impossible to show a character thinking through a problem on TV, and commercials tend to give the message that there is no problem that can't be solved by artificial means—that is, by buying something.

- There's a link between watching television and obesity. I'm not putting all the blame on television—poor diet and lack of exercise are the main causes of obesity. But there's no question that watching TV contributes to the problem, first, by sucking up time that might otherwise have been spent playing outside, and second, because kids tend to sit motionless in front of the tube, snacking.

- There's a link between watching television and developing behavior problems. The more toddlers watch, the more likely they are to be diagnosed with ADHD (attention deficit/hyperactivity disorder) later in life. Hundreds of studies have explored the connection between exposure to media violence and violent behavior in real life. That connection is real. There's a startling amount of violence on TV and in movies—including those aimed at young children. A lot of that violence is committed by "good guys" beating up "bad guys." And children often imitate what their TV and movie heroes do.

- Commercials are problematic too. Young children don't understand that commercials are trying to sell them something, and they can't tell the difference between commercials and programming.
- The messages kids get from TV are flawed. Most fathers, for example, whether in commercials or in programming, seem to be portrayed as clueless, incompetent boobs.

There are, of course, exceptions to the above-mentioned drawbacks, and you're probably not planning to toss your television out the window anytime soon. So if you're going to put your child in front of a TV screen, at least try to keep the following guidelines in mind:

- **If there's a television in your toddler's room, take it out**.
- **Set some basic rules**. For example, no watching during meals or in the middle of family time. And don't just leave the TV on as background noise; turn it off when your show is done.
- **Set a good example**. Limit your own screen time, and make sure your child sees you doing other things, like reading or exercising.
- **Don't use television or movies as a babysitter**. From experience I can tell you that this is an incredibly easy trap to fall into, and one your child won't be in any hurry to get out of.
- **Don't use TV/screen time as a bribe**. That makes is seem much more important than it is.
- **Make sure that whatever your child watches is made specifically for toddlers**. You may love sci-fi thrillers, but watch them after he's down for the night.
- **Watch together**. As mentioned above, your toddler can't tell the difference between reality and what's happening on the screen, and he may become frightened or confused. So use whatever you're watching as the topic for a discussion.
- **Fast-forward through commercials** (if you have the technology to do so) or watch commercial-free programming.
- **Monitor the media**. This does not mean turn it off. Watching television and movies with your child can be a great way to talk about issues of morality, right and wrong, politics, and more. And despite everything I just said about the connection between make-believe violence in the media and real-world violence,

fantasy violence may have some redeeming values, at least according to media critic Gerard Jones. "Instead of banning head-bonking TV shows and gory games like *Doom*, we should harness the tremendous power of fantasy to help our kids better navigate the world around them," he writes. It's an interesting argument, one that's worth investigating further. In the meantime, while your child is so young, I suggest that you avoid media violence as much as possible and use your TV- and/or video-watching time to cuddle and talk about what's on the screen. If you need a few suggestions about what to watch, the Parents Television Council (www.parentstv.org) has extensive listings and reviews.

Play: Getting Physical

One of the biggest myths about play is that extremely active entertainment, especially roughhousing, teaches kids to be violent. The evidence, however, supports the exact opposite conclusion. Anthony DeBenedet and Larry Cohen sum it up nicely in their book *The Art of Roughhousing*, writing that roughhousing "makes kids smart, emotionally intelligent, lovable and likable, ethical, physically fit, and joyful." Here are some of the details:

- Physical play teaches kids about morality, right and wrong, and following rules. John Snarey, who spent several decades studying fathers' impact on their children, writes that children who roughhouse with their fathers "usually quickly learn that biting, kicking, and other forms of physical violence are not acceptable." Those lessons help them learn to read people and their reactions and teach them the difference between playful aggression and real aggression. Roughhousing also demonstrates the proper way to use force and the importance of setting boundaries.
- Physical play teaches about compassion and how to treat others. As the grown-up, you could easily "win" every time you wrestle with your child. But that wouldn't be fun for either of you. So you'll probably let him or her win once in a while (but not too often, because that wouldn't be fun either). By doing so, you're showing your child that, as Uncle Ben told Peter Parker (before he became Spiderman), with great power comes great responsibility. In other words, because you're bigger and stronger, you have an obligation to treat other people fairly and with compassion.
- Children who play with their fathers tend to be more helpful, cooperative, and likely to share. They also have better communication and leadership skills, according to pioneering fatherhood researcher Ross Parke.
- Parke and his colleagues also found that for girls, high levels of physical play are associated with such desirable social attributes as positive emotional expressiveness and clarity of communication as well as originality, novelty, and

creativity. Boys become more empathetic, more popular among their peers, and less likely to be hyperactive or sad.

- Roughhousing makes kids smarter. Kids who do it at home get better grades in school. During rough play, the brain releases brain-derived neurotrophic factor (BDNF). BDNF is essential for healthy brain development and growth and is responsible for stimulating neuron growth throughout the brain. Those neurons, in turn, are associated with improving memory and learning.

- Roughhousing helps kids learn to take risks and boosts resilience. In a safe play environment, kids get a chance to try out new things. They learn from their failures and successes what works and what doesn't, and they apply those lessons to other areas of their life. Resilient children are more likely to see failure as a challenge and to try again, rather than give up.

- Physical play builds children's—especially girls'—confidence, assertiveness, and academic achievement, and increases the chances that they'll stand up for their friends. Several studies of successful women have shown that almost all had fathers who engaged in a lot of physical play with them.

- Physical play teaches children about how to deal with minor pains and discomforts. Dads often allow their children to take risks during rough play. Sometimes those risks produce bruises, bumps, rug burns, scrapes, and other minor injuries. Your quick response will help your children learn some valuable lessons in self-soothing and confidence in their ability to overcome problems on their own.

- As we've discussed before, fathers and mothers generally play very differently with their boys and girls. And this serves to reinforce children's "socially acceptable" (that is, gender-stereotyped) behavior, especially for boys. So if you're interested in reducing the chances that your child will end up trapped in a set of gender-based behaviors, play with him or her actively and frequently, and in a wide range of ways. Wrestling and physical play are great, but leave some time for quieter activities like art, reading, dress-up, and tea parties. For you and your child's mother, the point is to play with boys the same way as you'd play with girls, and vice versa.

- Roughhousing is great exercise. This is particularly important since a majority of school districts have drastically reduced (or in some cases completely eliminated) recess in schools.

- Lack of rough-and-tumble play is associated with a number of negative developmental, emotional, and physical problems, according to researchers Rafe Kelley and Beth Kelley. These include social isolation, aggressive behavior, depression, difficulty forming relationships with others, difficulty adapting to change, and poor self-control. And researchers Stuart Brown and Christopher

Vaughan found that lack of childhood roughhousing was an accurate predictor of future risk of drug or alcohol addiction and criminal behavior in adulthood. The "lack of experience with rough-and-tumble play hampers the normal give-and-take necessary for social mastery," they write, "and has been linked with poor control of violent impulses later in life."

Sounds like rolling around on the floor with your kids just about guarantees that they'll grow up confident, strong, and smart, doesn't it? Well, lots of physical play may increase the chances, but you've got to do more than wrestle with your child or turn yourself into a human jungle gym. Be sure to spend plenty of time talking, reading, teaching, changing diapers, and so on.

That said, here are some basic guidelines to keep in mind as you're wrestling and roughhousing:

- **Safety first**. Minimize injury risk by making sure you're on a soft surface and are far away from hard furniture, low ceilings, doorways, or anything else that could be a banging hazard. And be gentle, especially at first.
- **Don't do it too close to bedtime**. Rough play may seem like a great way to tire out a child, especially one who's been cooped up all day. But it can often get him or her even more wired.
- **If you have a daughter, don't hold back**. Dads tend to play more gently with their daughters than their sons. There's absolutely no reason to do that. Girls are just as hardy as boys, and as the evidence I've cited in this chapter shows, they benefit enormously from having a close, physically playful relationship with Dad.
- **Don't force your children to play with you if they don't want to**; it can actually do more harm than good. Research consistently shows that children whose fathers are overly "directive" (meaning they give too many commands) may become socially withdrawn, have fewer friends, are more likely to watch activities than get involved, and have more behavioral problems.
- **Listen carefully**. When you're playing with your children (especially when roughhousing), you should hear shrieks of laughter and happiness, not cries of pain or frustration.

All Kinds of Fun

FUN PHYSICAL PLAY

- Roughhouse
  - "Bet you can't get up." You lie on the floor and try to get up while your child tries to hold you down. Then reverse the roles.

- Good, old-fashioned wrestling.
- Sock wrestling. You and your child try to snatch each other's socks off. Watch out for flailing feet.
- Sleeping monster. You lie on the floor, and your child sits on you, pretending that you're a piece of furniture. But you're really a dragon ...
- Climb Mount Dad. Stand with your child facing you and hold his hands as he tries to climb up your legs to your belly and beyond.
- Stair surf. Slide down the stairs on a small mattress or cardboard box. Try this yourself first to make sure no one will get hurt.
- Bucking bronco. You can figure this one out for yourself, but be sure to hold on to your child until you're sure he can hold on by himself.
- Take a walk on a balance beam, along the curb, or even down a line on the sidewalk.
- Play catch (start with a large, slightly deflated ball).
- Jump over things (anything more than a few inches high, though, will be too much for most kids this age).
- Throw, kick, roll, and toss balls of all sizes.
- Ride a tricycle or possibly a scooter (the kind with three or four wheels).
- Spin around till you drop.
- Pound, push, pull, and kick (but not other people).
- Make music using drums (or buckets), xylophones, flutes, and anything else you have handy.
- Play Twister.

SMALL MOTOR SKILLS

- Puzzles (fewer than twenty pieces is probably best). You might even cut up a simple picture from a magazine and see whether your toddler can put it back together.
- Take-apart (and put-back-together) toys.
- Blocks and building sets.
- Draw, on paper or with chalk on the sidewalk.
- Sculpt with clay or another molding substance.
- Finger paint.
- Tambourines, drums, xylophones, and other noisemaking instruments.
- Play with string and large beads.
- Pour water or sand or seeds from one container to another.
- Get a big box (from a dishwasher or refrigerator), then build, paint, and decorate a house together.

BRAIN DEVELOPMENT

- Matching games (match baby animals with their parents, top halves of animals or objects with the bottom halves, or the old fashioned turn-over-the-card-and-find-the-match game).
- Alphabet and number games (put colorful magnetic letters and numbers on the fridge and leave them low enough for the child to reach).
- Dolls of all kinds (including action figures).
- Imaginary driving trips where you talk about all the things you see on the road. Be sure to let your toddler drive part of the way.
- Sorting games (put all the pennies, or all the triangles, or all the cups together).
- Arranging games (big, bigger, biggest).
- Smelling games: blindfold your toddler and have him identify things by their scent.
- Pattern games (lay out coins in a pattern—say, nickel, dime, quarter—and have your child match the pattern; do the same with blocks—square, rectangle, circle; or with cups—small, big, small, big—or anything else).
- Counting and other "math" games. (How many pencils are there? If I take one away, how many will there be?)
- Do science experiments (build ramps and see how fast toy cars will go down them; use mirrors to redirect lights.)
- Checkers (or chess, if your child is interested).

BUILDING IMAGINATION

- Pretending games with "real" things (phones, computer keyboards).
- Pretending games in which you act out different animals or vehicles or stars and planets, or that the floor is hot lava.
- Dress-up clothes.
- Art projects: the bigger and messier, the better.

A FEW FUN THINGS FOR RAINY DAYS (OR ANYTIME)

- Have pillow fights.
- Cook something—kneading bread or pizza dough is especially good, as is roasting marshmallows on the stove. (See pages 238–44 for more cooking ideas.)
- Go baby bowling (gently toss your toddler onto your bed).
- Acrobatics (airplane rides: you're on your back, feet up in the air, your toddler's tummy on your feet, and you and he are holding hands).
- Dance and/or sing.
- Stage a puppet show.

PLAYING OUTSIDE

- Play hide-and-seek.
- If it's not too cold, strip down to your underwear and paint each other, top to bottom, with nontoxic, water-based paints.
- Get bundled up and go for a long, wet, sloppy, muddy stomp in the rain. If you don't feel like getting wet, get in the car and drive through puddles.
- Run through sprinklers.
- Roll down a hill.
- Play tag (make a tree or paving stone "safe").
- Set up an obstacle course.
- Go on a nature hunt and collect pebbles or leaves or insects (which you'll release later).
- Build castles in a sandbox.

Group Activities

If you haven't already done so, it's a good idea to start getting your child involved in some regular group activities. Actually, it's a good idea for both of you: It'll give

It's All in Their Heads

In the movie *Harvey*, Jimmy Stewart (in the lead role) had an imaginary friend (a six-foot-tall rabbit), and there's little doubt that he was more than a bit nuts. But if your child has an imaginary playmate, there's nothing to worry about. Having imaginary playmates is a normal part of growing up—especially in the toddler years—and they serve several important functions:

- They can be wonderful companions for pretend play, which is an important way to stimulate creativity and imagination. Having an invisible friend can make those long trips to the moon or traveling back in time a little less lonely.
- They can act as a child's trusted confidant when there's no one else to tell his secrets to. Even small children have issues that are too private to tell us.
- They can help kids figure out the difference between right and wrong. Kids sometimes have a tough time stopping themselves from doing things they know are wrong. Blaming the imaginary friend for eating cookies before dinner is often a sign that the child understands right vs. wrong distinctions but isn't quite ready to assume complete responsibility for his actions.
- They can give you some valuable insights into your child's feelings. Listening to your child bravely comfort an invisible friend who's about to get a shot may be a clue that he's more afraid than he's letting on.

your child an opportunity to meet some new people and to practice his budding social skills. And while he's playing, you'll have a great opportunity to spend time with some adults who probably have many of the same questions and concerns about fatherhood that you do.

If you're interested in joining an ongoing group or an organized activity, you'll probably find a dozen options within a few miles of your house. Here are a few places to start looking:

- Your local YMCA has classes and get-togethers for toddlers and their parents, and there's most likely a place nearby that offers music or movement participation or other gatherings. Many churches, synagogues, and community centers have similar offerings.
- Your local parenting newspaper will have listings of activities, as will Meetup (meetup.com).
- Zoos, museums, planetariums, science centers, and others often have activities geared for toddlers.
- The National At-Home Dad Network (athomedad.org) has listings of dads' groups all over the country.

While it's generally perfectly fine to humor your child and go along with his claims about the existence of an imaginary friend, there are a few ground rules.

- **Don't let the "friend" be your child's only companion**. Kids need to socialize with others their own age. If your child seems to have no flesh-and-blood human friends or has no interest in being with his peers, talk to your pediatrician.
- **Don't let your child shift responsibility for everything bad to the friend**. Saying that the friend is the one responsible for a nighttime accident is okay. Blaming the friend for scribbling on the wall with lipstick or for committing a string of bank robberies isn't.
- **Treat the friend with respect**. This means remembering his name, greeting him when you meet, and apologizing when you sit on him.
- **Don't use the friend to manipulate your child**. That means no comments like, "Maggie finished her dinner, why don't you finish yours?"

Most kids lose their imaginary friends between their third and fifth birthdays. Sometimes the friends are forgotten, sometimes they're sent on a distant—and permanent—trip, and other times they're killed in a horrible accident.

If you're adventurous and want to start a group of your own, here are some things to consider:

- **Find a place where you can easily keep an eye on the kids while you're talking to the grown-ups**. A fenced park with benches can be great.
- **Don't let the group get too large**. Even if each adult keeps track of his or her own kids, any more than six is pushing it. And try to keep it to an even number so the kids can pair up without excluding anyone.
- **Meet regularly**. As you well know, kids love routines.
- **Bring some of your toddler's own toys**. This should help reduce the amount of grabbing, shoving, and tears.
- **Bring some food**. Your child will probably prefer to eat someone else's, but another kid will eat what you bring.
- **Don't hover**. Let the kids do what they want, as long as it's safe.
- **Play with the other kids—but not too much**. If the other little ones seem to be having too much fun with you, your child may get very jealous. Toddlers this age aren't too thrilled about sharing their daddies.
- **Don't push togetherness**. Kids may not want to play with one another all the time. They need plenty of time to play alone too.
- **Have a backup plan in case you get rained out of your regular place**. Places like Chuck E. Cheese are hot foul-weather destinations, as are museums and any other indoor spaces that have plenty of bathrooms and safe play equipment. If your backup meeting place is your house, be prepared for a bit more friction than usual. Having to share his house and his toys may be more than your child bargained for.
- **Keep your sick kid at home**. Although chances are good that whatever he's got has already been passed around, the other parents will be nervous anyway.

Music

During the second half of your child's third year, his language skills make a sudden, often dramatic spurt forward. You'll see this development in two distinct yet connected ways.

First, you'll notice that his imitation skills have become quite sharp: he can now repeat nearly any word or two-word phrase. He can also tell when he's imitating something correctly and when he's not.

Second, now that he's got a good grasp of the sounds that make up his native language, he'll begin using them as toys, amusing himself, and you, by making up his own words. Musically, a similar development is taking place. "Once they've acquired a simple vocabulary of tonal patterns and rhythms, [young children] can start creating their own songs," says music educator Edwin Gordon.

After a while your toddler will combine all these skills, and by his third birthday he may be able to sing all the words of a short song (like "Happy Birthday") or entire phrases of longer, familiar songs ("Baa, baa, black sheep, have you any wool? Yes, sir. Yes, sir. Three bags full," for example). But he won't be able to sing the whole song for another few months. He may also make deliberate changes to songs he already knows ("Baa, baa, blue sheep..."), just for the fun of it.

Your child's sense of rhythm has also been developing nicely. You'll notice that when he hears music he likes, he's now rocking, bobbing, clapping, and stomping in time with the beat, as opposed to making the seemingly random movements you saw just a few months ago.

This is a great time to try some imitation games with your child. Sing a note, then wait for him to repeat it. If he does that pretty well, try two notes, then three (a lot of kids can't do three-note patterns until well after they turn three, so don't get your hopes too high). Also try tapping out various rhythms and asking your child to repeat them.

The Rhythm of Reading

There's a fascinating connection between rhythm, language, and reading. Kali Woodruff Carr and her colleagues note that the rhythm of whatever language your child is hearing gives him cues about boundaries between words and syllables. (If you pay attention to your own speech when you're speaking to your toddler, you'll notice that you emphasize certain syllables more than others.) Children who can synchronize themselves to an external beat (say, from a song they're listening to) score higher on tests of language skills and reading readiness. Conversely, children who have trouble finding and staying with the beat are more likely to have language processing and, later on, reading difficulties, such as dyslexia, which Usha Goswami, director of the Centre for Neuroscience in Education at the University of Cambridge, has described as being "in tune but out of time."

If your toddler doesn't seem able to stay on beat when listening to music, you might want to do a simple experiment, which is similar to the musical imitation game described on this page, above. Using your hand or hands, tap or clap once and ask your child to do the same. Then tap twice, slowly, again asking him to imitate. If he can do that, add a third tap. Try different patterns—two fast and one slow, three fast, one slow and two fast, and so on. If your toddler has trouble with this, it's worth mentioning to your pediatrician.

Keep exposing your child to a wide variety of music and play it wherever you are. You can get children's CDs, but whatever you're listening to will work just as well. Just keep a lid on the volume. Loud music can damage his hearing. If you play an instrument, let your child see you in action. If he wants to participate, and your instrument isn't too fragile, let him. And if you don't have a musical keyboard around, now's the time to get one for your child.

Cooking with Kids

Although it might seem like a lot of trouble, cooking with your toddler can be a wonderful experience for both of you. Your child, of course, gets to make a huge mess (for you to clean up). But there are a few things kids get out of cooking:

- Early experience with math skills—measuring, counting, timing, fractions, and other real-world math applications.
- Exercise of coordination and fine motor skills.
- A greater understanding of cause and effect, such as: What happens to flour and other ingredients when you add milk or water to them? How do things change when you put them in the oven?
- An understanding of experimentation. What happens if you leave out ingredients such as baking powder, or add too much of something else, like yeast?
- Literacy exposure. Words in books aren't only about stories; they also give instructions and tell us how to do things.
- An appreciation of the importance of following directions.
- Practice working as a team, not only making the recipe but also, perhaps, cleaning up afterward.
- Expression of creativity. Once you've made a favorite recipe a few times, ask your child to improvise.
- Confidence, self-esteem, and a feeling of accomplishment.
- Opportunity to try new foods. At the least, it may encourage your child to be more open to expanding his palate.
- Enjoyment. It's just plain fun.

And if you aren't already your family's cook and bottle washer, your kids also get the added benefit of seeing you involved in a nontraditional task, which will help your child keep an open mind when considering careers and household roles of his own.

You, of course, benefit in very different ways. First of all, you get to use your time more efficiently—having fun and cooking dinner (or part of it) for the whole family simultaneously. It's not unlike taking a college course that satisfies a science requirement and a humanities requirement at the same time. Second, there's a good chance that your child will eat some of the food he makes, thereby expanding his food repertoire beyond plain pasta and white rice with soy sauce.

No matter what you're making, your child can participate in at least some part of the preparation. How long he'll actually stay in the kitchen with you depends on how much of a mess you'll let him make and whether or not what he's making is worth licking off a spoon. If you're willing to cooperate, just about any almost-three-year-old can:

- Stir (my kids loved this)
- Tear up leaves for salad (they hated salad, but they loved destroying things, so this worked out nicely)
- Knead and roll out dough (my kids' absolute favorite kitchen activity)
- Break eggs (actually, this may be their favorite)
- Measure ingredients and dump them into bowls (if this isn't the favorite, it's certainly a close second or third)
- Sprinkle toppings (hmmm … that's a lot of favorites)
- Cut things (using a dull plastic knife, of course)

Below are some fun, simple, quick recipes that you and your child can make together. In fact, he can probably handle most of the tasks by himself if you let him. But first, a few rules to keep in mind before you get started:

- **Read the "Cooking Safety" section (page 241) very carefully**.
- **Don't force**. If he doesn't want to do a particular step, let him alone.
- **Allow the fun to happen**. Yes, he'll get flour all over the floor (and the walls and his clothes). And yes, he'll get broken eggshells in the batter. If you're not in the mood to deal with these things, save your cooking adventure for another day.

KIDSICLES

What you'll need:
    1 cup fresh or frozen fruit
    1 cup milk or yogurt
    Ice-pop molds (or ice cube trays and sticks)
    A blender

1. Blend the fruit and milk or yogurt.
2. Pour into molds or tray.
3. Freeze for at least four hours; overnight is best.

Let your toddler get as involved as possible, but keep him away from the blender itself. If he wants to help pour, transfer some liquid from the blender into a smaller, easy-pouring container.

LIZ'S EGG IN THE NEST

What you'll need (per serving):

    1 egg

    1 piece of toast

    Cookie cutters (optional)

    Butter, for greasing the skillet

1. Cut a hole about the size of a golf ball in the middle of the piece of toast. If you've got some cookie cutters with simple shapes like animals or hearts, cut the hole with one of them instead.
2. Turn a small skillet on low, and add some butter
3. When the butter is melted, put the toast into the skillet.
4. Crack the egg into the hole.
5. Cook until the egg is the way your child likes it.

MILKSHAKE

What you'll need:

    1 cup milk

    Large piece of your child's favorite (non-citrus) fruit

    Several ice cubes

    1 to 2 drops vanilla extract (optional)

    1 to 2 teaspoons chocolate syrup (optional)

1. Put all the ingredients in a blender.
2. Cover and blend until smooth.

FRENCH TOAST

What you'll need:

    4 eggs

    1 cup milk

    1 teaspoon vanilla extract (optional)

    Pinch of cinnamon

    6–8 slices of bread (Stale bread is fine; moldy is not. If you want to make this even more fun, cut the bread into animal shapes, cars, or faces before you start.)

    1 tablespoon butter

    Syrup, jam, sour cream, or any other kind of topping

1. Combine eggs, milk, vanilla, and cinnamon in a bowl.
2. Stir (or whisk, if you have one) until mixed thoroughly.
3. Pour the mixture into a pie pan or shallow bowl or dish that's large enough to hold a slice of bread.

4. Drop a slice of bread in the mixture, let it soak for a few seconds, flip it over, and soak the other side.
5. Heat a skillet to medium and add some of the butter.
6. When the butter melts, spread it around and then add a slice or two of the batter-soaked bread (as many as can fit on the surface of the skillet without overlapping).
7. Cook until the bread is light brown on the bottom. Be careful about this—most kids will refuse to eat anything that's anywhere close to being burned.

Cooking Safety

Cooking with kids can be a huge amount of fun. But because it involves dealing with knives and flames, there's also the potential for getting hurt. Following these safety rules should help you get through the process with a minimum of bloodshed (or other bad outcomes).

- **Wash your hands and your child's hands before you start**. No explanation necessary, right?
- **Work at your child's level**—either at the kitchen table or, better yet, at your child's very own table. This reduces the chances that he'll slip off the stool he's been standing on or that he'll pull a heavy bowl off the counter and onto his head.
- **Keep sharp knives, blenders, and other potentially dangerous implements far, far away from your child**. If he's interested in using some tools, whisks, spoons, and measuring cups should keep him pretty busy. See the Resources section for info on safe cooking gear.
- **Use back burners and keep pot and pan handles pointed toward the back of the stove**. This reduces the chances that hot dishes will get pulled off the stovetop.
- **Remind your child to be careful about touching anything that used to be hot**. Electric stove tops stay hot even after they're turned off, and so do pots and pans. Repeat the reminder every ten minutes, as necessary.
- **Opening ovens, closing them, putting things into them, and taking things out are adult-only jobs**. Don't even think about letting an almost three-year-old try any of them.
- **Dress appropriately**. Long sleeves can get dragged through batter or yanked into blenders. Short sleeves are better. Topless is better still, and the most fun.

8. Flip over and cook until light brown on the other side (or somewhat less, if you happen to have overcooked the first side). Repeat until all slices are cooked.

9. Serve with your child's favorite topping.

PANCAKE ART

What you'll need:
- Bisquick or other pancake mix
- All the additional ingredients listed on the box
- Cookie cutters (optional)
- Pastry tube (optional)

1. Make the pancake batter following the recipe on the package.
2. If you've got a steady hand, drizzle the batter into the heated pan, making whatever shapes or letters your child wants. Alternatively, put the batter in the pastry tube and "draw" shapes, or place a cookie cutter (metal only) in the pan and pour batter into it.
3. When bubbles appear in the batter, it's time to turn the pancake over. If using, remove the cookie cutter first, being very careful, since it will be extremely hot. Cook until light brown on the bottom.

POPCORN BALLS

What you'll need:
- 10–12 cups popped popcorn
- 1 cup corn syrup, or one 10-ounce package of marshmallows
- ¼ cup butter or margarine (only if using marshmallows instead of the syrup)
- 1 or 2 packages of gelatin, any flavor(s) you like

1. Half fill several large bowls with the popcorn.
2. Put the corn syrup, or the marshmallows and butter, in a pan and melt over low heat.
3. Add the gelatin. Stir until it's completely dissolved.
4. Remove the mixture from the heat and pour it over the popcorn. Stir quickly so that the popcorn gets covered evenly.
5. Shape the popcorn into baseball-size balls.
6. Place the balls on a sheet of waxed paper and refrigerate until firm.

PRETZELS

What you'll need:
- 1 package yeast
- 1½ cups warm water
- 1 tablespoon sugar

1 tablespoon salt

4 cups flour

1 egg, beaten

1. Preheat the oven to 425° F.
2. Mix the yeast, water, sugar, and salt until everything is completely dissolved.
3. Stir in the flour.
4. Knead into a soft dough.
5. Roll into long ropes about the thickness of your finger.
6. Shape into pretzel shapes, numbers, letters, or anything your child feels like making.
7. Brush the beaten egg on the shaped dough.
8. Bake for 12 to 15 minutes.
9. Take out and let cool before eating.

QUESADILLA

What you'll need (per serving):

Cooking spray or 1 tablespoon butter, margarine, or oil

Two 6-inch tortillas (Wheat tortillas are usually softer, but if your child is allergic to wheat, corn is fine.)

Nice-size handful of your child's favorite cheese, grated

Several tablespoons of refried beans (optional)

Several tablespoons of steamed rice

Several tablespoons of cooked fresh or frozen vegetables (optional)

1. Put the cooking spray, butter, margarine, or oil in a skillet and place over medium heat.
2. Drop a single tortilla into the skillet and sprinkle some of the grated cheese all over it.
3. If you think your child will eat them, add the refried beans, rice, and/or vegetables.
4. Cover the first tortilla with a second one.
5. Cook for 30 to 45 seconds, or until the cheese has melted enough to keep the two tortillas stuck together.
6. Flip over and cook for another 30 to 45 seconds. If you can flip the tortilla sandwich in the skillet, your child and all her friends will consider you the absolute coolest guy in the neighborhood. If you can't, practice.

EVE'S CHOCOLATE LEAVES

What you'll need:

16-ounce package chocolate chips

New ¼-inch paintbrush

Cookie sheet covered with waxed paper

Some thick leaves with stems, gently washed and completely dry (Check
with your local garden shop to make absolutely sure they're not toxic;
camellia and magnolia leaves are pretty widely available and are fine.)

1. Melt the chocolate chips over low to medium heat or in the top of a double
boiler.
2. Paint the surface of the leaves with a thick coat of the melted chocolate.
3. Put the painted leaves on the waxed-paper-covered cookie sheet.
4. When you've painted as many leaves as your child thinks is fun, put the cookie
sheet into the refrigerator. Remove it when the chocolate has hardened (20–30
minutes).
5. Hold a leaf chocolate-side down, and with your other hand gently pull up the
stem and carefully remove the leaf from the chocolate.
6. Show your child the way the stem and vein pattern of the real leaf has been
replicated in the chocolate.

YOU AND YOUR PARTNER

Helping Her Cope with Being a Stepmom

On pages 217–21 we talked about you becoming a stepfather. But what if the situation is reversed, and your partner is a brand-new stepmother? Most of what I
said earlier applies here—just reverse the genders.

In short, you're the single most important factor in determining how your partner will deal with her new role. You're the one who has to welcome her into your
family, and you're the one who has to make sure your children understand her role.
Like just about anyone stepping into a preexisting family unit, she's going to feel a
little insecure. Here are some ways you can help her through this tough transition:

- **Let her know that she shouldn't try to be your child's mother**. In fact, she
probably *can't* be—unless you're a widower, your child already has a mother.
What she can and should do, however, is treat your child with love and respect.
After a while she'll get the same back.
- **Give her plenty of time to develop her own relationship with your child**. This
means letting things happen at their own pace and not forcing her to take on
more responsibility than she's able to.
- **Give her some feedback**. She may not say so, but she really wants to know that
the kids like her and that she's doing a good job. So if they say something nice
to you about her, pass it on. Compliment her when she does something great

with the kids, and give her some gentle pointers if she does something you don't agree with. But don't correct her while she's doing it—unless it's putting your child in danger—wait until the two of you are alone. Hovering over her shoulder puts way too much pressure on her. Instead, let her discover how to do most things for herself the same way you did: by making mistakes.

- **Talk to your kids**. Make sure they know what her authority is, and that they know what you expect from them in relation to her.
- **Encourage her to tell you how she's feeling**. She may be having the time of her life, or she may be frustrated, exasperated, and annoyed. Help her celebrate the joys, and be supportive when she needs to cry on your shoulder.
- **Help her deal with your ex**. Your new partner and your ex probably won't have all that much to do with each other. But they might bump into each other at family, school, or other events. You can help minimize potential conflicts by being balanced in the way you talk about your ex. If you've been saying nothing but bad things, your new partner is probably going to be somewhat hostile. But if you've been nothing but complimentary, she may be jealous.
- **Set up some ground rules**. It's critical that you and your new partner reach a clear understanding about the following issues:
  - **Discipline**. Who's going to do it, and how? This can be especially important if your partner has kids of her own and an established way of handling them. Generally speaking, you should handle disciplining your own children for at least a few years.
  - **Other involvement**. To make her feel part of the family, you have to give her some authority over the kids and back her up when she uses it. At the same time, you don't want her stepping in and telling you how to run your (and your kids') life. Also, will you expect her to take the kids shopping? Drive them to and/or from day care? Attend parent-teacher conferences?
  - **Money**. How will you handle household finances? Will any of her income be used to pay for day care or other expenses for your children? Or worse, for child support or alimony? If she has children of her own, will any of your income be used to pay for them?

FAMILY MATTERS

Getting Ready for a Second Child

According to *Parenting* magazine, the most common age gap between children in the United States is two to three years. That means there's a good chance you'll be welcoming a new baby into your home before you finish this book. As adults, you and your partner have all sorts of resources (including, I hope, *The Expectant Father*) to help you through the pregnancy and birth. But your child is depending on you to prepare him for the day his world turns upside down.

BEFORE THE BIRTH

- **Don't start too early**. Wait until your child asks some questions about his mother's physical changes, or about why you're moving furniture around, to open the discussion.
- **Don't make too big a deal about how great it's going to be to become a big brother or sister**. And don't try to force your child to get excited about the prospect.
- **Take your toddler to prenatal doctor visits**. If he's interested, have him hold the Doppler to hear the baby's heartbeat, and take him to see the ultrasound pictures. If he's not interested, leave him alone.
- **Read age-appropriate books about pregnancy and childbirth**. We've listed several on pages 164 and 226.
- **Enroll him in older-sibling prep classes**. Some hospitals offer classes in which kids learn the basics of what their mothers are going to go through during the birth; the kinds of things they can and can't do with their new sibling; and that Dad and Mom still love them very much, even though they aren't going to be the center of the universe anymore.
- **Expose him to other babies you know**. If you don't know any, the nursery at the hospital should have plenty of extras. (Although, with the understandably tight security at most hospitals, it may be hard to visit babies that aren't your own.)
- **Don't make too many changes at once**. If you're moving the older child out of a crib, moving to a new house, or making any other major changes, do it long before the baby arrives. Otherwise, your older child will think he's being moved out to make room for the new baby, which will only lead to resentment and sibling rivalry—before there's even a sibling to have a rivalry with.

AFTER THE BIRTH

Handling your older children's reactions to the new baby requires an extra touch of gentleness and sensitivity. Although kids are usually wildly excited (initially, at least) about their new status as big brother or big sister, when it hits them that the baby is going to be a permanent visitor, things change. Psychologist Henry Biller found that most kids show some negative reactions, such as being more disobedient and demanding. A lot of brand-new older siblings also exhibit some regressive behavior. For example, older children who are already toilet trained may start wetting themselves again (my oldest daughter did this). They may become clingy, start using "baby talk," crawl or demand to be carried instead of walking, or have crying jags for no reason at all. It's as if your older child is saying, "If all you wanted was a crying baby, why didn't you say so? I can do that."

These behavioral changes are perfectly normal and are really the result of the older child's feeling that the baby has stolen something that was exclusively his: your love and affection. Interestingly, Biller also found that children who have close relationships with their father adjust much better to the birth of a new sibling and have fewer ongoing problems.

Here are a few things you can do to ease the transition for your older kid:

- **As soon as the new baby is born, call the older child and tell him first**. Let him make the announcement (if he wants to) that he's a big brother to other members of the family.
- **Have the older child come to the hospital right away** (even if it's past his bedtime). Take a few pictures of him holding the baby.
- **Don't expect your older child to love the baby instantly**. It can take a long, long time. Really long. A friend of mine told me that for years, every time he drove by the hospital the second baby had been born in, his older son would ask, "Can we take her back yet?"
- **Don't make a big fuss about the new baby or smother her with gifts in front of the older child**. That will only make your toddler feel left out, jealous, and resentful. It could also result in the older child trying to hurt the baby. Have everyone who comes to visit the baby spend a few private minutes with the older child first, at least in part talking about something other than what he thinks of being a big brother.
- **Make sure you and your partner each spend some regular time alone with your toddler**, doing special activities, going to special places, reading his favorite books, or whatever he wants. He's going to need constant reminders that he's as important to you as the new baby. Just telling him so won't do the trick.
- **Don't blame yourself**. Friction between your older and younger kids is normal. Saying "If only I'd done_____, he'd love the baby" is a waste of time.
- **Get some special gifts for your toddler**.
- **Watch a few "becoming a big brother or sister" videos or read some of the books** listed on pages 164 and 226.
- **Go through your photo albums**, reminding your toddler what a wonderful baby he was.
- **Encourage your toddler to get involved**. Let him help as much as possible with "his" baby—holding, feeding, diapering, clothing, singing or talking, and running errands around the house. And be sure to be extra appreciative.
- **Do some shameless ego boosting**. It can help a lot if you say things like, "The

baby's so happy when she sees you," or "See how he stops crying when you hold him? Could you teach me how to do that?" or "Thanks for bringing me that bottle—you're a great big sibling!"

- **Teach your toddler how to play with the baby**. It might be fun to show him how to elicit reflex actions from the baby (I've got a big section on this in *The New Father: A Dad's Guide to the First Year*, pages 60–61). But never leave the baby alone with your older child, not even for a second (unless, of course, your older one is over twelve). Your primary consideration is, of course, to keep the new baby alive and uninjured. And you'll need to remind the older child (dozens of times) that hurting the baby is simply not allowed. Make it clear that doing so will result not only in his not being allowed to play with the baby for a while but also in the loss of some special big-kid privileges.
- **Give your toddler some space of his own that's completely off-limits to the baby**.
- **Allow him to have things he doesn't have to share at all**. With toys that must be shared, be meticulous about giving each child equal time—set a timer with a loud beep.
- **Give your toddler plenty of opportunity to be out of the home regularly—** sleepovers at friends' and grandparents', off with you or his mother or the babysitter, and so on. Otherwise, he'll feel like he's competing with the baby all day. Be careful, though, not to do too much of this—you don't want to give the child the impression that you're booting him out.
- **Give your toddler a few privileges**—a later bedtime, perhaps.
- **Encourage your toddler to express his emotions**. Ask a lot of questions about how he feels. Keep the questions focused on him—not on the baby. And be sure to let him know that those feelings are okay, by saying things like, "Being a big sibling can be hard and sometimes you can get mad. That's okay."
- **Treat negative feelings as positives**. You can't force a child to feel love if he doesn't feel it. And it's far better for him to say something hurtful than to express the idea physically. If he needs to burn off some hostility, make sure he gets plenty of exercise.
- **Empathize**. Every once in a while, let your toddler see you expressing your own occasional annoyance with the baby's demands, but not so often that he gets the idea that the new sibling is a permanent nuisance. Express your joy too. And talk about your own experience as an older child (if you were one).
- **Look at the world from the older child's perspective**. Imagine how it feels to your toddler when he sees his younger sibling wearing something that used to

be his—even if he outgrew it long ago. To him it can seem like there's nothing left of him.

- **For a child, the expression "It's not fair" really means, "It's not the same."** So get two of everything, and make sure your toddler gets first pick—one of the privileges of being the big sibling.

- **Be prepared**. When older children are forced not to hit younger siblings (life is tough, isn't it?), their aggression doesn't just disappear. It has to come out somewhere, and frequently it's reborn as a temper tantrum.

- **Be thoughtful of half-siblings**. If the new baby is the first for you and your new partner, and the older child doesn't live with you full-time, it's important to address that issue head-on. A lot of children in this situation see the new baby as replacing them and worry that you're starting a new family without them. It's important to reassure your child that you'll always love him and to help him understand that he's part of two families and that your family definitely includes him. A Venn diagram can help, with one circle showing your older child and the parent (and siblings, if any) he lives with when he's not with you, the other circle showing you, your partner, him, and the new baby. Be sure your older child is the sole occupant of the place where the two circles overlap.

Learning to Let Go

33–36 MONTHS

WHAT'S GOING ON WITH YOUR TODDLER

Physically

- Over the course of this last year, your toddler has put on only a few pounds. But she's getting longer and longer, especially in the legs and torso.
- She throws, catches, pedals her trike, and loves to jump off things.
- If it wasn't already, it should be fairly clear by now whether your child is left- or right-handed.
- Her hand coordination is constantly improving. She tries to imitate your writing and can draw a pretty passable circle (or at least a swirl).
- She very neatly lays out her clothes for the next day the night before and has no trouble putting on her own pants, socks, T-shirt, and jacket. Buttons, snaps, and zippers may still give her some trouble, though.

Intellectually

- As she approaches her third birthday, your toddler will be quite comfortable with many short-term time concepts. She regularly uses "soon," "in a minute," and the endearing "this day" (instead of "today").
- She's also deepening her understanding of spatial relationships—she's mastered *in* and *out*, but the more abstract *near* has eluded her until now.
- She's very concerned that every object has its own special place, and she may get quite upset if things aren't where they're supposed to be.
- Her attention span continues to grow, and she can now focus on an activity for as long as five to eight minutes. This means she's ready for longer-lasting games such as hide-and-seek.

- Her sorting skills are very well developed, and she loves to help you by separating the laundry into whites and colors, matching up pairs of socks, or putting away the silverware (with supervision, of course).
- She can now count up to three. (She may be able to say her numbers up to ten, but she doesn't really know what they mean.)

Verbally

- By her third birthday, your child will understand the majority of the conversational language she'll use for the rest of her life. About 80 percent of what she says can be understood, even by strangers.
- Boys' verbal skills and vocabularies are still lagging a bit behind girls'. Boys generally tell shorter stories whose main characters are usually themselves. Girls' stories are longer, and their main characters are more likely to be adults.
- Your toddler is finally able to use tenses (although not always completely accurately). My mother fell down and tore a ligament in her knee, and we told my youngest daughter about it the next day. For months afterward, she would look up and announce, "Grandma fell down boom and hurt her leg yesterday."
- Kids acquire most of their understanding of time words in the six months between ages two and a half and three.

Emotionally and Socially

- Like their teenage counterparts, "first adolescents" (see page 215) are incredible know-it-alls. But the veneer of confidence is pretty thin. "It helps to remember that the child is bossy not because he is sure, but actually because he is unsure," write child-development experts Louise Bates Ames and Frances Ilg. "The world still seems big and dangerous to him. If he can command even a small part of it (his parents), it helps him to feel secure." As your toddler's language

"You have to let them make their own mistakes."

251

skills improve, thus enabling her to gain some control over her impulses, the world will become (in her eyes) much less dangerous.

- Your toddler may still be quite negative and contrary. But it's critical to keep in mind that this is part of an important developmental stage. "The first step toward a positive self-identity and sense of selfhood is a negative self-identity, a negation of the values and desires of his parents," writes psychologist Fitzhugh Dodson. "A negative self-identity must precede positive self-identity."

- It's taken a while, but your toddler is finally beginning to interact regularly with her playmates. She loves the act of sharing but will often grab back whatever she's given someone. And she still spends a lot of time protecting her toys and her territory from intruders.

- Although her sense of humor is getting more sophisticated, it's still the incongruous that gets the biggest laughs: try to slip your feet into her shoes or wear her pants on your head, and you're likely to reduce your toddler to hysterical laughter. Other things that are usually good for a laugh include mishaps and minor accidents (unless someone is injured), silly questions ("Where are your wings?"), and adults imitating baby talk or pretending to throw a tantrum.

WHAT YOU'RE GOING THROUGH

Speaking Up

I was second in line to buy stamps at the post office when a young woman came into the lobby, dragging a three-year-old boy behind her. "Now just sit down over there and shut up," she snapped, pointing the boy to an empty seat on a nearby bench. But instead of sitting, the boy began to run around the lobby. That's when his mother grabbed him. "I'm sick and tired of you," she said as she slapped his face, hard. "And you better quit that crying, or I'll—"

He didn't. She did, this time knocking him to the floor.

I was stunned. Whatever that little boy had done, it certainly didn't warrant the treatment he was getting. At first I wanted to say something to the woman, but I couldn't bring myself to do it. Then I looked around the post office, hoping that maybe someone else would say something. But everyone seemed to be concentrating on the return addresses on the envelopes they'd brought. The woman was still chastising her child when my turn came. I bought my stamps, exchanged helpless looks and shoulder shrugs with the clerk, and quickly left. I sat outside in my car for a while, furious—not only at that woman for hitting her child, but also at myself and at everyone else in that post office. How could a bunch of responsible adults have stood by so silently? Certainly, seeing an adult abuse a child is something that bothers just about everyone. But to parents concerned about the safety and welfare of their own children, it's especially disturbing. Unfortunately, though, it happens all the time. And since we're spending time in places where there are other families around, we're likely to see more than our share.

WHY WE DON'T SPEAK UP

Most of us know what we'd do (or at least what we *think* we'd do) if someone tried to hurt our children. So why are we so hesitant to speak up when someone else's kids are being abused? Are we just uncaring and insensitive? Not at all. Until fairly recently, "children were mostly still viewed as the personal property or extensions of their parents with few or no legal rights whatsoever," according to Hanita Kosher and her colleagues. Parents were allowed to treat them any way they liked, and "corporal punishment was almost universal and was accepted as appropriate."

Another reason we don't speak up when we see someone treating a child inappropriately is that most of us try to stay in the background, hoping that someone else will take the lead. But when no one does, explains Dr. Ervin Staub, an expert in bystander behavior, "we downplay our own reactions and convince ourselves that what we initially thought was abusive behavior really wasn't that bad after all." Staub refers to this very common phenomenon as "pluralistic ignorance."

But hesitating to "butt in" and taking one's cues from others are definitely not the only factors that keep us silent. Imagine this scenario: You're walking home alone at night when you see a large man coming out the door of a house, carrying a screaming child. He quickly stuffs her into the back seat of a car and gets ready to drive away. He sees you staring suspiciously at him and glares back. Are you face to face with a violent kidnapper or just a frantic father taking a sick child to the hospital? If you play it safe and say nothing, you may experience one or both of the other feelings most likely to keep people from speaking up: fear of putting oneself in physical danger and fear of making things worse for the child.

WHEN TO GET INVOLVED . . .

For better or worse, passersby almost never have a legal obligation to do anything. (Doctors, teachers, social workers, childcare workers, and, in some states, the people who process photos at the local drugstore, however, are "mandated reporters," meaning that they're required to report suspected abuse to the proper authority.) But there are clearly times when all of us have a moral obligation to do something. Looking for some guidance about when, exactly, to jump in, I spoke with several experts, who helped me craft the following general guidelines:

- If you see that an adult is causing a child serious or life-threatening injury (hitting hard enough to leave a mark or actually drawing blood), do something.

- If you see that a child has been abandoned or negligently left in a dangerous situation (locked in a car in hot weather with the windows closed), do something.
- If the child's actions make it reasonably clear that he or she is scared, or that the person doing the suspected abuse is a stranger to her, do something.

... AND HOW TO DO IT

Okay, to sum it up, if you see something, do something. Sounds simple enough, but what, exactly, does "do something" mean? For some of us, confronting others is no problem. "I'd rather risk embarrassing myself to save a child," a friend of mine once told me, "than have to live with myself knowing that I could have done something but didn't." Of course, "confronting" doesn't have to mean "attacking." And there's a big difference between risking embarrassing yourself and risking your own or your family's safety. Here are a few approaches that might help defuse a potentially dangerous situation:

- **Make eye contact in the kindest way possible**. Looking disapproving or threatening could produce an effect exactly opposite to the one you're hoping for.
- **Strike up a conversation**. Perhaps say something completely out of the blue, such as, "What an incredibly beautiful child." Your interruption could be enough to break the rhythm and give the adult time to regain her senses.
- **Be sympathetic**. Commiserate, saying something like, "Kids can really push your buttons, can't they?" or "I know just how you feel. My daughter did exactly the same thing last week." This makes you the angry adult's ally and increases the chances that she'll stop what she's doing.
- **Keep it positive**. Dirty looks or negative remarks (for example, telling the person she's doing something wrong or is a bad parent) are likely to increase her anger and could make the situation worse for everyone.
- **Ask if you can help**. But ask quietly and politely. The last thing you want to do is make an already angry parent feel like he's being publicly chastised.
- **Make a loud noise or knock something over**. Again, sometimes all it takes to diffuse a hot situation is a momentary diversion.
- **Divert the child's attention**. Make a silly face, talk to her, or point out something of interest.
- **Take the first step**. People tend to adapt their behavior to that of the people around them. Most of the other bystanders are just as bothered as you are, but everyone's waiting for someone else to take the first step. If you jump in, chances are good that someone else will join you.
- **Ask for help**. You might say to another witness, "Did you see that? We need to do something to stop this."
- **Make the call**. For many of us, approaching a stranger—even to do something

as simple as ask directions—is simply too embarrassing or daunting. So if, after assessing the situation, you feel that there's no way to intervene safely, pull out your phone and call either 911 or the Childhelp National Child Abuse Hotline, 1-800-4-A-CHILD (1-800-422-4453). If the adult is in or gets into a car, try to get the license plate number while you call 911. If you're concerned about a neighbor, call your county child protective services and give them the address.

THE FEAR OF MAKING A MISTAKE

Sometimes it's obvious there's a problem: a child is getting beaten right in front of you, or you're driving down the highway and see that the woman driving the car next to you is breastfeeding a baby (don't laugh—this actually happens). But what should you do when the situation is not so clear-cut, or when you're seeing something that might be a flash of temper rather than a case of prolonged abuse? After all, as parents we've all come close to losing it on a particularly bad day. But what about that kid you know who's always covered with bruises?

Before calling the police, take a good, careful look at the situation and make sure your suspicions are reasonable. As you well know, children are always having accidents, and a few bruises and cuts are usually not an indication of abuse. If you need help evaluating what you've seen, or if you want to know how to make a report in your area, the Childhelp National Child Abuse Hotline is the place to call (again, 1-800-4-A-CHILD/1-800-422-4453). The hotline operator can either take a report from you directly or refer you to the appropriate agency in your area. The hotline is also a place to call if *you're* feeling out of control and need someone to talk to; see also "Parental Stress" in the Resources guide.

YOU AND YOUR TODDLER

A Different Kind of Playtime

As you know by now, the toddler years are the age of exploration, a time when your child investigates her world and learns about all the great things she can do with her body. Giving your child as much freedom as possible to explore is critical to her developing sense of autonomy and self-confidence. And most parents are perfectly willing to let their children explore whatever they want to—as long as they keep their hands out of their pants.

Like it or not, almost all toddlers go through a genital self-exploration phase, and it's especially common right around the time when they start making the transition from diapers to big-kid underwear. After all, when they were wearing diapers all the time, their genitals were pretty hard to grab hold of. But now that they're accessible nearly all the time . . . (Reminds me a little of the old joke: Why do dogs lick their crotches? Because they can.)

Still, it's a little discomfiting to watch a child play with his or her own genitals, and it's hard to resist pulling the child's hand away or snapping, "Stop that!" Maybe it's all those stories we heard about how masturbation causes blindness or hairy palms or turns kids into perverts.

Whatever the reason, it's important that you resist the urge to step between your child and her genitals. Making a big deal out of it can give your child the message that that part of her body is dirty or that touching it is somehow wrong. For a little boy, "his penis is no more interesting than any other part of him," says Fitzhugh Dodson. "It is only when we react as though there is something bad or naughty about it that we teach him to become morbidly interested." The same obviously goes for little girls. The truth, of course, is that "our toddlers will only develop sex hang-ups if we teach them to," says Dodson.

At home, the best plan of action is to neither encourage nor discourage genital exploration. In public places, however, gently redirect your child to another activity, telling her that private touching should be done in a private place, such as her own room in her own home. Here are a few more things you can do:

- **Teach your child the correct names for human body parts**—including *penis*, *vagina*, and *rectum*—just as you did for belly button, nose, and elbow. Being able to name something makes it a lot less mysterious.
- **Explain physical differences between adults and children**. Adults' pubic hair (and the hair on your chest, legs, back, and elsewhere) and adult-size genitals are of special concern to kids. The simple answer (one that's perfectly adequate for kids this age) is that as you get bigger, everything gets bigger, and that when you get to be a grown-up, you get hairier.
- **Talk about touching**. It's simply not okay for anyone (adult or child) to touch a child in his or her private area—except if the adult is a doctor or a parent bathing a child or changing a diaper. Bathroom privacy (closing the door, knocking) is also a good topic to bring up now.
- **Empower your child**. Tell her that if someone other than her parents or a doctor touches her private areas, that she should tell you right away.
- **Stay away from intimate touching or sex in front of your child**. But be warned: your child will likely walk in on you one day. And scrambling around trying to cover up may make your child think there's something wrong with your (and, by extension, her) body. Instead, calmly put on some clothes and walk your child back to her room. Depending on what the child sees, you can talk about how adults may touch each other in certain ways.

- **Don't punish or chastise your child for her behavior or for touching herself or others**. Simply redirect her to another activity. Later on, have another conversation about appropriate places for that type of behavior and about the rule that it's not okay to touch anyone else.
- **Observe**. Your child's curiosity about sex and self-exploration are normal (plus, the latter feels good). So is playing "doctor" and wanting to examine other children's body parts or show them hers. Such behavior may seem sexual to you, but in most cases, children see it as play. However, if your child seems to be obsessed with touching herself or others, you may want to speak to her pediatrician about whether it's a behavioral problem or a sign of sexual abuse.

WHY IT MAY BE TIME TO KEEP YOUR PANTS ON

At about the same time as your child develops an interest in her own body, she may also suddenly become conscious of yours—and of the differences between yours and your partner's and between yours and hers (or his, if you've got a boy). This is most likely to come up if you have a habit of not wearing much clothing around the house. Generally speaking, there's nothing wrong with your child's seeing you or your partner naked. But how do you know when a little more modesty is in order? The answer, of course, depends on many factors—your attitudes

It Takes Balls to Be a Dad

While we're on the topic of what's going on below the waist: Have you looked at your balls lately? Do they look any different than they did before you became a dad? Several studies have found that low testosterone levels are associated with higher levels of paternal involvement. Researcher Jennifer Mascaro and her colleagues decided to take that body of research up a notch and began comparing the size of a father's testicles with his level of involvement in direct caregiving. Turns out that, like low testosterone levels, smaller testicles are associated with higher levels of caregiving and nurturing-related brain activity. However, which came first, the balls or the baby, isn't entirely clear. "We're assuming that testes size drives how involved the fathers are," said James Rilling, one of the study's coauthors. "But it could also be that when men become more involved as caregivers, their testes shrink." And just so you know, the study was published in the journal *PNAS* (despite the acronym's apparent pronunciation, it's just an abbreviation for *Proceedings of the National Academy of Sciences*).

and comfort levels about nudity (do you think the human body is something to be proud of or something that should be kept completely private?), your child's awareness of the physical differences between you, and much more.

In my case, my daughters basically told me when to get dressed. I used to take baths with them, until one day, when the older one was about three, she decided to grab my penis in the bathtub—a pretty serious hint that either I should wear a swimsuit or she should bathe alone.

With my middle daughter, the hint came a little earlier: One afternoon, just after she'd turned two, she and I spent about a half hour talking about all the

Hyperactivity Alert

One of the most common behavioral diagnoses these days is attention deficit/hyperactivity disorder, or ADHD. Nearly one in ten (9.4 percent) American children age two to seventeen have been diagnosed with ADHD, and boys are four to six times more likely to receive the diagnosis than girls. No one's quite sure what causes ADHD, although some neurologists suspect that it's the result of deficits of two brain chemicals, dopamine and acetylcholine, which help the brain focus on one thing at a time. ADHD may also run in families. In addition, children who were born prematurely or at low birthweight, or whose mothers smoked, drank, or used drugs during pregnancy, may be at higher risk.

Children with ADHD often have a short attention span, are easily distracted, behave impulsively, are fidgety and squirmy, and seem to be in constant motion. Coincidentally, that's a pretty good description of almost all toddlers, at least some of the time. For that reason, ADHD is overdiagnosed—often by day-care workers and teachers, who don't have the training or experience to make an accurate diagnosis but who naturally prefer children who obey and sit still to those who don't. Only a trained professional—in most cases a psychologist, psychiatrist, or neurologist—is qualified to make an actual diagnosis.

The natural consequence of this overdiagnosis is that it's becoming more and more common for kids—especially boys—to be drugged into submission. So if your babysitter, day-care provider, or preschool teacher tells you your child is hyperactive or suffers from ADHD, don't panic. Instead:

- **Be skeptical**. In some ways, diagnosing ADHD is akin to the late Supreme Court justice Potter Stewart's famous definition of pornography: "I shall not

different kinds of tails animals have and why people don't have them at all. The next morning, she strolled into the bathroom just as I was stepping out of the shower. We chatted for a second, but suddenly she gave me a stunned, betrayed look and pointed at my crotch. "Daddy has a tail," she announced.

More Adult Separation Problems

I don't think I'll ever forget the time I drove my older daughter a few blocks away from my house and abandoned her. Okay, I didn't really abandon her, I just took her to preschool. But it was my first time, and somehow I felt I'd done something wrong.

today attempt further to define [it] ... but I know it when I see it." Over the course of a few days, compare your child's behavior to that of others her age. Is she significantly more active and less focused, and does she behave this way every day? A lot of what is casually "diagnosed" as ADHD is nothing more than normal toddler behavior.

- **Think about your child's temperament**. Is she naturally active and/or distractible? If so, what looks like ADHD might be perfectly normal.
- **If you're still worried, take your child to her pediatrician**. Describe the symptoms carefully. If your pediatrician recommends it, have your child tested by a qualified child psychiatrist. According to the Mayo Clinic, children should not be diagnosed with ADHD "unless symptoms continue for more than six months and affect their ability to participate in age-appropriate activities."
- **If the child psychiatrist suggests drugs, get a second opinion**.

If your child is conclusively diagnosed with ADHD, take it seriously. While ADHD doesn't cause other conditions, having ADHD increases the chances that a child may also have or develop anxiety disorder, bipolar disorder, conduct disorder, depression, learning disabilities, or Tourette syndrome.

Fortunately, treating ADHD in toddlers usually begins with behavioral therapy, which is designed to help you help your child to better control her behavior. This may involve limiting screen time, increasing physical activity (to help the child burn off energy), listening to calming music, reinforcing good behavior through rewards and praise, creating consistent structure and routines, establishing clear rules and consequences, and so on.

When our first child was born, my wife and I both cut our workloads to three days a week so we could spend as much time with her as possible. And for the first two and a half years of her life, at least one of us was with her almost all the time. But as I sat in my car after dropping her off for her first day of preschool, I began to wonder what kind of parent I was, leaving her all alone with people I hardly knew. Would they read to her? Could anyone possibly teach her as well as my wife and I had? Who would encourage her? And who would love her? I was nearly overcome by the desire to run back to the school, grab her, and take her home where she belonged. After a few minutes of this sort of thinking, it became painfully clear that my wife and I had spent months preparing the wrong person for our daughter's first day of school.

Fighting the urge to go back to the school, I drove home and sat down in front of my computer. I tried to remind myself that up until then I actually had been looking forward to having my child in school, knowing I'd have a lot more time to write. But as I stared dumbly at the screen saver, I kept thinking that maybe my priorities were out of order. After all, what was more important, writing a few articles or making sure my child got the best possible education? Eventually, though, I had to admit that school was clearly the best place for my daughter, especially a school taught by teachers who were so gifted.

What it really comes down to, I guess, is that I knew I was going to miss my daughter while she was at school. I'd miss the wonderful times we had—the rainy-day matinees and museums and the sunny-day outings, the hours spent cuddling on the couch reading the same book ten times in a row, the time sitting at her table drawing. And most of all, I'd miss the long talks we had and the feeling of overflowing joy and pride I got from watching her learn new things and seeing how bright and articulate she'd become.

But missing her wasn't all there was. I was jealous too. It just didn't seem fair that my daughter's teachers—people who hardly knew her—were going to be the beneficiaries of so much of her company. Oh, sure, the two of us would still have plenty of afternoons together in the park, and we'd still make pizza dough and soak each other with the hose while watering the garden and hide under the covers in my bed, ready to scare my wife when she came home from work. But no matter how much time we'd spend together now, I knew it would never seem like enough, because I'd always remember the time when I didn't have to share her with anyone.

She was still so small and helpless, but at the same time already off on her own. It really seemed like the end of an era. I remembered then (and still do now) going into her room at night when she was a baby and marveling at her angelic, smiling face and her small, perfect body. It was always a struggle not to wake her up to cuddle or play with. Thinking about it now, I realize that I was jealous even of her dreams.

I guess I should have known what I was going to feel as I dropped her off on her first day of school. I remember going to pick her up from a playdate at the park a few months before. I stood outside the fence for a few minutes, watching her chat and play with her friends. She seemed so mature, so grown up, so independent. Until that moment, I'd felt that I knew her completely. I knew the characters she pretended to be, I knew what she liked and didn't like, and we told each other everything. But watching her interact with other people—sharing secrets I'd never hear—I realized that the process of separating from our parents doesn't begin when we move out of their house at seventeen, or join the Marines, as it did for me. It really begins at three, in a park, digging tunnels in the sand with a friend.

YOU AND YOUR PARTNER

More Communication Issues

As we've discussed throughout this book, you and your partner became parents at the same time but not in the same way. As a result, the two of you have very different needs and expectations. Here's how this plays out.

YOU NEED YOUR PARTNER TO:

- Truly understand how hard it is to be an involved father. She should also appreciate the commitment you've made to your family and the things you do for them—even if they aren't exactly what she wants.
- Understand that you and she will probably disagree on how you assess your level of support and involvement. Women tend to compare what their partners do to what they do, and the men usually come up short. But men measure what they do against what their fathers did or what the guy down the street is doing, and they look pretty good in comparison.
- Be patient. Adults develop at different rates, just as children do. In many families the mother acquires her skills faster; in others it's the father.
- Understand, and try to accommodate whenever possible, your desires for her attention and affection, your own space, time with friends, and a social life.
- Give you the freedom to do things your own way. "Many mothers, considering themselves the primary parent, have a difficult time watching their husbands parent differently from themselves, and take over to 'do it right,'" writes psychotherapist Jerrold Lee Shapiro. Men and women parent differently and make different—but equally important—contributions to their children's development.

"Yours!"   *"Yours!"*

If you give in and do everything your partner's way, your child will end up with Mommy and Mommy's little helper, not Mommy and Daddy, which is what she needs. Your partner has the right to determine exactly how the children are to be mothered. She has no right to determine how they're to be fathered.

- Support you in your efforts to balance work and family.
- Be your biggest fan. The more your partner supports you and your efforts to be a good dad, the more involved you'll be.
- Know you love her and your child, even if you don't show it the way she wants you to. Men and women have very different ways of expressing love. Men tend to do, while women tend to speak. So make an effort to say the words a little more often. Hopefully she'll meet you halfway and accept that sometimes a wink, a smile, a pat on the shoulder or the butt, having dinner ready for her when she comes home from work, or cleaning out the rain gutters is just as effective a way of saying "I love you" as actually saying the words.

YOUR PARTNER NEEDS YOU TO:

- Be a full participant in your home, not just mother's little helper. This means taking responsibility for things (housework, meal planning, and shopping, for example) without having to be asked and assuming a major role in childcare (including caregiving, arranging playdates, and doing clothes shopping).
- Understand that although she may occasionally neglect your emotional and physical needs in favor of the baby's, she doesn't mean to hurt you.

- Listen to her carefully when she wants to talk about her doubts and anxieties. It's "more important to have our needs heard than it is to have them met," says psychotherapist Brad Sachs. "Though the specific needs may not be met, the more general and overarching one—the need for support and connectedness—will be."
- Not make her feel guilty when she makes mistakes. She wasn't born knowing how to parent any more than you were.
- Support her in her efforts to regain her pre-pregnancy body.
- Support her in her efforts to balance work and family.
- Understand that she may be feeling tremendous guilt at not being able to live up to society's expectations of her (as a good wife or partner, mother, executive).
- Be sympathetic to her daytime loneliness and desire for adult company, if she's a stay-at-home mom.

PUTTING IT TOGETHER

Clearly, while there's some overlap between your needs and your partner's, there are also plenty of places where you're far apart. During your transition from coupledom to parenthood, those differences need to be reconciled, and the best way to do so is to learn to focus on the things you have in common rather than on your differences (although being aware of your differences is critical). "Couples who are able to focus their attention on what unites them and produces mutual joy usually end up at the end of the transition with a better, happier marriage," says researcher Jay Belsky.

Here, according to Belsky, are the things that can make a couple's transition to parenthood easier:

- **Surrender individual goals and needs** and work together as a team.
- **Resolve differences about divisions of labor** and work in a mutually satisfactory manner. And revisit the who-does-what-and-for-how-long discussion regularly to make sure you're both still satisfied with the breakdown.
- **Handle stresses in a way that doesn't overstress one partner or the entire marriage**.
- **Fight constructively and maintain a pool of common interests** despite diverging priorities.
- **Realize that however good a marriage becomes post-baby, it will not be good in the same way as it was pre-baby**.
- **Maintain the ability to communicate** in a way that continues to nurture the marriage. All couples have arguments. But the big issue is not who wins or whether you reach a compromise, it's that you keep talking to each other in a respectful, understanding, nonjudgmental way.

It's a tall order, but one that, if you're willing to put in the time and effort, will change for the better the lives of everyone around you.

If, in the end, you and your partner cannot resolve your differences, see the appendix "What to Do If Communication Breaks Down," pages 270–76.

FAMILY MATTERS

Teaching Your Toddler about Money

For many parents, the thought of teaching our preschoolers about money is almost as scary as imagining having to teach them about sex. We know we're going to have to do it sometime, but we'd like to put it off for a while.

But think about it: aside from food, there's not much else in our lives that we use as frequently as money—from paying the rent and the electric bill to giving charity to a homeless family—and there's nothing that causes us so many problems. Money issues, for example, are a leading cause of divorce.

The point of this section is to get you to start teaching your child about money—what it does and doesn't do—while she's still young. Unfortunately, your child already knows a few more things about money than you think she does. For example, she knows in a general sort of way that one needs money to get things, and she knows (or thinks, anyway) that you always have some. But most toddlers (and some adults) aren't able to grasp the idea that you actually have to work to get money, and they'll refuse to accept "I don't have any money with me" as an excuse for not buying them what they want when they want it. After all, everyone knows that if Daddy and Mommy want to buy something, all they have to do is take some money out of a machine or use one of those little cards.

It's going to be a while before you can explain the intricacies of the banking system to your child, but if you start talking and teaching about money now, in a very matter-of-fact way, you'll be able to keep it from seeming too magical and alluring. Here are a few ways to do just that:

- **Go to the store**. Stores provide a great opportunity to talk about lots of money-related things: how much things cost, how you know what the prices are, how you pay for things (check, credit card, or cash), and the mysteries of making change. All these themes reinforce the idea that things cost money.
- **Allow participation**. Let your child hand the money to the clerk and collect the change.
- **Talk about prioritizing**. Talk about which products your family needs and which ones you want. Having a firm grasp of the difference will help your child throughout her life.

- **Make comparisons**. Which products are better bargains? If the store you're in sells three oranges for a dollar, and the other store you go to has two oranges for a dollar, which is a better deal? Why do you go to the other store at all?

The Family Payroll

There are four things you can do with money: get it, spend it, save it, and give it away. And since you need to do the first one before any of the others, you'll have to give your toddler some money of her own. When she's older, you'll want to tie her allowance to the performance of certain household chores. But for now, make it unconditional.

As soon as each of my children turned three, I started paying them their age in dollars every week—a veritable fortune to those of us who had to make do on an extremely sporadic fifty cents a week. I recommend this approach. But don't worry, not all of it goes straight into your child's pocket. Here's how it works:

You pay out the three dollars as ten quarters and ten nickels, and the first thing your child does is take 10 percent of her money (one nickel and one quarter) and put it into a jar marked "Charity." She gets to decide what to do with this money (for example, give it directly to a homeless person or combine it with some of your money and send it by check to a deserving organization). She then divides the remaining coins into six neat piles—three with three quarters, three with three nickels. Next she drops a stack of quarters and a stack of nickels (ninety cents) into three different, labeled jars:

- Instant gratification. Bite your tongue. It's her money, so let her spend it however she wants—even if it's on candy. She'll learn awfully quickly that once it's gone, it's gone.
- Medium term. This one gets saved up for a few weeks or a month (anything longer than that and she'll forget what she was saving for) and can then be cashed in for a treat, toy, or book.
- Long term. Basically, she won't be seeing this money for a few years. Let it accumulate in the jar for a while, then take it (and your child) down to the bank and open up a savings account.

As wacky as this whole allowance scheme may sound, the opportunities for learning are amazing: counting, percentages, division, categorizing, the importance of helping others, the value of patience, the benefits of saving, and so much more.

- **Play categorizing games**. As you're going up and down the aisles of the supermarket, have your child help you spot round things, red things, boxed things, and so forth. Being able to organize items into groups is a critical math and money-handling skill.
- **Teach coin identification**. Get four jars and label each with the name of a coin: penny, nickel, dime, quarter. Take a few coins, tell your child what they are, and put the appropriate coin in each jar. Then give your child some coins and have her name them and put them in the correct jars.
- **Foster awareness**. Let your child look at the check in restaurants. Show her that the numbers on the check are (or should be) the same as the prices listed on the menu.
- **Play counting games**. Have your child count out the forks and spoons when you're setting the table. Have her help you make recipes, scooping out the right number of spoonfuls or cups of ingredients.
- **Play equivalence games**. Using real coins, show your child that a nickel is the same as a stack of five pennies, that five nickels are the same as a quarter, and that two nickels are the same as a dime, even though a nickel is bigger than a dime. Two dimes and a nickel for a quarter is too complex at this age.
- **Be patient**. It will take years for all these ideas to sink in.

Completing the Puzzle: Putting Together the Pieces of You

Before I became a dad, I worked as a commodities trader, a labor negotiator, and a trade consultant—the kind of jobs you get with an MBA, the diploma for which I have buried someplace deep in a storage locker. But before my first child was even born, I'd already reached the conclusion that having an executive job and being an involved dad—at least the way I wanted to do it—weren't entirely compatible. I'd published a few articles, and in a moment of feverish optimism, I quit my job to write full-time, which gave me the flexibility to spend plenty of time with my daughter. I realize that fatherhood isn't going have as big an impact on everyone's career as it did on mine. In fact, making that kind of career transition isn't practical, or even desirable, for most dads. For some, the changes are more subtle. Here's how a US postal worker, for example, reacted when he was told he'd have to work nights: "I told them I could not work nights because I had a ten-year-old son and I am a single parent.... Being with my son two days a week is not a good way to be a parent."

Not everyone responds to fatherhood by making changes at work. But of the hundreds of men I've interviewed, I've never met one who didn't change his life in at least some ways after becoming a father, ways he never would have considered if he hadn't had kids. Here are a few of the changes dads have made:

- Job choice. More and more people these days are making decisions about where to work based at least partly on whether a prospective job offers enough flexibility to allow for a healthy work-family mix.
- Moving to a larger (and usually more expensive) house. When you've got a child, suddenly having a backyard or a playroom or an extra bedroom or two becomes very important.
- Moving to a different neighborhood, city, or even state so the kids can have access to better schools. Sometimes this is a change the whole family is okay with. But often this kind of change involves moving farther away from friends, family, movies, theater, museums, and other things the parents enjoy.
- Becoming the sole breadwinner. A lot of women decide not to go back to work for a few years after having their babies. While it's great for the kids to have a parent around so much of the time, it puts a lot of financial pressure on Dad, including paying for that bigger house and its bigger mortgage.
- Becoming a stay-at-home dad.
- Rethinking insurance and finances. Parents have to worry about paying for college; they're probably a little more conservative in their investments in general, and they tend to take out more life insurance. Music lessons and private-school tuition bump up expenses even further.

267

- Reconsidering non-house purchasing decisions. Besides the new house, many dads buy other things they never would have considered: a minivan, backyard swing sets, video-game consoles, and on and on.
- Choosing staycations instead of vacations.

Because your roles as worker and father are such important parts of who you are, there's no way to keep them from spilling over onto each other. Whether that spillover is positive or negative depends on a lot of factors, including:

AT WORK

- Your schedule. People who work more than forty-five hours a week report more work-family problems, while those who work fewer than twenty say their work schedule improves their family relationships.
- Other job-related factors. How much time you clock isn't all there is to it. Dads who put in long hours, have no control over their schedule, don't like or aren't challenged by their job, or have to work weekends or nights are more likely to suffer from what is sometimes called "kick-the-cat syndrome." That is, they take out their frustration in ways (and on others) unrelated to the cause. On the other hand, dads who have more control over their schedule and enjoy their jobs have children who are healthier and exhibit fewer behavioral problems, according to researchers Stewart Friedman and Jeffrey Greenhaus. Other studies show that workers who have a lot of decision-making authority at work actually have longer life spans than those who don't.
- Money. Having a salary makes it possible to put shoes on everyone's feet, drive a car, and perhaps finance a vacation or some other luxuries now and then. Being able to afford all that certainly makes life at home easier. But working too hard for that money could have the opposite effect.
- Your age. Younger dads, especially those who are trying to make a name for themselves in the business world, sometimes find that the hours and energy they spend at work lead to increased stress at home.
- Social support. Dads who enjoy the people they work with and feel respected and appreciated are less likely to report that their family life interferes with work and have children who do better in school.

AT HOME

- Family. The more people you're responsible for, the more likely you are to have some negative spillover from family to work. Worrying about small children and/or caring for an elderly parent increases problems at work even more and leads to burnout. However, having positive relationships at home keeps men from feeling the kind of psychological distress they otherwise would feel when unhappy at work, according to researchers Rosalind Barnett and Janet Hyde. They also found that the more involved a dad is in childcare, the better his psychological well-being and the happier his wife or partner will be.

- Social life. Having friends and spending time with them makes it less likely that you'll have stresses at home that will carry over to work. On the other hand, cutting back on time spent with friends in order to have more family time increases negative family-work spillover.
- Your partner's schedule. The more flexible it is, the less worried you'll be about things at home and the less your family concerns will cause you trouble at work. Your schedule will have the same effect on her.
- Boundaries. Keeping work and family separate naturally reduces the spillover between the two. But checking your work voice-mail or e-mail from home, or dealing with personal issues while at work, can create problems in both places.

Trying to keep your work and family lives in balance is a feat of acrobatics you'll be working on for the rest of your life.

CONCLUSION

Throughout this book, we've talked about the amazing ways your toddler has grown and developed. We've also talked about the amazing ways *you* have grown and developed right along with her. It's probably hard to remember the way life was just two short years ago. But when you have a calm moment, spend a few minutes thinking about it. Better yet, dust off some of those photo albums and refresh your memory. It's incredible how far you've both come, isn't it?

Over the past two years, your child has gone from a little baby who was just learning to walk and talk to an independent person charging around your house, supremely confident in her own abilities. And you've made a similar journey, from a relatively new dad with lots to learn to the guy who can handle almost anything.

But your job isn't done, and it never will be. As you move from the toddler years to preschool, school, adolescence, and beyond, you and your child will continue to grow—individually and in relation to each other. Of course, there'll be plenty of ups and downs along the way. But a few years down the road you'll look back—just as you have now—and you'll be amazed at how far you've come and at how much more lies ahead.

Appendix

WHAT TO DO IF COMMUNICATION BREAKS DOWN

In several chapters of this book, I have discussed communication strategies for couples. Sadly, though, not all couples are able to communicate effectively, and in too many cases, communication breakdowns end relationships.

Next to the death of an immediate family member, ending a couple relationship (whether by divorce or breakup) is one of the most painful experiences you'll ever go through. And you certainly won't be alone; it'll be hard on your partner and hard on your children as well. For that reason, I urge you to do everything you can do get communication—and your relationship—back on track. That includes spending more time talking, getting counseling (individually and together), and, if necessary, a trial separation. (Be sure to review the communication discussions and strategies outlined on pages 90–94 and 261–64.)

If, after exploring every option for salvaging your relationship, a divorce or breakup is inevitable, the most important thing you can do is keep things civil between you and your soon-to-be ex. There are two reasons for this. First, maintaining a respectful, businesslike (or better) relationship will make it easier for you to reach equitable agreements on child custody and how to divide up your assets. Hopefully, you'll be able to do this without expensive lawyers and court costs (about 90 percent of divorcing couples nationwide are able to settle out of court). Second—and most important—the biggest predictor of how well children will cope with the divorce or breakup is the level of conflict between the parents, especially if that conflict puts the children in the middle and makes them feel torn between their mother and father.

The following advice may make the impending change in your identity from "father" to "single father" a little less unpleasant. Please keep in mind that what you're going to read here isn't an exhaustive treatment of the subject—you can find that in my book *The Single Father: A Dad's Guide to Parenting Without a Partner*.

- **Get a lawyer**. Yes, just a few sentences ago I said it would be great if you could avoid lawyers, and that's still true. Hiring a lawyer does *not* mean you're heading for the courtroom, however. Chances are good that you'll never even meet a judge. Nor does hiring a lawyer mean that you're expecting a confrontation with your soon-to-be ex. What you're doing is getting someone involved who, without any unpleasant emotional attachments, will protect your interests and make sure that your concerns are properly addressed. Most divorce lawyers have seen dozens of cases just like yours and know exactly what to look out for. Do you? You're going to be under stress; there are a thousand intense and scary feelings running through your head at the same time; and you'll probably want to avoid as much conflict as possible. That's good. But that desire leads a lot of men facing a breakup to make decisions that are bad for them and bad for their children. A lawyer can help you draft fair property settlements and custody arrangements that will (hopefully) avoid conflict in the future.

- **Consider alternatives to litigation**. If the two of you are getting along okay (not well enough to be married, just civil to each other), and you think you can continue to do so for a while, I strongly suggest that you consider mediation. In the overwhelming majority of cases, mediation is cheaper, takes less time, and is much less psychologically damaging for everyone, including the kids, than a knock-down, drag-out court battle. (In some states you don't have a choice: mediation is mandatory for parents who can't agree on a custody arrangement.) Another alternative is *collaborative divorce*. With this approach, you and your partner each retain a collaborative attorney and agree to settle your issues by negotiation or mediation rather than battling in court.

- **Understand that there's no such thing as "winning" custody**. When it comes to custody battles, everyone loses, especially the kids. If your partner gets sole or primary custody, your relationship with your children will suffer greatly, and your children will bear the many negative consequences associated with long-term father absence (poorer academic performance, poorer social skills, increased chance of abusing drugs or alcohol or of getting in trouble with the law, and a greater likelihood of starting sexual experimentation early). But if you get sole or primary custody, your ex will miss out on having a relationship with the kids. And while this may sound like the perfect way to hurt your partner, keep in mind that the negative consequences of mother absence are just as significant as those of father absence. The bottom line is that the best parent is both parents. See pages 274–76 for more on custody arrangements.

If you end up with limited access to your children, it's hard not to get depressed. The constant goodbyes are going to be incredibly painful, and in some cases seeing the kids may be a stinging reminder of the loss of your marriage. According to several studies, these two factors are among the major reasons some divorced fathers taper off contact with their kids. So before you decide you can't deal with the pain of seeing your kids, try to think of your kids first. Not getting to see them may be painful to you, but not seeing you will be much more painful to them.

Right now the most important thing you can do is try to make the transition from one family to two as smooth as possible. And the place to start is by striving to keep communication with your ex as civil as possible. You may not have been terribly successful before, but it's more crucial now than ever: the children who suffer the least when their parents split up are those whose parents have the lowest levels of conflict (or at least those whose parents keep their conflicts to themselves). This doesn't mean that you and your ex have to be best friends or even that you have to speak to each other very often. What it does mean, however, is that you both have to agree to keep your eyes on what's really most important: your child(ren).

- **Talk to your children**. One of the hardest things about a breakup is having to tell your child about it. If possible, you and your partner should do it together. At this age, your child is still too young to truly understand what's happening. What she really wants to know is, "How is this going to affect me?" Everything you say should answer that question.

Start with a short explanation of what divorce is: "Mommy and Daddy are going to be living in different houses. But we both love you, and we will always take care of you." Your child most likely won't ask many questions, but that doesn't mean she's not affected. So try to anticipate—and preemptively answer—as many of her concerns as possible. Tell her, for example: "You're going to have one room at Daddy's house and one at Mommy's." "You'll be able to bring your favorite blankie with you wherever you go." "Mommies and daddies can get divorced from each other, but they never get divorced from their children. We will always love you and take care of you." "No, this is not happening because of anything you did."

Let your child know that feelings—even strong ones—are okay. "Divorce is hard for mommies and daddies and kids too, and it's okay to be sad or mad. But no matter what happens, we'll always love you and be here to care for you." (Are you seeing the theme here?)

In Case of Allegations of Abuse

An accusation of child abuse is the atomic bomb of any divorce or custody case. If you're accused, you'll be presumed guilty—unless you can disprove the charges. And that's not easy. By the time you first hear that you've been accused, your child will probably have been seen by a therapist or a child protective services caseworker, many of whom believe that their role is to "validate" the accusation. And things move pretty quickly from there. The instant you're accused of having molested or harmed your child, all your contact with the child will be cut off until the question gets heard in court, and that could be anywhere from a few days to a few months later.

Assuming you're innocent (if you're not, please close this book immediately and turn yourself in), you'll probably feel like strangling your ex and her lawyer. Needless to say, that won't help. Most attorneys agree that aggressive behavior will just make the judge more suspicious and negatively inclined toward you. It's critical, then, to be as cooperative as possible.

And as hard as it might be for you, try to give your ex the benefit of the doubt—she may have seen something she genuinely thought was a symptom of abuse. Try to imagine how you'd behave if you'd seen something suspicious. And remember: your goal should be to get the truth out, not to get revenge.

An accusation of domestic violence may have nearly the same effect as an accusation of sex abuse: no access to your child until a judge rules on the charge. But keep in mind that, as strange as it sounds, men are the victims of domestic violence at least as often as women. The problem is that men rarely see their partner's shoves, slaps, or thrown dishes as violence. As a result, they rarely report those incidents. Now's the time to change your thinking. If your partner (whether you're in an opposite-sex or same-sex relationship) has been violent toward you or the kids, file charges immediately.

This does two things: it helps protect the kids from further abuse, and it helps protect you if your partner attempts to bring charges against you in retaliation.

You may also want to read your child a few of the excellent books out there that deal with divorce and how kids process it. My favorites include: *As the Crow Flies*, by Elizabeth Winthrop; *Dinosaurs Divorce*, by Marc Brown; *I Don't Want to Talk about It*, by Jeanie Franz Ransom; and *Let's Talk about It: Divorce*, by Fred Rogers.

- **Never badmouth your child's other parent or use your child as a spy**. Your child sees herself as being "half Daddy and half Mommy," and she'll take a criticism of her mother (or you) as a criticism of her. Asking her to spy puts her in the horrible position of having to side with one parent over the other.
- **Get more counseling**. Like it or not, you and your partner—even if you aren't partners anymore—will be your child's parents until the day you die. For that reason, it's to everyone's advantage, especially your child's, that you two get to a point where you can communicate civilly and reasonably and that you get there as soon as possible. One of the best ways to accomplish this is to go to joint counseling, which comes in two basic flavors: pre-divorce counseling and co-parent counseling. As you can probably guess, pre-divorce counseling takes place in the early stages of the divorce process, most likely before any kind of custody or separation arrangements have been finalized. Pre-divorce counseling is designed to help you and your partner dissipate some of the anger and hostility between you so you can build a better base of communication. Then, hopefully, you'll be able to make mature, informed, and rational decisions and not get tripped up by your own vindictiveness. Co-parent counseling is similar, except that it happens after initial custody and separation arrangements are in place. You and your partner may find that your counselor's office is a safe, neutral place to have discussions about the kids.

If your partner refuses to attend joint counseling with you, go by yourself. Hopefully you'll learn some skills that will help you in your lifelong relationship with each other. And if you do end up in court, the fact that you went to counseling is a clear demonstration of your desire to work together with your ex.

CUSTODY

The Language of Custody

Before you agree to a custody arrangement, it's critical to understand the terms. The parent with *legal custody* is legally responsible for making decisions about anything that affects the health, education, and welfare of the children. Ideally, you should have joint legal custody (the law in several states). *Physical custody* refers to where the children live. But watch out: Even with joint physical custody the child's primary residence can still be at one or the other parent's home. It's also possible to have joint legal custody—meaning the parents share responsibility for big decisions—but sole or primary physical custody with one parent.

Until the early 1990s, in 80 percent of divorce cases, mothers got sole custody. Dads got custody about 3 percent of the time, and custody was shared 20 percent

of the time. Over the past few decades, though, more and more states are moving to the model I support, in which shared custody is the default. According
to researchers Maria Cancian, Daniel Meyer, and their colleagues, sole mother
custody has dropped to about 52 percent, while shared custody has risen to 44
percent. Sole father custody has stayed about the same.

Although that sounds like an improvement, there are still some problems.
First, shared custody, while better than sole mother custody, isn't necessarily fifty-
fifty. Second, in those 52 percent of cases in which Mom has sole custody, many
father-child relationships are destroyed. According to researchers Donald A.
Gordon and Jack Arbuthnot, "only a third of children in sole residential homes see
their other parent at least once a month. Another third have contact less than
once a month. Half of these have contact less than once a year. A final third have
no contact at all with their non-custodial parent."

Joint Custody and Overnights with Dad

A lot of ill-informed people still believe that sole-mother custody is the best
arrangement for children—especially very young ones. They claim that going
back and forth between houses and spending overnights with the noncustodial
parent (almost always Dad) is bad for the children. This is absolutely false.

Psychologist Richard Warshak analyzed dozens of scientific studies on joint
custody (sometimes called shared parenting) and parenting plans, especially those
involving young children. His conclusion was quite clear: "The evidence shows
that shared parenting should be the norm for children of all ages, including sharing
the overnight care for very young children," he wrote. In addition, "Prohibitions
or warnings against infants and toddlers spending overnight time in their father's
care are inconsistent with our current understanding of child development." One
hundred and ten experts from around the world endorsed Washak's findings.

Whether or not you're married to the mother of your child, it's critical that you
do everything you can to seek fifty-fifty joint physical and legal custody of your
children. Except in cases in which children need protection from an abusive or
neglectful parent (which I'm assuming isn't applicable to your situation), children
in shared parenting (joint physical custody, or JPC) families do better than children in sole physical custody (SPC) families, according to Wake Forest University
researcher Linda Nielsen. After analyzing fifty-four studies comparing outcomes
of children in SPC and JPC situations, Nielsen found that JPC kids had better
outcomes in academic achievement, emotional health (anxiety, depression, self-
esteem, and overall satisfaction with life), behavioral problems (bullying, delinquency, misbehavior, drugs, alcohol, and smoking), physical health, stress-related
illnesses, and relationships with their parents and others.

Nielsen also found that even in cases where there was a high degree of conflict between the divorced parents, JPC children—even very young ones—still had better outcomes than those in SPC.

Child Support

If you owe child support, pay it; if you're supposed to receive it, collect it. Back in 1975, when the official child-support system was born, noncustodial parents (usually fathers) were ordered to pay a certain amount of money every month to help the custodial parents (usually mothers) cover child-related expenses. The idea was the children should never have to worry about whether their basic needs of food, shelter, care, and education are going to be taken care of. Since dads typically earned a lot more than moms (in large part because many moms didn't work outside the home), that made good sense.

As more women entered the workforce, the situation became more complicated, so states created formulas to calculate how much a noncustodial parent should have to pay. Those formulas took into account the incomes and expenses of both parents and the percentage of time the children spent with each parent. But because mothers still got sole custody most of the time, most fathers were ordered to pay child support. Unfortunately, some fathers were either unwilling or unable to pay, and the term *deadbeat dad* was born.

Today, however, joint custody is much more common, and more and more women are outearning their partners. As a result, more women are being obligated (either by a judge or by an agreement between the parties) to pay child support (although, even after controlling for income and other factors, women are less likely than men to be ordered to pay). And while some people might automatically assume that mothers would be more likely to pay what they owe, it turns out that they're actually *more* likely to be deadbeats than dads.

According to the US Census Bureau, 71.2 percent of mothers received some or all of the child support they were owed (44.9 percent received everything). Compare that to the 58.7 percent of dads who received some or all of their award (35.5 percent received everything). That means 28.9 percent of dads and 41.3 percent of moms paid nothing at all.

Bottom line: if you owe child support, make every attempt to pay it in full and on time. If you've lost your job or are serving in the military reserve or the National Guard, talk to your lawyer about getting your support order modified. But if your ex was ordered to pay you child support, stand up for yourself and do everything you can to collect it. Sure, you can probably scrape by without it, but why should you have to? The money is for your kids, not for you. So swallow your pride and do it for them. It's not the first time, and it won't be the last.

Acknowledgments

This book, like the others in the series, wouldn't have been possible without the contributions of many, many people. Some helped with the first edition, some with the second, some with the third, and some with some combination.

At Abbeville Press, over the course of more than twenty years, Bob Abrams has been unwavering in his confidence and support. David Fabricant has had his hand gently yet firmly on the tiller, while Louise Kurtz makes sure all the parts move in the right direction. Angela Taormina did the layout, and Celia Fuller and Misha Beletsky created the outstanding—and ever evolving and improving—design. In earlier editions, Jackie Decter and the late Susan Costello patiently and persistently edited, and in this edition, Amy K. Hughes did an amazing job of making me sound better than I would have without her. Thanks to Matt Garczynski and Amanda Killian for their help behind the scenes.

Justin Anderson advised on all things teeth. Sharon Braz helped refine the section on big-time communication breakdowns between partners. Gene and June Brott, my parents, read the early versions, babysat, and were a constant source of support. Jim Cameron and the folks at Temperament Talk generously shared their work on temperament, which opened my eyes to a whole new world. Ken Guilmartin and Edwin Gordon helped me learn about the importance of teaching music to children. My agent, Jim Levine, made all the right connections. Research on fathers done by Phil and Carolyn Cowan, Rob Palkovitz, Glen Palm, and Ross Parke was—and continues to be—an incredible inspiration. Finally—and most importantly—I'm forever indebted to the hundreds of fathers I've relied on over the years, who bravely and openly shared their insights, thoughts, fears, worries, advice, recommendations, and wisdom.

Selected Bibliography

Books

Ames, Louise Bates, and Carol Chase Haber. *Your One-Year-Old: The Fun-Loving, Fussy 12- to 24-Month-Old*. New York: Delta, 1982.

Ames, Louise Bates, and Frances L. Ilg. *Your Two-Year-Old: Terrible or Tender*. New York: Delta, 1980.

Austrian, Sonia G., ed. *Developmental Theories through the Life Cycle*. New York: Columbia University Press, 2002.

Baylies, Peter. *The Stay-at-Home Dad Handbook*. Chicago: Chicago Review Press, 2004.

Bekoff, Marc, and Jessica Pierce. *Wild Justice: The Moral Lives of Animals*. Chicago: University of Chicago Press, 2010.

Belsky, Jay, and John Kelly. *The Transition to Parenthood: How a First Child Changes a Marriage: Why Some Couples Grow Closer and Others Apart*. New York: Delacorte, 1994.

Berman, Phyllis W., and Frank A. Pedersen. *Men's Transitions to Parenthood: Longitudinal Studies of Early Family Experience*. Hillsdale, NJ: Erlbaum, 1987.

Bettelheim, Bruno. *A Good Enough Parent: A Book on Child-Rearing*. New York: Vintage, 1987.

Biller, Henry B. *Fathers and Families: Paternal Factors in Child Development*. Westport, CT: Greenwood Publishing Group, 1993.

Biller, Henry B., and Robert J. Trotter. *The Father Factor: What You Need to Know to Make a Difference*. New York: Pocket Books, 1994.

Bluestine, Eric. *The Ways Children Learn Music: An Introduction and Practical Guide to Music Learning Theory*. Chicago: GIA Publications, 1995.

Bowman, Barbara, Suzanne Donovan, et al., eds. *Eager to Learn: Educating Our Preschoolers*. Washington, DC: National Research Council, National Academies Press, 2000.

Brazelton, T. Berry, and Bertrand Cramer. *The Earliest Relationship: Parents, Infants, and the Drama of Early Attachment*. Reading, MA: Addison-Wesley, 1990.

Brenner, Mark. *Pacifiers, Blankets, Bottles, and Thumbs: What Every Parent Should Know about Starting and Stopping*. New York: Fireside, 2004.

Britton, James. *Language and Learning: The Importance of Speech in Children's Development*. New York: Penguin, 1970.

Bronstein, Phyllis, and Carolyn Pape Cowan, eds. *Fatherhood Today: Men's Changing Role in the Family*. New York: John Wiley & Sons, 1988.

Brott, Armin. *Father for Life: A Journey of Joy, Challenge, and Change*. New York: Abbeville Press, 2003.

——. *The New Father: A Dad's Guide to the First Year*. 3rd ed. New York: Abbeville Press, 2016.

Brown, Roger. *A First Language: The Early Stages*. London: George Allen & Unwin, 1973.

Brown, Stuart, and Christopher Vaughan. *Play: How It Shapes the Brain, Opens the Imagination and Invigorates the Soul*. New York: Penguin Random House, 2010.

Cantor, Ruth F., and Jeffrey A. Cantor. *Parents' Guide to Special Needs Schooling: Early Intervention Years*. Westport, CT: Auburn House, 1995.

Caplan, Frank, and Theresa Caplan. *The Second Twelve Months of Life*. New York: Bantam, 1982.

Carnoy, Martin, and David Carnoy. *Fathers of a Certain Age: The Joys and Problems of Middle-Aged Fatherhood*. Minneapolis: Fairview Press, 1997.

Cath, Stanley H., ed. *Father and Child: Developmental and Clinical Perspectives*. Hillsdale, NJ: Analytic Press, 1994.

Cohen, Lawrence. *Playful Parenting*. New York: Random House, 2002.

Connors, Abigail Flesch. *101 Rhythm Instrument Activities for Young Children*. Beltsville, MD: Gryphon House, 2004.

Cowan, Carolyn Pape, and Philip A. Cowan. *When Partners Become Parents: The Big Life Change for Couples*. New York: HarperCollins, 2000.

Cowan, Philip A., et al. "Mothers, Fathers, Sons, and Daughters: Gender Differences in Family Formation and Parenting Style." In *Family, Self, and Society: Toward a New Agenda for Family Research*, edited by Philip A. Cowan, Dorothy Field, and Donald A. Hansen, 165–95. Hillsdale, NJ: Erlbaum, 1993.

DeBenedet, Anthony T., and Lawrence J. Cohen. *The Art of Roughhousing: Good Old-Fashioned Horseplay and Why Every Kid Needs It*. Philadelphia, PA: Quirk Books, 2012.

Dodson, Fitzhugh. *How to Father*. New York: Signet, 1974.

Dweck, Carol. *Mindset: Changing the Way You Think to Fulfill Your Potential*. New York: Little, Brown, 2017.

———. *Mindset: The New Psychology of Success*. New York: Ballantine, 2006.

Faber, Adele, and Elaine Mazlish. *How to Talk So Kids Will Learn*. New York: Harper Perennial, 2002.

Finley, Gordon E. "Children of Adoptive Families." In *Developmental Issues in the Clinical Treatment of Children and Adolescents*, edited by W. K. Silverman and T. H. Ollendick, 358–70. Boston: Allyn and Bacon, 1999.

Flint (MI) Public Library. *Ring a Ring O'Roses: Finger Plays for Pre-School Children*. Flint, MI: Flint Public Library, 2000.

Fox, Mem. *Reading Magic: Why Reading Aloud to Our Children Will Change Their Lives Forever*. New York: Harcourt, 2001.

Fraiberg, Selma H. *The Magic Years: Understanding and Handling the Problems of Early Childhood*. New York: Scribner's, 1959.

Friedman, Stewart, and Jeffrey H. Greenhaus. *Work and Family: Allies or Enemies?* London: Oxford University Press, 2000.

Galinsky, Ellen. *Between Generations: The Six Stages of Parenthood*. New York: Times Books, 1981.

Garvis, Susan, and Narelle Lemon. *Understanding Digital Technologies and Young Children: An International Perspective*. New York, Routledge, 2016.

Gordon, Edwin E. *Learning Sequences in Music: Skill, Content, and Patterns*. Chicago: GIA Publications, 2013.

———. *A Music Learning Theory for Newborn and Young Children*. Chicago: GIA Publications, 1990.

Greenspan, Stanley, and Nancy Thorndike Greenspan. *First Feelings: Milestones in the Emotional Development of Your Baby and Child*. New York: Penguin, 1985.

Grunow, Richard F., Edwin E. Gordon, and Christopher D. Azzara. *Jump Right In: The Instrumental Series; Teachers Guide for Winds and Percussion*. Rev. ed. Chicago: GIA Publications, 2001.

Hass, Aaron. *The Gift of Fatherhood: How Men's Lives are Transformed by Their Children*. New York: Fireside, 1994.

Haugland, Susan W., and Daniel David Shade. *Developmental Evaluations of Software for Young Children*. Albany, NY: Delmar, 1990.

Healy, Jane M. *Failure to Connect: How Computers Affect Our Children's Minds for Better and Worse*. New York: Simon & Schuster, 1998.

Heddle, Rebecca. *Science in the Kitchen*. London: Usborne, 1992.

Hetherington, E. Mavis, and John Kelly. *For Better or for Worse: Divorce Reconsidered.* New York: W. W. Norton, 2002.

Holtzman, Debra. *The Safe Baby: A Do-It-Yourself Guide to Home Safety.* Boulder, CO: Sentient Publications, 2004.

Hoppenhauer, Denise Harris. *Adopting a Toddler.* Lincoln, NE: iUniverse, 2004.

Jensen, Amy Hillyard. *Healing Grief.* Redmond, WA: Medical Publishing, 1980.

Jones, Gerard. *Killing Monsters: Our Children's Need for Fantasy, Heroism, and Make-Believe Violence.* New York: Basic Books, 2000.

Katzen, Mollie, and Ann Henderson. *Pretend Soup and Other Real Recipes: A Cookbook for Preschoolers and Up.* Berkeley, CA: Tricycle Press, 1994.

Kellog, Rhoda. *The Psychology of Children's Art.* New York: Random House, 1967.

Kohl, MaryAnn F. *First Art: Art Experiences for Toddlers and Twos.* Beltsville, MD: Gryphon House, 2002.

Kohl, MaryAnn F., and Jean Potter. *Cooking Art: Easy Edible Art for Young Children.* Beltsville, MD: Gryphon House, 1997.

Kosher, Hanita, et al. *Children's Rights and Social Work.* Cham, Switzerland: Springer, 2016.

Kutner, Lawrence. *Toddlers and Preschoolers.* New York: William Morrow, 1994.

Kvols, Kathryn J. *Redirecting Children's Behavior.* Chicago: Parenting Press, 1998.

Lamb, Michael E., ed. *The Role of the Father in Child Development.* New York: John Wiley & Sons, 1997.

Lamb, Michael E., J. H. Pleck, E. L. Charnov, and J. A. Levine. "A Biosocial Perspective on Paternal Behavior and Involvement." In *Parenting across the Lifespan: Biosocial Perspectives,* edited by J. B. Lanaster, J. Altmann, A. S. Rossi, and L. R. Sherrod, 111–42. Hawthorne, NY: Aldine, 1987.

Leach, Penelope. *Babyhood.* 2nd ed. New York: Knopf, 2016.

Linn, Susan. *Consuming Kids: The Hostile Takeover of Childhood,* New York: New Press, 2004.

McCoy, Bill. *Father's Day: Notes from a New Dad in the Real World.* New York: Times Books, 1995.

McMahon, Robert J., and Rex L. Forehand. *Helping the Noncompliant Child.* 2nd ed. New York: Guilford Press, 2005.

Minnesota Fathering Alliance. *Working with Fathers: Methods and Perspectives.* Stillwater, MN: Nu Ink, 1992.

Newman, Barbara M., and Philip R. Newman. *Development through Life: A Psychosocial Approach.* 6th ed. Pacific Grove, CA: Brooks/Cole, 1994.

O'Brien, Maureen. *Watch Me Grow: I'm One-Two-Three.* New York: Quill, 2002.

Odean, Kathleen. *Great Books for Babies and Toddlers.* New York: Ballantine, 2003.

Owens, Robert Jr. *Help Your Baby Talk: Introducing the New Shared Communication Method to Jump-Start Language and Have a Smarter and Happier Baby.* New York: Perigee, 2004.

Palkovitz, Rob. *Involved Fathering and Men's Adult Development: Provisional Balances.* Mahwah, NJ: Lawrence Erlbaum, 2002.

Parke, Ross. *Fathers.* Rev. ed. Cambridge, MA: Harvard University Press, 1996.

———. "Fathers and Families." In *Handbook of Parenting,* vol. 3, edited by M. H. Bornstein, 27–74. Hillsdale, NJ: Erlbaum, 1995.

Pasley, Kay. "Stepfathers." In *Dimensions of Fatherhood,* edited by S.M.H. Hanson and F.F.W Bozett, 283–306. Beverly Hills, CA: Sage, 1985.

Pleck, Joseph H. (2010). "Paternal Involvement: Revised Conceptualization and Theoretical Linkages with Child Outcomes." In *The Role of the Father in Child Development,* edited by Michael E. Lamb, 5th ed., 58–93. Hoboken, NJ: John Wiley.

Pleck, Joseph H., and B. P. Masciadrelli (2007). "Paternal Involvement by U.S. Residential Fathers: Levels, Sources and Consequences." In *The Role of the Father in Child Development,* edited by Michael E. Lamb, 4th ed., 222–71. Hoboken, NJ: Wiley.

Pruett, Kyle. *Fatherneed: Why Father Care Is as Essential as Mother Care for Your Child.* New York: Free Press, 2000.

Radin, Norma, and Graeme Russell. "Increased Father Participation and Child Development Outcomes." In *Fatherhood and Family Policy,* edited by Michael E. Lamb and Abraham Sagi, 191–218. New York: Routledge, 1983.

Roehlkepartain, Eugene. *Building Strong Families: An In-Depth Report on a Preliminary Survey on What Parents Need to*

Succeed. Chicago: YMCA of the USA / Minneapolis: The Search Institute, 2002.

Roopnarine, Jaipaul, and Brent Miller. "Prelude: Pregnancy and Birth." In *Dimensions of Fatherhood*, edited by Shirley Hanson and Frederick W. Bozett, 49–63. Beverly Hills, CA: Sage Publications, 1985.

Rosemond, John. *Making the "Terrible" Twos Terrific!* Kansas City, MO: Andrews McMeel, 2013.

Ross, John Munder. *What Men Want: Mothers, Fathers, and Manhood.* Cambridge, MA: Harvard University Press, 1994.

Sachs, Brad E. *Things Just Haven't Been the Same: Making the Transition from Marriage to Parenthood.* New York: William Morrow, 1992.

Schatz, William. *Healing a Father's Grief.* Redmond, WA: Medical Publishing, 1984.

Schildhaus, Wendee Kim. *Marital Adaptation and Growth after the Death of a Child.* Boston: Boston University, 1997.

Shapiro, Jerrold Lee. *Becoming a Father.* New York: Springer, 1995.

Sheldon, S. H. "Sleep in Infants and Children." In *Sleep Medicine*, edited by T. L. Lee-Chiong, M. J. Sateia, and M. A. Carskadon, 99–103. Philadelphia: Hanley & Belfus, 2002.

Shopper, Moisy. "Toiletry Revisited: An Integration of Developing Concepts and the Father's Role in Toilet Training." In *Fathers and Their Families*, edited by Stanley H. Cath et al., 77–98. Hillsdale, NJ: Analytic Press, 1989.

Silvey, Anita. *100 Best Books for Children.* Boston: Houghton-Mifflin, 2004.

Singer, Dorothy, and Jerome Singer. *The House of Make-Believe.* Cambridge, MA: Harvard University Press, 1992.

Snarey, John. *How Fathers Care for the Next Generation: A Four-Decade Study.* Cambridge, MA: Harvard University Press, 1993.

Spangler, Doug. *Fatherhood: An Owner's Manual.* Richmond, CA: Fabus, 1994.

Staub, Ervin. *The Psychology of Good and Evil: Why Children, Adults, and Groups Help or Harm Others.* Cambridge: Cambridge University Press, 2003.

———. *The Roots of Evil: The Origins of Genocide and Other Group Violence.* New York: Cambridge University Press, 1989.

Striker, Susan. *Young at Art: Teaching Toddlers Self-Expression, Problem-Solving Skills, and an Appreciation of Art.* New York: Owl Books, 2001.

Tabors, Patton O. *One Child, Two Languages.* Baltimore: Paul H. Brookes, 1997.

Trelease, Jim. *The Read-Aloud Handbook.* 5th ed. New York: Penguin, 2001.

Tyson, Eric. *Personal Finance for Dummies.* 4th ed. New York: John Wiley & Sons, 2003.

Warshak, Richard. *The Custody Revolution: The Father Factor and the Motherhood Mystique.* New York: Poseidon, 1992.

White, Burton L. *The New First Three Years of Life.* New York: Prentice Hall, 1995.

Winnicott, D. W. *Playing and Reality.* New York: Basic Books, 1971.

Zweiback, Meg. *Keys to Preparing and Caring for Your Second Child.* New York: Barron's Educational, 1991.

Article, Papers, and Reports

Abkarian, G. G., et al. "Fathers' Speech to Their Children: Perfect Pitch or Tin Ear?" *Fathering* 1, no. 1 (February 2003): 27–50.

Adamsons, Kari Lee, Marion O'Brien, and Kay Pasley. "An Ecological Approach to Father Involvement in Biological and Stepfather Families." *Fathering* 5, no. 2 (May 2007): 129–47.

Agras, Stewart, et al. "Risk Factors for Childhood Overweight: A Prospective Study from Birth to 9.5 Years." *Journal of Pediatrics* 145, no. 1 (2004): 20–25.

American Academy of Pediatrics. "Handheld Screen Time Linked with Speech Delays in Young Children." Press release, May 4, 2017. Online at: https://eurekalert.org/pub_releases/2017-05/aaop-hst042617.php.

Antrilli, Nick K., and Su-hua Wang. "Toddlers on Touchscreens: Immediate Effects of Gaming and Physical Activity on Cognitive Flexibility of 2.5-year-olds in the US." *Journal of Children and Media* 12, no. 4 (2018): 496–513. doi:10.1080/17482798.2018.1486332.

Appleton, Katherine M., et al. "Repeated Exposure and Conditioning Strategies for Increasing Vegetable Liking and

Intake: Systematic Review and Meta-analyses of the Published Literature." *American Journal of Clinical Nutrition* 108, no. 4 (2018): 842–56.

Archer, Karin. "Infants, Toddlers and Mobile Technology: Examining Parental Choices and the Impact of Early Technology Introduction on Cognitive and Motor Development." PhD dissertation, Wilfrid Laurier University, Ontario, 2017. http://scholars.wlu.ca/etd/1925.

Azor-Martinez, Ernestina, et al. "Effectiveness of a Hand Hygiene Program at Child Care Centers: A Cluster Randomized Trial." *Pediatrics* 142, no. 5 (November 2018).

Bailey, William J. "A Longitudinal Study of Fathers' Involvement with Young Children: Infancy to Age Five Years." *Journal of Genetic Psychology* 155, no. 3 (1994): 331–39.

———. "Psychological Development in Men: Generativity and Involvement with Young Children." *Psychological Reports* 71 (1992): 929–30.

Barnett, Rosalind Chait, and Janet Shibley Hyde. "Women, Men, Work, and Family: An Expansionist Theory." *American Psychologist* 56 (2001): 781–96.

Bassok, Daphna, M. Fitzpatrick, E. Greenberg, and S. Loeb. "Within- and Between-Sector Quality Differences in Early Childhood Education and Care." *Child Development* 87, no. 5 (2016): 1627–45.

Baumrind, Diana. "Current Patterns of Parental Authority." *Developmental Psychology Monograph* 4, no. 1, pt. 2 (January 1971): 1–101.

Beaven, C. Martyn, and Johan Ekström. "A Comparison of Blue Light and Caffeine Effects on Cognitive Function and Alertness in Humans." *PLoS One* 8, no. 10 (2013): e76707.

Bedford, Rachael, Irati R. Saez de Urabain, Celeste H. M. Cheung, Annette Karmiloff-Smith, and Tim J. Smith. "Toddlers' Fine Motor Milestone Achievement Is Associated with Early Touchscreen Scrolling." *Frontiers in Psychology*, August 2, 2016: 1–8. doi:10.3389/fpsyg.2016.01108.

Bergström, Malin, Emma Fransson, and Bitte Modin. "Fifty Moves a Year: Is There an Association Between Joint Physical Custody and Psychosomatic Problems in Children?" *Journal of Epidemiology and Community Health* 69, no. 8 (April 2015): 769–74. doi:10.1136/jech-2014-205058.

Bornehag, C. "The Association Between Asthma and Allergic Symptoms in Children and Phthalates in House Dust: A Nested Case-Control Study." *Environmental Health Perspectives* 112 (October 2004): 1393–97.

British Psychological Society. "Lift-the-Flap Books May Hinder Kids from Learning New Words." *ScienceDaily*, September 14, 2016. www.sciencedaily.com/releases/2016/09/160914090452.htm.

Burke, Catherine. "Simple Technology Encourages Independence in Play and Communication for Infants and Toddlers with Disabilities." University of Alabama at Birmingham, Civitan International Research Center, n.d. Online at: http://www.floridahealth.gov/alternatesites/cms-kids/providers/early_steps/training/documents/simple_technology.pdf.

Bus, Adriana, et al. "Attachment and Bookreading Patterns: A Study of Mothers, Fathers, and Their Toddlers." *Early Childhood Research Quarterly* 12 (1997): 81–98.

Cancian, Maria, Daniel R. Meyer, Patricia R. Brown, et al. "Who Gets Custody Now? Dramatic Changes in Children's Living Arrangements after Divorce." *Demography* 51, no. 4 (2014): 1381–96. https://doi.org/10.1007/s13524-014-0307-8.

Cano, Thomas, Francisco Perales, et al. "A Matter of Time: Father Involvement and Child Cognitive Outcomes." *Journal of Marriage and Family* 81 (February 2019): 164–84.

Cantor, Patricia. "Computers and the Very Young." *Focus on Infants and Toddlers* 13, no. 4 (2001): 1–2, 4, 6.

Cartmill, Erica A., et al. "Quality of Early Parent Input Predicts Child Vocabulary 3 Years Later." *Proceedings of the National Academy of Sciences* 110, no. 28 (2013): 11278–83.

Chassiakos, Yolanda Reid, Jenny Radesky, Dimitri Christakis, Corrin Cross, and Megan Moreno. "Children and Adolescents and Digital Media." *Pediatrics* 138, no. 5 (2016): e20162593. doi:10.1542/peds.2016-2593.

Chess, Stella, and Thomas Alexander. "Temperamental Individuality from Childhood to Adolescence." *Journal of Child Psychiatry* 16 (1987): 218–26.

Christakis, Dimitri, et al. "How Early Media Exposure May Affect Cognitive Function." *Proceedings of the National Academy of Sciences* 115, no. 40 (2018): 9851–58.

Cohen, Jake Morgan. "A Naturalistic Observation Study of Paternal Nurturance and Child Emotional Expression." Unpublished thesis, University of Arizona, 2018.

Cohn, Deborah A., et al. "Mothers' and Fathers' Working Models of Childhood Attachment Relationships, Parenting Styles, and Child Behavior." Unpublished manuscript, 1997.

Conde-Agudelo, Agustin, et al. "Birth Spacing and Risk of Autism and Other Neurodevelopmental Disabilities: A Systematic Review." *Pediatrics* 137, no. 5 (May 2016).

Cooney, Teresa M., et al. "Timing of Fatherhood: Is 'On-Time' Optional?" *Journal of Marriage and the Family* 55 (February 1993): 205–15.

Dahl, R. E. "The Development and Disorders of Sleep." *Advances in Pediatrics* 45 (1998): 73–90.

Dauch, Carly, et al. "The Influence of the Number of Toys in the Environment on Toddlers' Play." *Infant Behavior and Development* 50 (February 2018): 78–87.

Davis, Clara. "Results of the Self-Selection of Diets by Young Children." *Canadian Medical Association Journal* 41, no. 3 (1939): 257–61.

———. "Self Selection of Diet by Newly Weaned Infants: An Experimental Study." *American Journal of Diseases in Children* 36, no. 4 (1928): 651–79.

DeLoache, Judy S., David H. Uttal, and Karl S. Rosengren. "Scale Errors Offer Evidence for a Perception-Action Dissociation Early in Life." *Science* 304 (May 2004): 1027–29.

DeLuccie, Mary F. "Mothers as Gatekeepers: A Model of Maternal Mediators of Father Involvement." *Journal of Genetic Psychology* 156, no. 1 (1995): 115–31.

———. "Predictors of Paternal Involvement and Satisfaction." *Psychological Reports* 79 (1996): 1351–59.

Duursma, Elisabeth. "The Effects of Fathers' and Mothers' Reading to Their Children on Language Outcomes of Children Participating in Early Head Start in the United States." *Fathering* 12, no. 3 (December 2014): 283–303.

Eaton, Michelle, and Bronwyn S. Fees. "Perceptions of Influence on Child's Competence among Fathers in the Military Context." *Psychological Reports* 90, no. 3, pt. 1 (December 2002): 703–10.

Eberle, Scott. "Better Learning Through Recess: Hands-on Play Switches on Minds." *Psychology Today*, March 6, 2017.

Eisenberg, Dan T. A., M. Geoffrey Hayes, and Christopher W. Kuzawa. "Delayed Paternal Age of Reproduction in Humans Is Associated with Longer Telomeres across Two Generations of Descendants." *Proceedings of the National Academy of Sciences* 109, no. 26 (June 2012): 10251–56.

Fagot, Beverly I. "Sex Differences in Toddlers' Behavior and Parental Reaction." *Developmental Psychology* 10, no. 4 (1974): 554–58.

Fagot, Beverly, and Richard Hagan. "Aggression in Toddlers: Responses to the Assertive Acts of Boys and Girls." *Sex Roles* 12, nos. 3–4 (1985): 341–51.

Fletcher, Richard, Jennifer St. George, and Emily Freeman. "Rough and Tumble Play Quality: Theoretical Foundations for a New Measure of Father-Child Interaction." *Early Child Development and Care* 183, no. 6 (2012): 746–59.

Ganong, Lawrence H., Marilyn Coleman, and Tyler Jamison. "Patterns of Stepchild-Stepparent Relationship Development." *Journal of Marriage and Family* 73 (2011): 396–413.

Garfield, Craig F., et al. "Longitudinal Study of Body Mass Index in Young Males and the Transition to Fatherhood." *American Journal of Men's Health* 10, no. 6 (2016): N158–67.

Gershoff, Elizabeth, and Andrew Grogan-Kaylor. "Spanking and Child Outcomes: Old Controversies and New Meta-Analyses." *Journal of Family Psychology* 30, no. 4 (June 2016): 453–69. doi:10.1037/fam0000191.

Gosselin, Marie-Pierre, and D. R. Forman. Attention-Seeking during Caregiver Unavailability and Collaboration at Age 2. *Child Development* 83, no. 2 (March–April 2012): 712–27.

Gordon, Donald A., and Jack Arbuthnot. "How Often Do Non-Custodial Parents See Their Children?" *Divorce Magazine*, updated March 21, 2018. https://www.divorcemag.com/articles/how-often-do-non-custodial-parents-see-their-children.

Goswami, Usha. "Dyslexia—In Tune but Out of Time." *Psychologist* 26, no. 2 (2013): 106–9.

Grall, Timothy. *Custodial Mothers and Fathers and Their Child Support: 2015 Current Population Reports*. US Department of Commerce, United States Census Bureau, January 2018. https://www.census.gov/content/dam/Census/library/publications/2018/demo/P60-262.pdf.

Green, Frances L., John H. Flavell, and Eleanor R. Flavell. "Development of Children's Awareness of Their Own Thoughts." *Journal of Cognitive Development* 1 (2000): 97–112.

Grossman, Karin, et al. "The Uniqueness of the Child–Father Attachment Relationship: Fathers' Sensitive and Challenging Play as a Pivotal Variable in a 16-Year Longitudinal Study." *Social Development* 11, no. 3 (2002): 301–37.

Hadaway, Nancy, et al. "Poetry for Language Development of English Language Learners." *Dragon Lode* 20, no. 2 (2002).

Hale, Lauren, et al. "Youth Screen Media Habits and Sleep: Sleep-Friendly Screen Behavior Recommendations for Clinicians, Educators, and Parents." *Child and Adolescent Psychiatric Clinics of North America* 27, no. 2 (2018): 229–45.

Halle, Tamara. *Charting Parenthood: A Statistical Portrait of Fathers and Mothers in America*. Washington, DC: Child Trends, 2002. http://www.childtrends.org/publications/charting-parenthood-a-statistical-portrait-of-fathers-and-mothers-in-america/.

Hardesty, Constance, DeeAnn Wenk, et al. "The Influence of Parental Involvement on the Well-Being of Sons and Daughters." *Journal of Marriage and Family* 56, no. 1 (February 1994): 229.

Harper, Mairi, Rory E. O'Connor, and Ronan C. O'Carroll. "Increased Mortality in Parents Bereaved in the First Year of Their Child's Life." *BMJ Supportive and Palliative Care* 1, no. 3 (December 2011): 306–9. doi:10.1136/bmjspcare-2011-000025.

Haugland, Susan W. "What Role Should Technology Play in Young Children's Learning?" Pt. 1. *Young Children* 54, no. 6 (1999): 26–31.

Haun, Daniel B. M., Yvonne Rekers, and Michael Tomasello. "Children Conform to the Behavior of Peers; Other Great Apes Stick with What They Know." *Psychological Science* 25, no. 12 (2014): 2160–67. https://doi.org/10.1177/0956797614553235.

Hawthorne, Dawn M., JoAnne M. Youngblut, and Dorothy Brooten. "Parent Spirituality, Grief, and Mental Health at 1 and 3 Months after Their Infant's/Child's Death in an Intensive Care Unit." *Journal of Pediatric Nursing* 31, no. 1 (2016): 73. doi:10.1016/j.pedn.2015.07.008.

Heath, D. Terri. "The Impact of Delayed Fatherhood on the Father-Child Relationship." *Journal of Genetic Psychology* 155, no. 4 (1994): 511–30.

Hirsh-Pasek, Kathy, Jennnifer M. Zosh, et al. "Putting Education in 'Educational' Apps: Lessons from the Science of Learning." *Psychological Science in the Public Interest* 16, no. 1 (May 2015).

Holley, Clare E., Claire Farrow, and Emma Haycraft. "A Systematic Review of Methods for Increasing Vegetable Consumption in Early Childhood." *Current Nutrition Reports* 6, no. 2 (2017): 157–70.

Holley, Clare E., Emma Haycraft, and Claire Farrow. "'Why Don't You Try It Again?' A Comparison of Parent Led, Home Based Interventions Aimed at Increasing Children's Consumption of a Disliked Vegetable." *Appetite* 87 (2015): 215. doi:10.1016/j.appet.2014.12.216.

Hummer, Robert A., and Elaine M. Hernandez. "The Effect of Educational Attainment on Adult Mortality in the United States." *Population Bulletin* 68, no. 1 (2013): 1–16.

Huttenlocher, Janellen, W. Haight, A. Bryk, M. Seltzer, and T. Lyons. "Early Vocabulary Growth: Relation to Language Input and Gender." *Developmental Psychology* 27, no. 2 (1991): 236–48.

Huttenlocher, Janellen, M. Vasilyeva, E. Cymerman, and S. Levine. "Language

Input and Child Syntax." *Cognitive Psychology* 45, no. 3 (2002): 337–45.

Janecka, Magdalena, C.M.A. Hawthorn, et al. "Paternal Age Alters Social Development in Offspring." *Journal of the American Academy of Child and Adolescent Psychiatry* 56, no. 5 (2017): 383. doi:10.1016/j.jaac.2017.02.006.

Janecka, Magdalena, F. Rijsdijk, et al. "Advantageous Developmental Outcomes of Advancing Paternal Age." *Translational Psychiatry* 7, no. 6 (June 2017): e1156. doi:10.1038/tp.2017.125.

Jeng, S. F., et al. "Prognostic Factors for Walking Attainment in Very Low-Birthweight Preterm Infants." *Early Human Development* 59, no. 3 (2000): 159–73.

Jewett, Don L., et al. "A Double-Blind Study of Symptom Provocation to Determine Food Sensitivity." *New England Journal of Medicine* 323 (August 1990): 429–33.

Katzev, Aphra R., "Girls or Boys: Relationship of Child Gender to Marital Instability." *Journal of Marriage and the Family* 56 (February 1994): 89–100.

Kazdin, Alan, and Corina Benjet. "Spanking Children: Evidence and Issues." *Current Directions in Psychological Science* 12, no. 3 (2003): 99.

Kelley, Rafe, and Beth Kelley. "Just Wrestle: How We Evolved Through Rough and Tumble Play." *Journal of Evolution and Health* 2, no. 3 (2018): article 9. https://doi.org/10.15310/2334-3591.1073.

Keogh, Barbara K., et al. "Children with Developmental Delays Twenty Years Later: Where Are They? How Are They?" *American Journal on Mental Retardation* 109, no. 3 (May 2004): 219–30.

Kirkorian, Heather L. "When and How Do Interactive Digital Media Help Children Connect What They See on and off the Screen?" *Child Development Perspectives* 12, no. 3 (September 2018): 210–14.

Koren, Gideon, and Ari Nachmani. "Drugs That Can Kill a Toddler with One Tablet or Teaspoonful: A 2018 Updated List." *Clinical Drug Investigation*, published online November 15, 2018. https://doi.org/10.1007/s40261-018-0726-1.

Kutiper, Karen, and P. Wilson. "Updating Poetry Preferences: A Look at the Poetry Children Really Like." *Reading Teacher* 47, no. 1 (1993): 28–34.

Kwok, Chun Shing, et al. "Self-Reported Sleep Duration and Quality and Cardiovascular Disease and Mortality: A Dose-Response Meta-Analysis." *Journal of the American Heart Association* 7, no. 15 (2018): e008552.

Ladge, Jamie J., Beth Humberd, et al. "Updating the Organization Man: An Examination of Involved Fathering in the Workplace." *Academy of Management Perspectives* 29, no. 1 (January 2015): 152–71.

Lapierre, Matthew A., Jessica T. Piotrowski, and Deborah L. Linebarger. "Background Television in the Homes of US Children." *Pediatrics* 130 (2012): 839–46. doi:10.1542/peds.2011-2581.

Leech, Kathryn A., et al. "Father Input and Child Vocabulary Development: The Importance of *Wh*- Questions and Clarification Requests." *Seminars in Speech and Language* 34, no. 4 (2013): 249–59.

Li, Jiong. "Mortality in Parents after Death of a Child in Denmark: A Nationwide Follow-up Study." *Lancet* 361, no. 9355 (2003): 363–67.

Li, Jiong, et al. "Cancer Incidence in Parents Who Lost a Child." *Cancer* 95, no. 10 (December 2002): 2237–42.

Lin, Ling-Yi, R. J. Cherng, Y. J. Chen, Y. J. Chen, and H. M. Yang. "Effects of Television Exposure on Developmental Skills among Young Children." *Infant Behavior and Development* 38 (2015): 20–26.

Ma, Julia, M. van den Heuvel, J. Maguire, P. Parkin, and Catherine Birken. "Is Handheld Screen Time Use Associated with Language Delay in Infants?" Presented at the Pediatric Academic Societies Meeting, San Francisco, CA, 2017.

MacDonald, Kevin, and Ross D. Parke. "Bridging the Gap: Parent-Child Play Interaction and Peer Interactive Competence." *Child Development* 55 (1984): 1265–77.

———. "Parent-Child Physical Play: The Effects of Sex and Age of Children and Parents." *Sex Roles* 15, nos. 7–8 (1986): 367–78.

Margalit, Malka, Amiram Raviv, and Dee B. Ankonina. "Coping and Coherence among Parents with Disabled Children." *Journal of Clinical Child Psychology* 21, no. 3 (1992): 202–9. doi:10.1207/s15374424jccp2103.

Margetts, Kay. "Children Bring More to School Than Their Backpacks." *European Early Childhood Education Research Journal* 11, supplement (February 2003): 5–14.

Marsiglio, William. "Contemporary Scholarship on Fatherhood: Culture, Identity, and Conduct." *Journal of Family Issues* 14 (December 1993): 484–509.

Mascaro, Jennifer S., Patrick D. Hackett, and James K. Rilling. "Testicular Volume Is Inversely Correlated with Nurturing-Related Brain Activity in Human Fathers." *Proceedings of the National Academy of Sciences* 110, no. 39 (September 2013): 15746–51. doi:10.1073/pnas.1305579110.

Mascaro, Jennifer S., Kelly E. Rentscher, Patrick D. Hackett, Matthias R. Mehl, and James K. Rilling. "Child Gender Influences Paternal Behavior, Language, and Brain Function." *Behavioral Neuroscience* 131, no. 3 (June 2017): 262–73.

McBride, Brent A., and Gail Mills. "A Comparison of Mother and Father Involvement with Their Preschool-Age Children." *Early Childhood Research Quarterly* 8 (1993): 457–77.

McDonald, Ellie, D. Gartland, Rhonda Small, and Stephanie Brown. "Dyspareunia and Childbirth: A Prospective Cohort Study." *BJOG: An International Journal of Obstetrics and Gynaecology* 122, no. 5 (January 2015): 672–79.

McMunn, Anne, et al. "Fathers' Involvement: Correlates and Consequences for Child Socioemotional Behavior in the United Kingdom." *Journal of Family Issues* 38, no. 8 (2015): 1109–31.

Montag, Jessica L., et al. "The Words Children Hear: Picture Books and the Statistics for Language Learning." *Psychological Science* 26, no. 9 (2015): 1489–96.

Myers, Lauren J., Rachel B. LeWitt, Renee E. Gallo, Nicole M. Maselli. "Baby FaceTime: Can Toddlers Learn from Online Video Chat?" *Developmental Science* 20, no. 4 (July 2017): e12430. doi:10.1111/desc.12430.

National Institute of Child Health and Human Development. "Characteristics and Quality of Child Care for Toddlers and Preschoolers." *Applied Developmental Science* 4, no. 3 (2000): 116–35.

Newman, Philip R., and Barbara Newman. "Parenthood and Adult Development." *Marriage and Family Review* 12, nos. 3–4 (1988): 313–37.

Nielsen, Linda. "Re-Examining the Research on Parental Conflict, Coparenting, and Custody Arrangements." *Psychology, Public Policy, and Law* 23, no. 2 (2017): 211–31.

Palkovitz, Rob, Marcella A. Copes, and Tara N. Woolfolk. "'It's Like … You Discover a New Sense of Being': Involved Fathering as an Evoker of Adult Development." *Men and Masculinities* 1 (July 2001): 49–69.

Palm, Glen. "Involved Fatherhood: A Second Chance." *Journal of Men's Studies* 2 (1993): 139–54.

Papadakis, Stamatios J., and Michail Kalogiannakis. "Mobile Educational Applications for Children: What Educators and Parents Need to Know." *International Journal of Mobile Learning and Organisation* 11, no. 2 (January 2017): 1.

Perry, Nicole B., et al. "Childhood Self-Regulation as a Mechanism Through Which Early Overcontrolling Parenting Is Associated with Adjustment in Preadolescence." *Developmental Psychology* 54, no. 8 (2018): 1542–54. http://dx.doi.org/10.1037/dev0000536.

Pew Research Center. "Modern Parenthood: Roles of Moms and Dads Converge as They Balance Work and Family." March 14, 2013. http://www.pewsocialtrends.org/2013/03/14/modern-parenthood-roles-of-moms-and-dads-converge-as-they-balance-work-and-family/.

Pleck, Joseph. "Integrating Father Involvement in Parenting Research." *Parenting: Science and Practice* 12 (2012): 2–3, 243–53.

Porter, Megan E., "Perceptions Fathers Have on Time Spent with Preschool Children and Its Impact on Language Outcome Measures." *Rehabilitation, Human Resources and Communication Disorders Undergraduate Honors Theses* 46 (2016). https://scholarworks.uark.edu/rhrcuht/46.

Power, Thomas G. "Compliance and Self-Assertion: Young Children's Responses to Mothers versus Fathers." *Developmental Psychology* 30, no. 6 (1994): 980–89.

Pulkki-Råback, Laura, et al. "Living Alone and Antidepressant Medication Use: A Prospective Study in a Working-Age Population." *BMC Public Health* 12 (March 2012): 236. doi:10.1186/1471-2458-12-236.

Radesky Jenny S., C. Kistin, S. Eisenberg, J. Gross, G. Block, B. Zuckerman, and M. Silverstein. "Parent Perspectives on Their Mobile Technology Use: The Excitement and Exhaustion of Parenting while Connected." *Journal of Developmental and Behavioral Pediatrics* 37, no. 9 (November–December 2016): 694–701.

Radesky, Jenny S., Jayna Schumacher, and Barry Zuckerman. "Mobile and Interactive Media Use by Young Children: The Good, the Bad, and the Unknown." *Pediatrics* 135, no. 1 (January 2015): 1–3.

Radin, Norma. "Father-Child Interaction and the Intellectual Functioning of Four-Year-Old Boys." *Developmental Psychology* 6 (1972): 353–61.

Rauscher, Frances, et al. "Music Training Causes Long-term Enhancement of Preschool Children's Spatial-Temporal Reasoning." *Neurological Research* 19 (February 1997): 2–8.

Reis, Myrna, and Dolores Gold. "Relationship of Paternal Availability to Problem Solving and Sex-Role Orientation in Young Boys." *Psychological Reports* 40 (1977): 823–29.

Rescorla, Leslie. "Language and Reading Outcomes to Age Nine in Late-Talking Toddlers." *Journal of Speech, Language, and Hearing Research* 45 (April 2002): 360–71.

Rohner, Ronald P., and Robert A. Veneziano. "The Importance of Father Love: History and Contemporary Evidence." *Review of General Psychology* 54 (December 2001): 382–405.

Ross, Hildy, Ori Friedman, and Aimee Field. "Toddlers Assert and Acknowledge Ownership Rights." *Social Development* 24, no. 2 (November 2014): 341–56.

Rowe, Meredith L. "A Longitudinal Investigation of the Role of Quantity and Quality of Child-Directed Speech in Vocabulary Development." *Child Development* 83, no. 5 (2012): 1762–74.

Rowe, Meredith L., David Coker, and Barbara Alexander Pan. "A Comparison of Fathers' and Mothers' Talk to Toddlers in Low Income Families." *Social Development* 13, no. 2 (May 2004): 278–91.

St. George, Jennifer, Richard Fletcher, and Kerrin Palazzi. "Comparing Fathers' Physical and Toy Play and Links to Child Behaviour: An Exploratory Study." *Infant and Child Development* 26, no. 1 (2017).

Samuels, Andrew. "The Good Enough Father of Whatever Sex." Unpublished manuscript, n.d.

Scholastic. *Kids and Family Reading Report: The Rise of Read-Aloud*, 7th ed. Scholastic, 2019. https://www.scholastic.com/content/dam/KFRR/Read_Aloud_Temp/KFRR_The_Rise_of_%20Read_Aloud.pdf.

Sethna, Vaheshta, et al. "Father-Child Interactions at 3 Months and 24 Months: Contributions to Children's Cognitive Development at 24 Months." *Infant Mental Health Journal* 38, no. 3 (2017): 378–90.

Shapiro, Danielle N., and Abigail J. Stewart. "Dyadic Support in Stepfamilies: Buffering Against Depressive Symptoms among More and Less Experienced Stepparents." *Journal of Family Psychology* 26, no. 5 (2012): 833–38.

Sharrow, Elizabeth, Jesse H. Rhodes, et al. "The First-Daughter Effect: The Impact of Fathering Daughters on Men's Preferences for Gender-Equality Policies." *Public Opinion Quarterly* 82, no. 3 (October 2018): 493–523.

Shinskey, Jeanne L. "Manipulative Features in Educational Picture Books Hinder Word Learning in Toddlers." Paper presented at conference of British Psychological Society, Developmental Section, Belfast, September 2016.

Singer, Jerome L., and Dorothy G. Singer. "Preschoolers' Imaginative Play as Precursor of Narrative Consciousness." *Imagination, Cognition and Personality* 25, no. 2 (2005): 97–117.

Sorce, James F., et al. "Maternal Emotional Signaling: Its Effect on the Visual Cliff Behavior of One-Year-Olds." *Developmental Psychology* 21, no. 1 (1985): 195–200.

Straus, Murray A., and Carolyn J. Field. "Psychological Aggression by American Parents: National Data on Prevalence, Chronicity, and Severity." *Journal of Marriage and Family* 65 (November 2003): 795–808.

Stroebe, Margaret, et al. "Partner-Oriented Self-Regulation among Bereaved Parents: The Costs of Holding in Grief for the Partner's Sake." *Psychological Science* 24, no. 4 (2013): 395–402. doi:10.1177/0956797612457383.

Sziron, Monika, and Elisabeth Hildt. "Digital Media, the Right to an Open Future, and Children 0–5." *Frontiers in Psychology* 9 (2018): 2137.

Thomas, Alexander, Stella Chess, and Herbert G. Birch. "The Origin of Personality." *Scientific American* 223 (August 1970): 102–9.

Tomopoulos, Suzy, et al. "Children under the Age of Two Are More Likely to Watch Inappropriate Background Media Than Older Children." *Acta Paediatrica* 103, no. 5 (2014): 546–52.

US Department of Health and Human Services, National Institutes of Health, and Eunice Kennedy Shriver National Institute of Child Health and Human Development. "NICHD Study of Early Child Care and Youth Development: Phase IV, 2005–2007 [United States]." Inter-university Consortium for Political and Social Research, Ann Arbor, MI, June 25, 2018. https://doi.org/10.3886/ICPSR22361.v5

Vadasy, Patricia, Rebecca Fewell, et al. "Follow-up Evaluation of the Effects of Involvement in the Fathers Program." *Topics in Early Childhood Education* 6, no. 2 (1986): 16–31.

Vaish, Amrisha, and Tricia Striano. "Is Visual Reference Necessary? Contributions of Facial versus Vocal Cues in Twelve-Month-Olds' Social Referencing Behavior." *Developmental Science* 7, no. 3 (2004): 261–69.

Vliegen, Nicole, Sara Casalin, and Patrick Luyten. "The Course of Postpartum Depression: A Review of Longitudinal Studies." *Harvard Review of Psychiatry* 22, no. 1 (January–February 2014): 1–22.

Warshak, Richard A. "Social Science and Parenting Plans for Young Children: A Consensus Report." *Psychology, Public Policy, and Law* 20, no. 1 (February 2014): 46. doi:10.1037/law0000005.

Wartella, Ellen, Vicky Rideout, A. J. Lauricella, and S. L. Connell. "Parenting in the Age of Digital Technology: A National Survey." Revised. Center on Media and Human Development, School of Communication, Northwestern University, 2014.

Weisleder, Adriana, and Anne Fernald. "Talking to Children Matters: Early Language Experience Strengthens Processing and Builds Vocabulary" *Psychological Science* 24, no. 11 (2013): 2143–52.

Whaley, Kimberlee K. "The Emergence of Social Play in Infancy: A Proposed Developmental Sequence of Infant-Adult Social Play." *Early Childhood Research Quarterly* 5 (1990): 347–58.

Whitehurst, Grover J., et al. "Accelerating Language Development Through Picture Book Reading." *Developmental Psychology* 24, no. 4 (1988): 552–59.

Williams, Edith, and Norma Radin. "Effects of Father Participation in Child Rearing: Twenty-Year Follow-up." *American Journal of Orthopsychiatry*, 69, no. 3 (July 1999): 328–36.

Woodruff Carr, Kali, et al. "Beat Synchronization Predicts Neural Speech Encoding and Reading Readiness in Preschoolers." *Proceedings of the National Academy of Sciences* 111, no. 40 (2014): 14559–64.

Resources

This list of resources is by no means comprehensive. Rather, it's designed to offer some immediate answers to your questions and to steer you in the right direction. That said, because old resources sometimes fade away and new ones appear as if by magic, you'll find a more updated list on my website, at https://mrdad. com/resources. But we need your help. If you know of a resource that can benefit dads and their families, please send an email to armin@mrdad.com.

Adoption

Adoption.com has a huge number of resources on adoption, finding adoption agencies, and much more.
https://adoption.com

Adoptive Families has lots of great info on the adoption process as well as on parenting an adopted child.
https://www.adoptivefamilies.com

National Adoption Center is dedicated to creating families and a community of adoptive parents.
www.adopt.org

National Council for Adoption believes that every child deserves to thrive in a nurturing, permanent family. The council works with individual families, government, and the media to raise awareness.
https://www.adoptioncouncil.org

Advice, General

There are literally dozens of parenting resources out there. Among my favorites:

Zero to Three's mission is to ensure that all babies and toddlers have a strong start in life. The organization does that by supporting the caring adults who touch the lives of infants and toddlers.
https://www.zerotothree.org

Kids in the House is the largest parenting video library in the world and aims to help parents and caregivers become better at parenting by educating, inspiring, and entertaining.
https://www.kidsinthehouse.com

Parenting.com has advice and resources on every conceivable parenting topic and has special sections for dads, adoptive parents, single parents, and relationships.
https://www.parenting.com

At-Home Dads

City Dads Group was started by two at-home dads who wanted to create a community that would provide the same kind of parental camaraderie and network that mothers so often build and rely upon.
https://citydadsgroup.com

National At-Home Dad Network provides advocacy, community, education, and support for families in which fathers are the primary caregivers of their children.
http://athomedad.org

Child Abuse Reporting

Childhelp has a state-by-state list of phone numbers.
(1-800) 4-A-CHILD (422-4453)
www.childhelp.org

Childcare

Child Care Aware is a nationwide campaign created to help parents identify quality childcare in their communities.
www.childcareaware.org

Child Care Resources' mission is to help kids grow into successful adults by enriching the learning environment of their crucial early years. The website has extensive information for families and providers.
https://www.childcareresources.org

Head Start. For information on Head Start programs in your area, visit:
https://www.acf.hhs.gov/ohs
https://www.nhsa.org
https://www.nhsa.org/why-head-start/head-start-locator

National Association for the Education of Young Children (NAEYC) accredits childcare programs that meet its standards and gives referrals to accredited providers in your area.
www.naeyc.org

National Resource Center for Health and Safety in Child Care is a wonderful general resource. Plus, it has listings of childcare regulations for all fifty states.
http://nrckids.org

Cooking and Other Messy Things

Cooking with Kids educates and empowers children and families to make healthful food choices through hands-on learning with fresh, affordable foods.
https://cookingwithkids.org

Curious Chef has a wide variety of kitchen tools specially designed for children.
https://curiouschef.com

Blakey, Nancy. *Lotions, Potions, and Slime: Mudpies and More!* Berkeley, CA: Tricycle Press, 1996.

Karmel, Annabel. *The Toddler Cookbook*. New York: DK Children, 2008.

Katzen, Mollie, and Ann Henderson. *Pretend Soup and Other Real Recipes: A Cookbook for Preschoolers and Up*. Berkeley, CA: Tricycle Press, 1994.

Wheeler-Toppen, Jodie. *Edible Science: Experiments You Can Eat*. Washington, DC: National Geographic Children's Books, 2015

Woolmer, Annabel. *The Tickle Fingers Toddler Cookbook*. London: Ebury Digital, 2016

Developmental and Physical Disabilities

Assistive Technology Industry Association is a great resource if you're looking for equipment and other assistive tools.
https://www.atia.org

Association for Children with Down Syndrome trains and educates children with Down syndrome.
www.acds.org

Center for Parent Information and Resources has a series of fact sheets that describe specific disabilities' characteristics and offer tips for parents on specialized care.
https://www.parentcenterhub.org/specific-disabilities

Christopher and Dana Reeve Foundation has a special report, "Parenting with a Disability: Know Your Rights Toolkit," that's filled with extremely important and valuable

information and resources for parents with disabilities.
https://ncd.gov/sites/default/files/Documents/Final%20508_Parenting%20Toolkit_Plain%20Language_0.pdf

Dads Appreciating Down Syndrome assists and supports fathers and families of children with Down syndrome.
https://www.dadsnational.org

Dads 4 Special Kids is an organization dedicated to helping men who have a child with special needs in their lives.
http://d4sk.org

Family Resource Center on Disabilities provides caregivers of children with disabilities information, training, and assistance with assistive technology, disability laws, and medical needs.
http://frcd.org/resources

PACER Center bills itself as "Champions for Children with Disabilities."
https://www.pacer.org

Yellow Pages for Kids with Disabilities has state-by-state listings of consultants, psychologists, tutors, therapists, coaches, and other professionals who serve children with disabilities.
https://www.yellowpagesforkids.com

Harrison, Jill, Matthew Henderson, and Rob Leonard, eds. *Different Dads: Fathers' Stories of Parenting Disabled Children.* London and Philadelphia: Jessica Kingsley Publishers, 2007. A collection of inspiring personal testimonies written by fathers of children with a disability, who reflect on their own experiences and offer advice to other fathers and families on the challenges of raising a child with a disability.

Fathers, Divorced or Single

American Coalition for Fathers and Children, with chapters nationwide, believes that equal, shared parenting time or joint custody is the optimal custody situation.
e-mail: info@acfc.org
www.acfc.org

Children's Rights, with chapters in most states, has a well-stocked catalog of

resources, including a listing of great books on the subject for kids and their parents.
www.childrensrights.org

Making Lemonade is an online resource community for single parents of all kinds. Find support, information, referrals to experts, and a good laugh.
www.makinglemonade.com

Fathers, Military

Military Onesource offers a full range of services 24/7, 365 days a year.
(1-800) 342-9647 from the United States
https://www.militaryonesource.mil

National Military Family Association has many resources for military families.
https://www.militaryfamily.org

Brott, Armin. *The Military Father: A Hands-on Guide for Deployed Dads.* New York, NY: Abbeville Press, 2009.

Fathers, Step

Cyberparent.com is a good source of information and referrals.
www.cyberparent.com

National Stepfamily Resource Center (NSRC) is a division of Auburn University's Center for Children, Youth, and Families (CCYF). Its primary objective is to serve as a clearinghouse of information, linking family science research on stepfamilies with best practices for couples and children in stepfamilies.
www.stepfamilies.info

Stepdadding has info, resources, and a blog on stepfathering.
http://stepdadding.com

LeBey, Barbara. *Remarried with Children: Ten Secrets for Successfully Blending and Extending Your Family.* New York: Bantam, 2004.

Massimo, Matthew. *Stepparenting: Becoming a Stepparent; A Blended Family Guide to Parenting, Raising Children, Family Relationships and Step Families.* N.p.: Amazon Digital Services, 2014.

Pickhardt, Carl. *Keys to Successful Stepfathering.* New York: BES Publishing, 2010.

Fatherhood, General

Families and Work Institute is a nonprofit research organization focusing on work-family issues.
www.familiesandwork.org

MrDad.com is my site, which has hundreds of articles, blogs, podcasts, and other materials on all aspects of fatherhood.
https://mrdad.com

National Center for Fathering has resources designed to help men become more aware of their own fathering style and then work toward improving their skills.
www.fathers.com

National Fatherhood Initiative offers membership that includes the quarterly newsletter *Fatherhood Today*; updates on family issues and political/legislative developments; and the Fatherhood Resource Center catalog of books, videos, and audiotapes.
https://www.fatherhood.org

Health Issues

American Academy of Pediatrics (AAP) has one of the biggest collections of resources for parents who need basic information fast on everything from colic and treating diaper rash to sleep problems and introducing solid foods.
www.aap.org

Healthychildren.org is powered by the American Academy of Pediatrics and is a bit more user-friendly than the AAP's site.
https://www.healthychildren.org

Kids Health has a full range of doctor-approved information.
www.kidshealth.org

Healthy Living

The Green Guide is a wonderful newsletter (and website) filled with tips for healthy, organic living.
www.thegreenguide.com

Men, General

Men's Health Network is a national education organization that recognizes men's health as a specific social concern. The site has a fantastic database of articles, resources, and links on every conceivable fatherhood issue.
www.menshealthnetwork.org

Menstuff is a huge collection of resources on men, men's health, fatherhood, parenting, relationships, and more.
www.menstuff.org

Music

Kindermusik
https://www.kindermusik.com

Music Together
https://www.musictogether.com

Both companies offer music and movement programs for infants and their parents. CDs and songbooks are available. Classes in each method are offered throughout the United States. Listings are available on the websites.

Parental Stress

Childhelp USA
(1-800) 4-A-CHILD (422-4453)
CRISISTEXTLINE.org
Text HOME to 741741

Parental Stress Line has trained volunteer counselors who can help you through any problem, large or small.
(1-800) 632-8188

Reading, Finding Good Books

American Library Association has reviews of children's books and lists of award winners.
www.ala.org

The Children's Book Review has good-quality reviews of books by subject and age, interviews with authors, and more.
https://www.thechildrensbookreview.com

Children's Literature provides a searchable database of reviews of the latest kids' books.
www.childrenslit.com

Children's Literature Web Guide has a wealth of information on children's books, recommendations, and links to other good sites.
www.ucalgary.ca/~dkbrown

RESOURCESgment>

The Horn Book has lists of children's classics, medal winners, and other resources for parents.
www.hbook.com

Through the Looking Glass Children's Book Reviews seeks to help parents, teachers, and others find exceptional books for the young people in their lives.
http://lookingglassreview.com/books

Codell, Esme. *How to Get Your Child to Love Reading.* Chapel Hill, NC: Algonquin, 2003.

Coon, Cheryl. *Books to Grow With: A Guide to Using the Best Children's Fiction for Everyday Issues and Tough Challenges.* Portland, OR: Lutra Press, 2004.

Lewis, Valerie, and Walter Mayes. *Valerie and Walter's Best Books for Children.* New York: Quill, 2004.

Silvey, Anita. *Children's Book-a-Day Almanac.* New York: Roaring Brook Press, 2012

Safety

Public Playground Safety Checklist, from the US Consumer Product Safety Commission.
https://www.cpsc.gov/safety-education/safety-guides/playgrounds/public-playground-safety-checklist

Sign Language

Baby Sign Language has everything you need get started in about five minutes.
https://www.babysignlanguage.com

Baby Signs Too offers videos and books based on the work of Linda Acredolo and Susan Goodwyn.
https://babysignstoo.com

My Baby Can Talk is a system designed to be used with children starting at about ten months.
www.mybabycantalk.com

Signing Time is a subscription service with a focus on teaching sign language to toddlers.
https://www.signingtime.com

Temperament

The Preventive Ounce develops programs designed to help parents recognize and understand their child's emerging temperament and manage the issues that are normal for that child's temperament.
https://www.preventiveoz.org

Toy and Game Reviews

Parents@Play is my weekly, nationally syndicated column, where we review only the best toys, games, and activities that families can do together.
www.parentsatplay.com

TTPM.com has written and video reviews of toys, games, and more. Also check out TTPM's YouTube channel.
https://ttpm.com

Twins and More

Dad's Guide to Twins is exactly what the name would indicate.
https://dadsguidetotwins.com

Twins Magazine offers advice, anecdotes, facts, support, and resources for parents of twins.
www.twinsmagazine.com

Twiniversity has everything you could possibly want to know about raising and parenting twins.
https://www.twiniversity.com

We're constantly revising and updating this book and are always looking for ways to improve it. So if you have any comments or suggestions, please e-mail them to: armin@mrdad.com.

Please also connect with us on social media:
- Instagram: https://www.instagram.com/officialmrdad/
- Facebook: https://www.facebook.com/MrDad/
- Twitter: https://twitter.com/mrdad
- LinkedIn: https://www.linkedin.com/in/mrdad
- Pinterest: https://www.pinterest.com/mrdad/

293

Index

B

baby, new. See new baby
babysitters. See sitters
baby talk, 76, 77, 247, 252
bachelor's degree, salary and, 205
balance, developing, 27, 55, 95, 149
balanced meals, 78–79
balloons, safety concerns and, 30
ball play: catching, 26, 56, 213, 232, 250; kicking, 27, 56, 95, 126, 182, 232; rolling, 26–27; throwing, 13, 26, 56, 95, 126, 232, 250
Band-Aids, 214, 223
bankruptcy, 207
Barnett, Rosalind, 104, 269
basement, safety concerns and, 53
Bassok, Daphna, 170
bath, fear of, 17, 64, 68–69
bathroom privacy, 256
Baumrind, Diana, 133, 137
Beaven, C. Martyn, 194
bedtime: physical play before, 231; restricting liquids before, 158; restricting technology devices before, 194; routines and rituals for, 46, 56, 72, 156, 189; toddler's excuses to put off, 156
bedtime stories, 28, 37, 46, 72, 189, 214
Belsky, Jay, 90, 263
beverages, 200–201; before bedtime, 158
bilingual toddlers, 78
Biller, Henry, 246, 247
biological dad vs. stepdad, 219, 220
Birken, Catherine, 33
birth defects, 167
birth order, 221; of disabled child, 86
blaming imaginary companion, 234, 235
blanket sledding, 27
block building, 14, 27, 33, 95, 149, 213
blowing bubbles, 26, 28
body: genital self-exploration and, 97, 152, 222, 255–57; identifying parts of, 16, 29, 110, 256; of parents, toddler's interest in, 256, 257–59
body painting, 234
books: concept, 41, 111, 165, 225; lift-the-flap and pop-up, 37; suggested (lists), 39–41, 110–11, 163–66, 224–26; turning pages of, 13, 15, 37, 56, 57, 96, 149. See also reading
bookshelves, toddler-accessible, 37
boredom: indications of, 43; reading same book and, 109

bossiness, 129, 251–52
bottle: putting child to bed with, 82; weaning from, 81
bowel movements, 152, 157
brain activity, during sleep, 156
brain development, 230, 233
Brazelton, T. Berry, 115
breast, weaning from, 81
breath-holding, in tantrums, 116–17
bribes, 138, 139, 228; using dessert as, 80, 199
Britton, James, 97
Brown, Marc, 273
Brown, Stuart, 230–31
brushing teeth, 81–82, 95, 127
bubbles, blowing, 26, 28
buckets, drownings in, 49
Burke, Catherine, 34, 35
Burton, Tim, 130

C

caffeine, 201
Cameron, Jim, 116–17, 139–40, 202
cancer, 19, 79, 89, 100, 105, 154, 155, 201
Cancian, Maria, 275
Caplan, Frank and Theresa, 57
carpooling, 204
Carr, Kali Woodruff, 237
car-seat safety, 48
Cartmill, Erica, 74
Casalin, Sara, 60
catching, 26, 56, 213, 232, 250
categorizing, 25, 26, 265, 266
cause and effect, 35, 36, 56, 75, 150, 184, 238
Center for Human Development, 118, 119
chairs for toddlers, 106; high chairs, 51, 199, 202
charging, 205–6. See also credit cards
charity, 264, 265
Chess, Stella, 118
child abuse: allegations of, in divorce proceedings, 273; outrage at, 188; by partner, 273; resources for, 290; speaking up about, 252–55
childbearing decisions. See family planning
child care: resources for, 290. See also preschools
Child Care Action Campaign (CCAC), 180
Child Care Aware, 173, 174, 290

National Institute of Child Health and
  Human Development, 172
nature walks, 113, 176
negatives, adults' use of, 198
negativism, 96, 123, 128, 214–15, 252
neglectful parents, 86, 133, 275
new baby, 245–49; and easing transition
  for older sibling, 246–49; family planning and, 166–69; preparing older sibling
  for, 246; toddler's reactions to, 168, 169,
  246–47
Newman, Barbara and Philip, 152–53, 173, 187
newspaper, "teachable moments" in, 218
Nielsen, Linda, 275–76
night-lights, 17, 69, 71, 156
nightmares, 56–57, 72–73, 156
night terrors, 73
no, 198, 214
noises, fear of, 64
nonsense syllables, 214
nudity, 257–59
number games, 233
nursery rhymes, 76, 128, 214

O

obesity and overweight, 33, 79, 142, 191, 227
object permanence, 46, 96
O'Brien, Marion, 219–20
observation skills, 26, 113
obstacle courses, 27
older siblings: books for, 164, 226; new baby
  and, 246–49; walking and, 14
Oobleck, 113
oral sex, 60
outrage, 188
overprotectiveness, 22
overweight. See obesity and overweight
ownership of objects, 56, 96, 127

P

pain, physical, 18, 230
painting, 42, 43, 44, 150, 190, 232, 234
Palkovitz, Rob, 103, 131
Palm, Glen, 186, 187
Pancake Art (recipe), 242
Papadakis, Stamatios, 192
parallel play, 23
Parent Advocacy Coalition for Educational
  Rights (PACER), 34–35, 291
parenting styles, 133–39; discipline and,
  133–39; identifying, 133, 134, 136–37
Parke, Ross, 216, 229
partner, relationship with. See relationship
  with partner
Pasley, Kay, 219–20
passing out, in tantrums, 116
patience: fatherhood and, 130; toddler's
  struggles speaking and, 177–78
pattern games, 233
peer pressure, 128
penis, 258; genital self-exploration and, 97,
  152, 222, 255–57; holding during toilet
  training, 161, 162; teaching correct word
  for, 256
peripheral vision, 149, 151
permissive parenting style, 133, 134, 137
Perry, Nicole B., 22
persistence level, 119, 121, 125
physical development: at 12—15 months,
  13–14; at 15—18 months, 55–56; at 18—21
  months, 95–96; at 21—24 months, 126; at
  24—27 months, 149; at 27—30 months,
  182; at 30—33 months, 213; at 33—36
  months, 250
physical exhaustion, of father, 17, 63, 90, 105
physical play, 30, 229–32; cognitive flexibility
  and, 191–94
play: at 12—15 months, 14, 23–28; at 15—18
  months, 28–31; at 18—21 months, 102–7; at
  30—33 months, 229–34; alone, 102, 106–7;
  alongside other toddlers, 59; fantasy, 25,
  183, 196; fun educational activities and,
  112–13; group activities and, 234–36; outside, 234; parallel, 23; with peers, 102–6,
  151; physical, 30, 191–94, 229–32; at preschools, 176–77; pretend, 28, 38, 56, 107,
  173, 232, 233, 234–35; rainy day activities,
  233; of toddler with new baby, 248. *See
  also* toys

ABOUT THE AUTHOR

A nationally recognized parenting expert, Armin A. Brott is the author of more than twenty books, including The Expectant Father: The Ultimate Guide for Dads-to-Be and The New Father: A Dad's Guide to the First Year. He has also written on parenting for the New York Times Magazine, the Washington Post, Sports Illustrated, and Newsweek, among many other publication. He writes the nationally syndicated column "Ask Mr. Dad" and hosts Positive Parenting, a syndicated weekly talk show. Brott lives with his family in the San Francisco Bay area. To learn more, visit his website, **mrdad.com**.

CARTOON CREDITS

**FATHERING YOUR
SCHOOL-AGE CHILD**
*A Dad's Guide to the Wonder
Years: 3 to 9*
By Armin A. Brott
Paper · **$12.95**
ISBN 978-0-7892-0924-5
Hardcover · **$24.95**
ISBN 978-0-7892-0923-8

THE MILITARY FATHER
*A Hands-on Guide for
Deployed Dads*
By Armin A. Brott
Hardcover · **$24.95**
ISBN 978-0-7892-1030-2

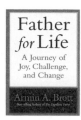

FATHER FOR LIFE
*A Journey of Joy, Challenge,
and Change*
By Armin A. Brott
Hardcover · **$24.95**
ISBN 978-0-7892-0784-5

**THE EXPECTANT AND
FIRST YEAR FATHER**
2-BOOK BOXED SET
THE EXPECTANT FATHER
The Ultimate Guide for Dads-to-Be
THE NEW FATHER
A Dad's Guide to the First Year
$29.95 · ISBN 978-0-7892-1221-4

FAQ FOR EXPECTANT FATHERS
By Armin A. Brott
Paper · **$9.95**
ISBN 978-0-7892-1269-6

FAQ FOR NEW FATHERS
By Armin A. Brott
Paper · **$9.95**
ISBN 978-0-7892-1270-2

For more information on the *New Father* series and a complete list of titles,
visit **www.abbeville.com/newfather**

*Available from your favorite bookstore or online retailer,
or by calling* 1-800-ARTBOOK

OVER 2,000,000 FATHERHOOD BOOKS IN PRINT!

An information-packed, month-by-month guide to all the emotional, financial, and yes, even physical changes the father-to-be may experience during the course of his partner's pregnancy—now significantly updated and expanded. Incorporating the wisdom of top experts in the field, from obstetricians and birth-class instructors to psychologists and sociologists, the fourth edition of *The Expectant Father* includes the latest research about assisted reproductive technologies (ART) and many other topics, and is filled with sound advice and practical tips for men, such as:

- Ways to support and encourage your partner throughout pregnancy
- Overcoming infertility
- What childbirth classes don't teach you
- How to make sense of your conflicting emotions
- How to juggle your work and family roles
- Special ways to prepare if you're adopting a baby
- How to become the father you really want to be

THE EXPECTANT FATHER
FOURTH EDITION
The Ultimate Guide for Dads-to-Be
By Armin A. Brott and
Jennifer Ash
Paper · $13.95
ISBN 978-0-7892-1213-9
Hardcover · $24.95
978-0-7892-1212-2

An indispensable, month-by-month handbook on all aspects of fatherhood during the first year—now fully updated and expanded—by the author of *The Expectant Father*. Incorporating a wealth of knowledge from top experts, the latest scientific research, and the author's and other fathers' personal experiences, *The New Father* presents invaluable information and practical tips on such issues as:

- Charting the baby's physical, intellectual, verbal, and social development
- Understanding your own emotional and psychological development
- Planning your finances and choosing the right life insurance policy
- Understanding how your partner is feeling and dealing with changes in your relationship
- How to understand what your baby is telling you

THE NEW FATHER
THIRD EDITION
A Dad's Guide to the First Year
By Armin A. Brott
Paper · $13.95
ISBN 978-0-7892-1177-4
Hardcover · $24.95
ISBN 978-0-7892-1176-7

For more information on the *New Father* series and a complete list of titles, visit **www.abbeville.com/newfather**

Available from your favorite bookstore or online retailer, or by calling 1-800-ARTBOOK